Machine Learning with
SAS® Viya®

SAS Institute Inc.

sas.com/books

Contents

About This Book

What Is This Book About?

The focus of this book is to explore data using SAS® Viya®—the latest extension of the SAS Platform—to build, validate, and deploy models into production to augment business decision making. We call this the analytics life cycle. This is at the heart of the SAS Platform, and it is a series of phases: **Data, Discovery, Deployment**, with the goal to extract value from raw data.

Analytics Life Cycle

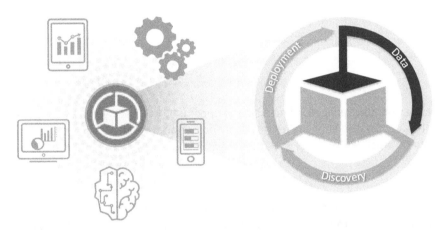

SAS Drive is a common interface for the SAS Viya applications that supports all three phases of the analytics life cycle. It enables you to view, organize, and share your content from one place.

Screen Shot of SAS Drive

Application Bar (1)
Toolbar (2)
Quick Access area (3)
Tabs (4)
Canvas (5)
Information Pane (6)

SAS Drive is available from the Applications menu in the upper left. The displayed tabs depend on the products that are installed at your site. This book focuses on the Build Models action that launches Model Studio pipelines.

What Is Required to Create Good Machine Learning Systems?

In most business problems, you need to go from data to decisions as quickly as possible. Machine learning models are at the heart of critical business decisions. They can identify new opportunities and enable you to manage uncertainty and risks. To create these models, you need to wrangle your data into shape and quickly create many accurate predictive models. You also need to manage your analytical models for optimal performance throughout their lifespan. All good machine learning systems need to consider the following:

- Data preparation
- Algorithms
- Automation and iterative processes
- Scalability
- Ensemble modeling

In this book, we will illustrate each of these processes and how to do them using SAS Model Studio. We will also present just enough theory so that you can understand the techniques and algorithms used enough to be able to choose the correct model for each business problem and fine-tune the models in an efficient and insightful way.

Is This Book for You?

Building representative machine learning models that generalize well on new data requires careful consideration of both the data used for the model to train, and the assumptions about the various training algorithms. It is important to choose the right algorithm for both the data that you will be modeling and the business problem that you are trying to solve.

SAS graphical user interfaces help you build machine learning models and implement an iterative machine learning process. You don't have to be an advanced statistician. The comprehensive selection of machine learning algorithms can help you quickly get value from your big data and are included in many SAS products.

What Should You Know about the Examples?

This book includes worked demonstrations and practices for you to follow to gain hands-on experience with SAS Model Studio.

Software Used to Develop the Book's Content

Model Studio is included in SAS Viya. It is an integrated visual environment that provides a suite of analytic data mining tools that enable you to explore and build models. It is part of the **Discovery** phase of the analytic life cycle. The data mining tools provided in Model Studio enable you to deliver and distribute analytic model data mining champion models, score code, and results. Model Studio contains the following SAS solutions:

- SAS Visual Forecasting
- SAS Visual Data Mining and Machine Learning
- SAS Visual Text Analytics

The visual analytic data mining tools that appear in Model Studio are determined by your site's licensing agreement. Model Studio operates with one, two, or all three of the web-based analytic tools as components of the software.

Model Studio comes with SAS Data Preparation. SAS Data Preparation is a software offering that adds data quality transformations and other advanced features. There are several options that enable you to perform specific data preparation tasks for applications, such as SAS Environment Manager, SAS Visual Analytics, Model Studio, and SAS Decision Manager. You can perform some of the basic data preparation tasks through Model Studio, as we will describe in this book.

Example Code and Data

The data sets used in the book's demonstrations and practices are provided to download.

You can access the example code and data for this book by linking to its author page at support.sas.com/sasinstitute.

We Want to Hear from You

SAS Press books are written *by* SAS Users *for* SAS Users. We welcome your participation in their development and your feedback on SAS Press books that you are using. Please visit sas.com/books to do the following:

- Sign up to review a book

- Recommend a topic

- Request information on how to become a SAS Press author

- Provide feedback on a book

Do you have questions about a SAS Press book that you are reading? Contact the author through saspress@sas.com or https://support.sas.com/author_feedback.

SAS has many resources to help you find answers and expand your knowledge. If you need additional help, see our list of resources: sas.com/books.

Acknowledgments

This book is based on the SAS training course, *Machine Learning Using SAS® Viya®*, developed by Carlos Pinheiro, Andy Ravenna, Sharad Saxena, Jeff Thompson, Marya Ilgen-Lieth, and Cat Truxillo. Additional content and editing was made by Sian Roberts. Design, editing, and production support was provided by the SAS Press team: Robert Harris, Lauree Shepard, Suzanne Morgen, and Denise Jones.

Preface

What Is Machine Learning?

Machine learning is a branch of artificial intelligence (AI) that automates the building of models that learn from data, identify patterns, and predict future results—with minimal human intervention.

Machine learning is not all science fiction. Common examples in use today include self-driving cars, online recommenders such as movies that you might like on Netflix or products from Amazon, sentiment detection on Twitter, or real-time credit card fraud detection.

Statistical Modeling Versus Machine Learning

Just like statistical models, the goal of machine learning is to understand the structure of the data. In statistics, you fit theoretical distributions to the data that are well understood. So, with statistical models there is a theory behind the model that is mathematically proven, but this requires that data meets certain strong assumptions too. Machine learning has developed based on the ability to use computers to probe the data for structure without having a theory of what that structure looks like. The test for a machine learning model is a validation error on new data, not a theoretical test that proves a null hypothesis. Because machine learning often uses an iterative approach to learn from data, the learning can be easily automated. Passes are run through the data until a robust pattern is found.

Algorithms

Building representative machine learning models that generalize well on new data requires careful consideration of both the data used for the model to train and the assumptions about the various training algorithms. It is important to choose the right algorithm for both the data that you will be modeling and the business problem that you are trying to solve. For example, if you are building a model to detect tumors, then it would be important to choose a model with a high accuracy, as it would be more important not to miss any possible tumors. On the other hand, if you were looking to build a model to predict who best to send an offer to in a marketing campaign with a limited budget, you would want the model that is best at predicting rank, or the top 100 or so customers most likely to use the offer. In Chapter 2, we discuss different measures of model performance and when they should be used in more detail.

While many machine learning algorithms have been around for a long time, advances in computer power and parallel processing have allowed the ability to automatically apply complex mathematical calculations to big data faster and faster, making them a lot more useful.

Most industries working with large amounts of data recognize the value in machine learning technology to gain insights and automate decisioning. Common application areas include:

- Fraud
- Targeted Marketing
- Financial Risk
- Churn

Fraud

Fraud detection methods attempt to detect or impede illegal activity that involves financial transactions. Anomaly detection is one of the ways to detect fraud. You look to predict an event that occurs rarely and identify patterns in the data that do not conform to expected behavior, such as an abnormally high purchase made on a credit card.

Targeted Marketing

Targeted marketing is another common application area. Most companies rely on some form of direct marketing to acquire new customers and generate additional revenue from existing customers. Predictive modeling generally accomplishes this by helping companies answer crucial questions such as: Who should I contact? What should I offer? When should I make the offer? How should I make the offer?

Financial Risk

Financial risk management models attempt to predict monetary events such as credit default, loan prepayment, and insurance claim. Banks use multiple models to meet a variety of regulations (such as CCAR and Basel III). With increased scrutiny on model risk, bankers must establish a model risk management program for regulatory compliance and business benefits. Models are useful things to have around, and bankers have come to rely on them for certain applications, some of which expose the bank to significant risks. Predictive models fall into this category. Examples include loan approval using credit scoring and hedging models using swaps and options to manage the balance sheet while protecting liquidity and determining capital adequacy.

Churn

Customer churn is one of the main problems in many businesses. Churn or attrition is the turnover of customers of a product or users of a service. Studies have shown that attracting new customers is much more expensive than retaining existing ones. Consequently, companies focus on developing accurate and reliable predictive models to identify potential customers who will churn soon.

What Is SAS Viya?

SAS Viya is an open, cloud-enabled, analytic run-time environment with a number of supporting services, including SAS Cloud Analytic Services (CAS). CAS is the in-memory engine on the SAS Platform.

> *Run-time environment* refers to the combination of hardware and software in which data management and analytics occur.

CAS is designed to run in a single-machine symmetric multiprocessing (SMP) or multi-machine massively parallel processing (MPP) configuration. CAS supports multiple platform and infrastructure configurations. CAS also has a communications layer that supports fault tolerance. When CAS is running in an MPP configuration, it can continue processing requests even if it loses connectivity to some nodes. This communication layer also enables you to remove or add nodes while the server is running.

Distributed Server: Massively Parallel Processing (MPP)

A distributed server uses multiple machines to perform massively parallel processing. The figure below depicts the server topology for a distributed server. Of the multiple machines used, one machine acts as the controller and other machines act as workers to process data.

Distributed Server: Massively Parallel Processing (MPP)

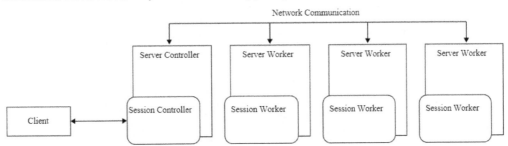

Client applications communicate with the controller, and the controller coordinates the processing that is performed by the worker nodes. One or more machines are designated as worker nodes. Each worker node performs data analysis on the rows of data that are in-memory on the node. The server scales horizontally. If processing times are unacceptably long due to large data volumes, more machines can be added as workers to distribute the workload. Distributed servers are fault tolerant. If communication with a worker node is lost, a surviving worker node uses a redundant copy of the data to complete the data analysis. Whenever possible, distributed servers load data into memory in parallel. This provides the fastest load times.

Single-Machine Server: Symmetric Multiprocessing (SMP)

The figure below depicts the server topology for a single-machine server. The single machine is designated as the controller. Because there are no worker nodes, the controller node performs data analysis on the rows of data that are in-memory. The single machine uses multiple CPUs and threads to speed up data analysis.

Single-Machine Server: Symmetric Multiprocessing (SMP)

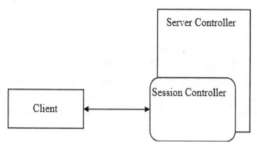

This architecture is often referred to as symmetric multi-processing (SMP). All the in-memory analytic features of a distributed server are available to the single-machine server. Single-machine servers cannot load data into memory in parallel from any data source.

Using Cloud Analytic Services (CAS)

Leveraging the CAS server that is part of the SAS Viya release includes a whole host of tangible benefits. The main reason is represented by a simple three-word phrase: tremendous performance gains. Because processes run so much faster, you can complete your work faster. This means that you can complete more work, and even entire projects, in a significantly reduced time frame.

Processing Type	Multi-threaded, Single Machine (SAS Viya SMP)	Multi-threaded, Multiple Machines (SAS Viya MPP)
Distributed, parallel processing?	Yes	Yes
In-memory data persistence?	Yes	Yes
Common performance speed-up	10x–20x	Up to 100x*

* Increase depends on many factors including hardware allocation. Performance could be higher.

See Appendix A.1 for information about working with CAS, CAS-supported data types, and loading data into CAS.

The Mindset Shift

There are some differences that you need to be aware off when working with SAS Viya. In SAS Viya, you might have nondeterministic results or might not get reproducible results, essentially because of two reasons:

- distributed computing environment
- nondeterministic algorithms

In distributed computing, cases are divided over compute nodes, and there could be variation in the results. You might get slightly different results even in the same server when the controllers/workers are more manageable. In different servers, this is even more expectable. A CAS server represents pooled memory and runs code multi-threaded. Multi-threading tends to distribute the same instructions to other available threads for execution, creating many different queues on many different cores using separate allocations or subsets of data. Most of the time, multiple threads perform operations on isolated collections of data that are independent of one another but part of a larger table. For that reason, it is possible to have a counter (for example, n+1;) operating on one thread to produce a result that might be different from a counter operating on another thread because each thread is working on a different subset of the data.

Therefore, results can be different from thread to thread unless and until the individual results from multiple threads are summed together. It is not as complicated as it might sound. That is because SAS Viya automatically takes care of most collation and reassembly of processing results, with a few minor exceptions where you must further specify how to combine results from multiple threads.

A nondeterministic algorithm is an algorithm that, even for the same input, can exhibit different behaviors on different runs, as opposed to a deterministic algorithm. There are several ways an algorithm might behave differently from run to run. A concurrent algorithm can perform differently on different runs due to a race condition. A probabilistic algorithm's behaviors depend on a random number generator. The nondeterministic algorithms are often used to find an approximation to a solution when the exact solution would be too costly to obtain using a deterministic one (Wikipedia). Some SAS Visual Data Mining and Machine Learning models are created with a nondeterministic process. This means that you might experience different displayed results when you run a model, save that model, close the model, and re-open the report or print the report later.

Deterministic and Nondeterministic Algorithms

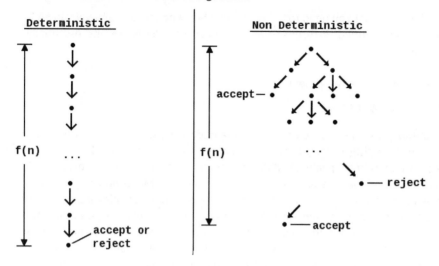

Image source: By Eleschinski2000—With a paint program, CC BY-SA 3.0,
https://commons.wikimedia.org/w/index.php?curid=43528132

A deterministic algorithm that performs $f(n)$ steps always finishes in $f(n)$ steps and always returns the same result. A nondeterministic algorithm that has $f(n)$ levels might not return the same result on different runs. A nondeterministic algorithm might never finish due to the potentially infinite size of the fixed height tree.

It is an altogether different mindset!

You are "converging" on a model or "estimating" a model, not exactly computing the parameters of the model. Bayesian models understand this when they look for convergence of parameters. They try to converge to a distribution, not a point. Maybe it would be interesting to try running the models 10 times across different samples and ensembling them to see the dominant signal. You cannot expect the results to be reproduced because some algorithms have randomness included in the process. However, the results do converge. This is a distinguished computing environment designed for big data, and this non-reproducibility is the price that we pay.

Note: "Data Science's Reproducibility Crisis" https://towardsdatascience.com/data-sciences-reproducibility-crisis-b87792d88513 is an interesting read.

SAS Visual Data Mining and Machine Learning:

A variety of products sit in SAS Viya. They enable users to perform their jobs as part of the analytics life cycle. In this book, you use SAS Visual Data Mining and Machine Learning.

> The Model Studio interface is superset of SAS Visual Data Mining and Machine Learning, SAS Visual Forecasting, and SAS Visual Text Analytics.

SAS Visual Data Mining and Machine Learning is a product offering in SAS Viya that contains:

1. underlying CAS actions and SAS procedures for data mining and machine learning applications
2. GUI-based applications for different levels and types of users.

These applications are as follows:

- **Programming interface**: a collection of SAS procedures for direct coding or access through tasks in SAS Studio.

- **Interactive modeling interface**: a collection of tasks in SAS Visual Analytics for creating models in an interactive manner with automated assessment visualizations

- **Automated modeling interface**: a pipeline application called Model Studio that enables you to construct automated flows consisting of various nodes for preprocessing and modeling, with automated model assessment and comparison, and direct model publishing and registration.

Each of these executes the same underlying actions in the CAS execution environment. In addition, there are supplementary interfaces for preparing your data (Data Studio) and managing and deploying your models (SAS Model Manager and SAS Decision Manager) to support all phases of a machine learning application.

> In this book, you primarily explore the Model Studio interface and its integration with other SAS Visual Data Mining and Machine Learning interfaces.

You use the SAS Visual Data Mining and Machine Learning web client to visually assemble, configure, build, and compare data mining models and pipelines for a wide range of analytic data mining tasks.

Chapter 1: Introduction to Machine Learning

Introduction

There are two main types of machine learning methods, *supervised learning* and *unsupervised learning*.

Supervised Learning

Supervised learning (also known as *predictive modeling*) starts with a training data set. The observations in a training data set are known as *training cases* (also known as *examples*, *instances*, or *records*). The variables are called *inputs* (also known as *predictors*, *features*, *explanatory variables*, or *independent variables*) and *targets* (also known as *responses*, *outcomes*, or *dependent variables*). The learning algorithm receives a set of inputs along with the corresponding correct outputs or targets, and the algorithm learns by comparing its actual output with correct outputs to find errors. It then modifies the model accordingly. Through methods like classification, regression, prediction, and gradient boosting, supervised learning uses patterns to predict the values of the label on additional unlabeled data. In other words, the purpose of the training data is to generate a predictive model. The *predictive model* is a concise representation of the association between the inputs and the target variables.

Supervised learning is commonly used in applications where historical data predicts likely future events. For example, it can anticipate when credit card transactions are likely to be fraudulent or which insurance customer is likely to file a claim.

Unsupervised Learning

Unsupervised learning is used against data that has no historical labels. In other words, the system is not told the "right answer" – there is no target data – the algorithm must figure out what is being shown. The goal is to explore the data and find some structure or pattern. Unsupervised learning works well on transactional data. For example, it can identify segments of customers with similar attributes who can then be treated similarly in marketing campaigns. Or it can find the main attributes that separate customer segments from each other. Popular techniques include self-organizing maps, nearest-neighbor mapping, k-means clustering, and singular value decomposition. These algorithms are also used to segment text topics, recommend items, and identify data outliers.

Semisupervised Learning and Reinforcement Learning

Other common methods include semisupervised learning and reinforcement learning. *Semisupervised learning* is used for similar applications as supervised learning. But it uses both labeled and unlabeled data for training – typically a small amount of labeled data with a large amount of unlabeled data (because unlabeled data is less expensive and takes less effort to acquire). This type of learning can be used with methods such as classification, regression, and prediction. Semisupervised learning is useful when the cost associated with labeling is too high to allow for a fully labeled training process. Early examples of this include identifying a person's face on a web cam.

Reinforcement learning is often used for robotics, gaming, and navigation. With reinforcement learning, the algorithm discovers through trial and error which actions yield the greatest rewards. This type of learning has three primary components: the agent (the learner or decision maker), the environment (everything the agent interacts with), and actions (what the agent can do). The objective is for the agent to choose actions that maximize the expected reward over a given amount of time. The agent will reach the goal much faster by following a good policy. So the goal in reinforcement learning is to learn the best policy.

In this book, we will be focusing on supervised learning or predictive modeling.

Supervised Learning Predictions

The outputs of the predictive model are referred to as *predictions*. Predictions represent your best guess for the target given a set of input measurements. The predictions are based on the associations learned from the training data by the predictive model.

The training data are used to construct a model (rule) that relates the inputs to the target. The predictions can be categorized into three distinct types:

- decisions
- rankings
- estimates

Decision Prediction

Decision predictions are the simplest type of prediction. Decisions usually are associated with some type of action (such as classifying a case as a churn or no-churn). For this reason, decisions are also known as *classifications*. Decision prediction examples include handwriting recognition, fraud detection, and direct mail solicitation.

Figure 1.1: Decision Predictions

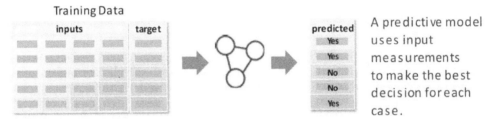

Decision predictions usually relate to a categorical target variable. For this reason, they are identified as primary, secondary, and tertiary in correspondence with the levels of the target.

> **Note:** Model assessment in Model Studio generally assumes decision predictions when the target variable has a categorical measurement level (binary, nominal, or ordinal).

Ranking Prediction

Ranking predictions order cases based on the input variables' relationships with the target variable. Using the training data, the prediction model attempts to rank *high value* cases higher than *low value* cases. It is assumed that a similar pattern exists in the scoring data so that *high value* cases have high scores. The actual produced scores are inconsequential. Only the relative order is important. The most common example of a ranking prediction is a credit score.

Figure 1.2: Ranking Predictions

Training Data

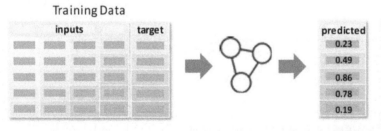

inputs	target		predicted
			720
			520
			590
			460
			610

A predictive model uses input measurements to optimally rank each case.

> Ranking predictions can be transformed into decision predictions by taking the primary decision for cases above a certain threshold while making secondary and tertiary decisions for cases below the correspondingly lower thresholds. In credit scoring, cases with a credit score above 700 can be called good risks, those with a score between 600 and 700 can be intermediate risks, and those below 600 can be considered poor risks.

Estimation Prediction

Estimation prediction uses the inputs to estimate a *value* for the dependent variable conditioned on some unobserved values of the independent variable. For cases with numeric targets, this can be thought of as the average value of the target for all cases having the observed input measurements. For cases with categorical targets, this number might equal the probability of a target outcome.

Figure 1.3: Estimate Prediction.

Training Data

inputs	target		predicted
			0.23
			0.49
			0.86
			0.78
			0.19

A predictive model uses input measurements to optimally estimate the target value.

Prediction estimates are most commonly used when their values are integrated into a mathematical expression. For example, two-stage modeling, where the probability of an event is combined with an estimate of profit or loss to form an estimate of unconditional expected profit or loss. Prediction estimates are also useful when you are not sure of the ultimate application of the model.

Estimate predictions can be transformed into both decision and ranking predictions. When in doubt, use this option. Most Model Studio modeling tools can be configured to produce estimate predictions.

Model Building and Selection

In order to choose the best model for the business problem and data, many models are built and compared in order to choose a *champion model*, which can then be deployed into production. We will discuss scoring and model selection in a later chapter. But before you start building models it is important to hold back some of the data to be used to help select the best model.

Model Complexity

Selecting model complexity is a balance between bias and variance. An insufficiently complex model might not be flexible enough, which leads to *underfitting*. An underfit model leads to biased inferences, which means that they are not the true ones in the population; for example, in the case of a decisioning model, they could predict "no" when the target should be "yes."

An overly complex model might be too flexible, which leads to *overfitting*. An overfit model includes the random noise in the sample, which can lead to models that have higher variance when applied to the population. This model would perform almost perfectly with the training data but is likely to have poor performance with the validation data.

A model with just enough flexibility gives the best generalization.

Figure 1.4: Accuracy Versus Generalizability

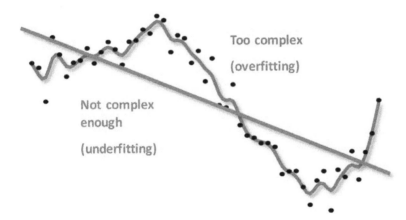

Too complex

(overfitting)

Not complex
enough

(underfitting)

Introducing Model Studio

Model Studio enables you to explore ideas and discover insights by preparing data and building models. It is part of the **discovery** piece of the analytics life cycle. Model Studio is a central, web-based application that includes a suite of integrated data mining tools. The data mining tools supported in Model Studio are designed to take advantage of the SAS Viya programming and cloud processing environments to deliver and distribute analytic model data mining champion models, score code, and results.

Demo 1.1: Creating a Project and Loading Data

In this demonstration, you will create a new project in Model Studio based on the **commsdata** data set. A project is a top-level container for your analytic work in Model Studio. The table is imported from a local drive. The type of project is defined. This project is used to predict churn for a fictitious telecommunications company. A target variable is selected for this table.

1. First, open SAS Drive on your machine and select **SAS Viya ▶ SAS Drive** from the bookmarks bar or from the link on the page.
2. Next, log on using your user ID and password.

   Note: Use caution when you enter the user ID and password because values can be case-sensitive.
3. Click **Sign In**.
4. Select **Yes** in the Assumable Groups window. The SAS Drive home page appears.

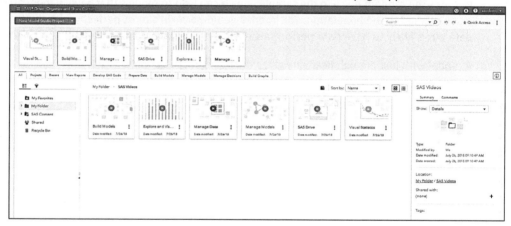

Note: The SAS Drive page on your computer might not have the same tiles as the image above.

5. Click the Applications menu in the upper left corner of the SAS Drive page. Select **Build Models**.

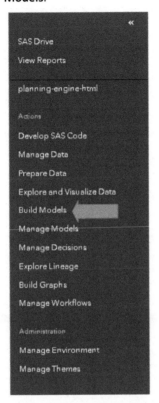

This launches Model Studio.

Note: Some of the top features in Model Studio in SAS Visual Data Mining and Machine Learning are presented in a paper titled "Playing Favorites: Our Top 10 Model Studio Features in SAS® Visual Data Mining and Machine Learning" at https://www.sas.com/content/dam/SAS/support/en/sas-global-forum-proceedings/2019/3236-2019.pdf.

Alternatively, click **New** in the upper left corner to reveal a menu to create a new item. Select **Model Studio project** from the menu.

Note: When this alternative process is used to go to Model Studio, it bypasses the Model Studio Projects page and immediately opens the window to create a new project as shown below in step 7 of this demonstration.

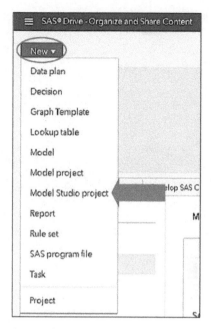

The Model Studio Projects page is now displayed.

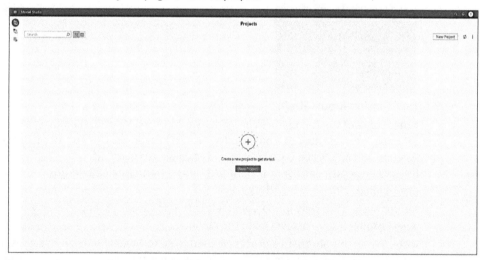

Note: On your computer, the Projects page might differ from the image above. There might be pre-existing projects on your computer.

From the Model Studio Projects page, you can view existing projects, create new projects, access the Exchange, and access Global Metadata. Model Studio projects can be one of three types (depending on the SAS licensing for your site): Forecasting projects, Data Mining and Machine Learning projects, and Text Analytics projects.

Note: The Exchange organizes your favorite settings and enables you to collaborate with others in one place. Find a recommended node template or create your own template for a streamlined workflow for your team. The Exchange is accessed later in this chapter.

6. Select **New Project** in the upper right corner of the Projects page.

7. Enter **Demo** as the name in the New Project window. Leave the default type of **Data Mining and Machine Learning.** Click **Browse** in the Data field.

Note: You can specify a pipeline template at project creation. Continue with a blank template. Pipeline templates are discussed soon.

8. Import a SAS data set into CAS.

    a. In the Choose Data window, click **Import**.

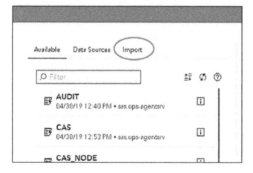

b. Under Import, select **Local File**.

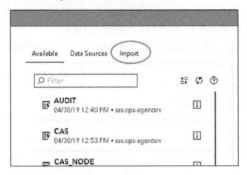

c. Navigate to the data folder.

d. Select the **commsdata.sas7bdat** table. Click **Open**.

e. Select **Import Item**. Model Studio parses the data set and pre-populates the window with data set configurations.

Note: When the data is in memory, it is available for other projects through the Available tab.

f. Click **OK** after the table is imported.

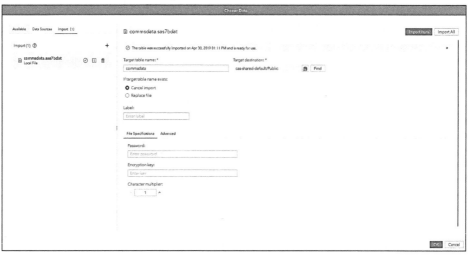

Note: Tables are imported to the CAS server and are available to use with SAS Visual Analytics. When the import is complete, you are returned to Model Studio. For more information about data types supported in CAS and how to load data into CAS, see the details section at the end of this demo.

9. Click **Advanced** in the New Project window.

10. The Advanced project settings appear. There are four groups of Advanced project settings: Advisor Options, Partition Data, Event-based Sampling, and Node Configuration.

Under the Advisor Options group, there are three options:

Maximum class levels specifies the threshold for rejecting categorical variables. If a categorical input has more levels than the specified maximum number, it is rejected.

Interval cutoff determines whether a numeric input is designated as interval or nominal. If a numeric input has more distinct values/levels than the interval cutoff value, it is declared interval. Otherwise, it is declared nominal.

Maximum percent missing specifies the threshold for rejecting inputs with missing values. If an input has a higher percentage of missing values than the specified maximum percent, it is rejected. This option can be turned on or off. It is on by default.

Note: This is the only place where these Advisor Options are seen and can be changed.

The Advanced project settings options for Partition Data and Event-Based Sampling are covered in the next chapter. And, along with Node Configuration, they are discussed in the next demo. You can access the Partition Data, Event-Based Sampling, and Node Configuration options here, and you can also access them after the project is created.

Click **Cancel** to return to the New Project window.

11. Click **Save**.

Note: After you create your new project, Model Studio takes you to the Data tab of your new project. Here, you can adjust data source variable role and level assignments and define certain metadata rules (for example, methods of imputation and transformation). You can also retrain a model with new data, if the target variable in the new data set is the same as the original data set.

Note: In Model Studio, *metadata* is defined as the set of variable roles, measurement levels, and other configurations that apply to your data set. When you need to create multiple projects using similar data sets (or when using a single data set), you might find it useful to store the metadata configurations for usage across projects. Model Studio enables you to do this by collecting the variables in a repository named Global Metadata. By storing your metadata configurations as global metadata, the configurations will apply to new data sets that contain variables with the same names.

12. When the project is created, you need to assign a target variable to run a pipeline. In Model Studio, you can create analytic process flow in the form of a pipeline.

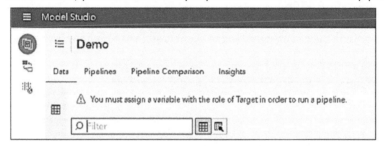

You can also have target variable roles already defined in your data. Model Studio provides several options for managing and modifying data. The Data tab enables you to modify variable assignments and manage global metadata.

13. In the variables window, select **churn** (Step 1). Then in the right pane, select **Target** under the Role property (Step 2). (You might need to scroll down in the variable list to see **churn**.)

The right pane enables you to specify several properties of the variables, including Role, Level, Order, Transform, Impute, Lower Limit, and Upper Limit**.**

For the Transform, Impute, Lower Limit, and Upper Limit properties, altering these values on the Data tab does not directly modify the variable. Instead, this sets metadata values for these properties. The Data Mining Preprocessing nodes that use metadata values (Transformations, Impute, Filter, and Replacement) might use these parameters if the corresponding action is requested. You see this in the next few demonstrations.

14. Click **Specify the Target Event Level**. You can specify the target event level here that needs to be modeled.

15. Click the drop-down arrow.

    Note that the churn rate is around 12%. By default, Model Studio considers alphanumerically the last category as the event, and therefore no change is required.

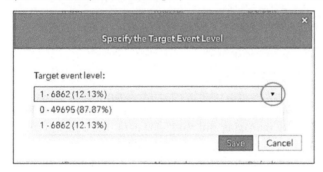

16. Close the Specify the Target Event Level window.

End of Demonstration

Model Studio: Analysis Elements

A **project** is a top-level container for your analytic work in Model Studio. A Model Studio project contains the **data source**, the **pipelines** that you create, and related **project metadata** (such as project type, project creator, share list, and last update history). If you create more than one pipeline in your project, analytic results that compare the performance of multiple pipelines are also stored in the project.

Model Studio: Analysis Elements

Figure 1.5: Analysis Events in Model Studio

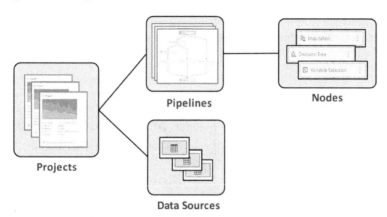

You can add nodes to the pipeline to create your modeling process flow. You can save results from SAS Visual Data Mining and Machine Learning nodes by inserting a SAS Code node after the node (and sometimes a Manage Variable node before the SAS Code Node). This enables you to write some specific DATA step or other Base SAS or CASL statements to save your desired outputs and data sets to a permanent library for further use.

If you want to capture the data being exported out of a node, you can simply attach a Save Data node anywhere on your pipeline and specify details of the table that you want to save. In addition, there is an output tab in the results of nodes that enables you to view the scored output table. From here, you can specify a sample if desired, as well as request to save the table. You can also save data other than the scored output tables. Further, you can download and save data from the tables and plots shown in the results of nodes. This is done by clicking the **Download Data** shortcut button in the upper right corner, which appears right next to the **Expand** shortcut button.

/opt/sas/viya/config/data/cas/default/projects				
Name	Size	Changed	Rights	Owner
..		12/20/2017 1:15:20 PM	rwxr-xr-x	cas
datamining-8eb9539b-95c3-46bc-807f-588213f7566c		3/9/2018 10:07:29 AM	rwxr-xr-x	cas
datamining-63e94ff6-07c7-4b64-9d79-87f777e66bc9		6/1/2018 3:01:21 AM	rwxr-xr-x	cas
datamining-a7976f72-a721-407c-af1c-a304067b1e69		5/29/2018 3:13:48 AM	rwxr-xr-x	cas
datamining-de12ceab-326f-49b9-aaf0-c82561a068f4		5/29/2018 6:18:34 AM	rwxr-xr-x	cas
datamining-f5428069-a643-4b2a-a567-d0da70c16ebe		6/8/2018 5:30:53 AM	rwxr-xr-x	cas
datamining-fad7c7d7-b67e-4d66-91b7-14b01e6939e6		5/28/2018 7:20:40 AM	rwxr-xr-x	cas
forecasting-50657c82-e4f2-41eb-8dcc-6501448dc47d		3/9/2018 10:40:13 AM	rwxr-xr-x	cas

Model Studio: Analysis Elements

You can view the list of projects (like above) by navigating to the location where it has been saved. Shown above is the path for a Linux OS using WinSCP (a File Transfer Protocol application on your client machine). Generally, the path is **/opt/sas/viya/config/data/cas/default/projects/**. You might have a different path if it is a Windows installation.

Figure 1.6: Pipeline

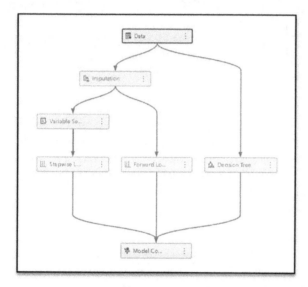

- Pipelines are structured flows of analytic actions.

- Pipelines contain the nodes that process data and create models.

- Custom pipelines can be saved to *the Exchange* for others to use.

A *pipeline* is an analytic process flow. After creating a new pipeline, you can create visual data mining functionality by adding nodes to the pipeline. Nodes can be added separately, or, to save time, templates can add several nodes at once. To create a pipeline from a template, specify the template in the New Pipeline window. You can add nodes to a pipeline in the following two ways:

1. Drag and drop from an expanded Nodes pane.
2. Right-click and select either **Add child node** or **Add parent node.**

Pipelines are grouped together in a top-level container (that is, in a project that also includes the data set that you want to model and a pipeline comparison tool). A project can contain multiple pipelines. You can create a new pipeline and modify an existing pipeline.

Pipelines can be saved to the *Exchange* where they become accessible to other users. All available nodes, along with descriptions, and all available pipeline templates, including pre-built and user-created, can be found here.

Model Studio: Analysis Elements

Templates

Model Studio supports templates as a method for creating statistical models quickly. A *template* is a special type of pipeline that is pre-populated with configurations that can be used to create a model. A template might consist of multiple nodes or a single node. Model Studio includes a set of templates that represent frequent use cases, but you can also create models themselves and save them as templates in the Exchange.

There are three levels of templates available, both for a class target as well as for an interval target. An intermediate template for class target was shown in Figure 1.6. You can create a new template from an existing pipeline, create a new template in the Exchange, and modify an existing template.

The advanced templates are also available with *autotuning* functionality. A large portion of the model-building process is taken up by experiments to identify the optimal set of parameters for the model algorithm. As algorithms get more complex (neural networks to deep neural networks, decision trees to forests and gradient boosting), the amount of time required to identify these parameters grows. There are several ways to support you in this cumbersome work of tuning machine learning model parameters. These approaches are called *hyperparameter optimization* and are discussed later in the book. The following pipeline templates are included with Model Studio:

Table 1.1: Pipeline Templates

Pipeline Template Name	Pipeline Template Description
Blank template	A data mining pipeline that contains only a Data node
Basic template for class target	A simple linear flow: Data, Imputation, Logistic Regression, Model Comparison
Basic template for interval target	A simple linear flow: Data, Imputation, Linear Regression, Model Comparison
Intermediate template for class target	Extends the basic template with a stepwise logistic regression model and a decision tree

Model Studio: Analysis Elements

Pipeline Template Name	Pipeline Template Description
Intermediate template for interval target	Extends the basic template with a stepwise linear regression model and a decision tree
Advanced template for class target	Extends the intermediate template for class target with neural network, forest, and gradient boosting models, as well as an ensemble
Advanced template for class target with autotuning	Advanced template for class target with autotuned tree, forest, neural network, and gradient boosting models

The next demo shows how to build a new pipeline from a basic template for a class target. This template is a simple linear flow and includes a logistic regression node as the predictive model. Chapter 5 includes a refresher on logistic regression for those who are not familiar with this technique.

Demo 1.2: Building a Pipeline from a Basic Template

Although it is nice to be able to build up your own pipelines from scratch, it is often convenient to start from a template that represents best practices in building predictive models. The application comes with a nice set of templates available for creating new pipelines. In this demonstration, to start simple, you build a new pipeline from a basic template for class target.

1. Click **+** next to the current pipeline tab in the upper left corner of the canvas.

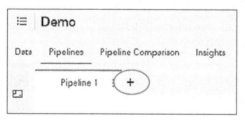

2. In the New Pipeline window, select **Browse templates** in the **Template** field.

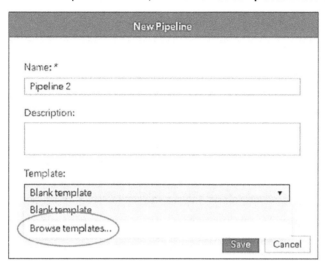

Note: Some of the options on the Template menu might be different on your computer from what is shown above.

3. In the Browse Templates window, select **Basic template for class target**. Click **OK**.

4. In the New Pipeline window, name the pipeline **Basic Template**.

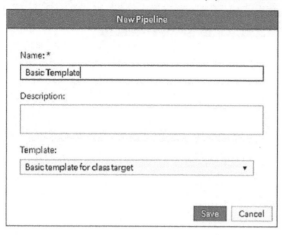

5. Click **Save**.

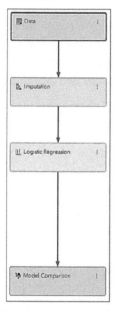

The *basic template for class target* is a simple linear flow and includes the following nodes: Data, Imputation, Logistic Regression, and Model Comparison. You can add nodes by right-clicking the existing nodes (or dragging and dropping from the Nodes pane.)

Different colors of nodes represent their respective groups in the Model Studio.

Note: Because a predicted response might be different for cases with a missing input value, a binary imputation indicator variable is often added to the training data. Adding this variable enables a model to adjust its predictions in the situation where "missingness" itself is correlated with the target.

6. Click **Run Pipeline** in the upper right corner.

7. After the pipeline has successfully run, right-click the **Logistic Regression** node and select **Results**.

The Results window contains two important tabs at the top: one for Node results and one for Assessment results.

Here are some of the windows included under the Node tab in the results from the Logistic Regression node:

○ t-values by Parameter plot

○ Parameter Estimates table

○ Selection Summary table

○ Output

Here are some of the windows included under the Assessment tab in the results from the Logistic Regression node:

○   Lift Reports plots

○   ROC Reports plots

○   Fit Statistics table

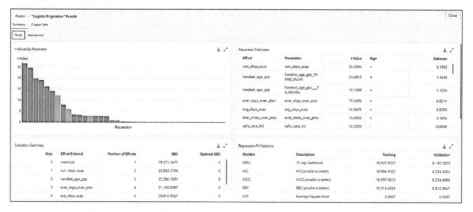

Explore the results as you see fit.

8.   Close the Results window by clicking **Close** in the upper right corner of the window.

9.   Right-click the **Model Comparison** node and select **Results**.

10.   Click to expand the **Model Comparison** table. Unless specified, the default fit statistic (KS) is used for selecting a champion model with a class target.

Note: To change the default fit statistic for just this comparison, change the class selection statistic of the Model Comparison properties in the right-hand pane when the node is selected in the pipeline. To change the default fit statistic for all projects, change the class selection statistic on the Project Settings menu. The default is the Kolmogorov-Smirnov statistic (KS).

A subset of the Model Comparison table is shown below.

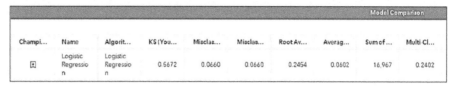

| | | | | | | | | | Model Comparison |
Champi...	Name	Algorit...	KS (You...	Misclas...	Misclas...	Root Av...	Averag...	Sum of ...	Multi-Cl...
⊞	Logistic Regressio n	Logistic Regressio n	0.5672	0.0660	0.0660	0.2454	0.0602	16.967	0.2402

Note: The Model Comparison node is always added by default when any model is contained in the pipeline. If the pipeline contains only a single model, the Model Comparison node summarizes performance of this one model.

11. Exit the maximized view by clicking **X** in the upper right corner of the window.

End of Demonstration

Quiz

1. After you create your new project, Model Studio takes you to the Data tab. What can you do in the Data tab? (Select all that apply.)
   a. Modify variable roles and measurement levels.
   b. Manage global metadata.
   c. Modify variable names and labels.
   d. Manage columns to display the Variables table.

Chapter 2: Preparing Your Data: Introduction

Introduction

Trash in—trash out! To be effective, machine learning models need to be built from well-prepared data. It is often said that 80% of the time spent in building a successful machine learning application is spent in data preparation (Dasu and Johnson 2003). Data preparation is not strictly about correctly transforming and cleaning existing data. It also includes a good understanding of the features that need to be considered and ensuring that the data that you are using are appropriate in the first place. This is known as the **Data** phase of the analytics cycle.

Explore the Data

Preparing any data for analysis should always start by exploring your data. Exploring data means getting an overall feel for the data, including knowledge of the variables by using both graphical and numerical methods, such as histograms, scatter plots, bar charts, and stem-and-leaf plots. There are also more modern graphical tools, such as heat maps and word clouds, that scale well to large data sets. Numerical summary methods are also used to explore data. These include summary statistics for measure of central tendency such as the mean, median, or mode. Numeric measures of variability such as variance, standard deviation, range, or interquartile-range are also used to explore data. Extreme values such as outliers, the minimum, or the maximum are used to explore data as well as counts or percentages of missing data. Bivariate measures such as correlation are also used.

Figure 2.1: Exploring the Data

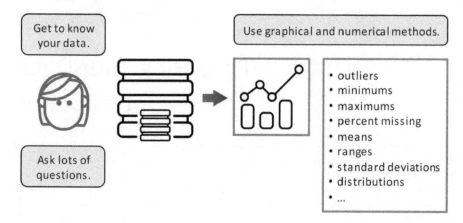

In order to prepare your data to train your model, the following essential tasks must be carried out:

- Divide the data
- Address rare events
- Manage missing values
- Add unstructured data
- Extract features
- Handle extreme or unusual values
- Select useful inputs

In the following sections, we will discuss each of these tasks.

Model Studio: Data Preprocessing

Data preprocessing can occur in several places throughout SAS Visual Data Mining and Machine Learning: in a dedicated application (Data Studio), during visual exploration (SAS Visual Analytics), and during execution of a pipeline (Model Studio). Here we use the Model Studio application, which provides data preprocessing capabilities in the form of pipeline nodes. These nodes form a group called Data Mining Preprocessing.

Model Studio: Data Preprocessing

Figure 2.2: Data Preprocessing with Model Studio

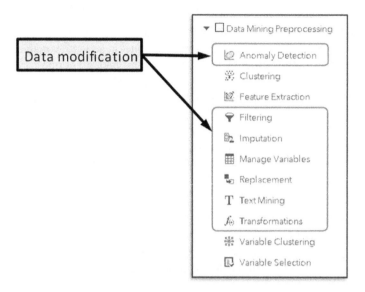

Data modification is a broad preprocessing category. Any operation that alters the data or data roles can be considered as a modification, including dimension reduction techniques. Model Studio provides several SAS Visual Data Mining and Machine Learning nodes to modify your data.

Table 2.1: Model Studio Data Modifying Nodes

Node Name	Node Description
Anomaly Detection	The Anomaly Detection node identifies and excludes anomalies using the support vector data description (SVDD). Briefly, the SVDD formulation identifies outliers by determining the smallest possible hypersphere (built using support vectors) that encapsulates the training data points. The SVDD then excludes those data points that lie outside of the sphere that is built from the training data. Anomaly detection with SVDD is useful for data sets where most of the data belongs to one class, and the other class is scarce or missing.
Filtering	The Filtering node excludes certain observations, such as rare values and outliers. Filtering extreme values from the training data tends to produce better models because the parameter estimates are more stable.

Model Studio: Data Preprocessing

Node Name	Node Description
Imputation	The Imputation node replaces missing values in data sets. Simple imputation schemes include replacing a missing value in an input variable with the mean or mode of that variable's nonmissing values. For non-normally distributed variables or variables that have a high proportion of missing values, simple imputation might be ineffective. Imputation might also fail to be effective for variables whose missingness is not at random. For ideal results, create missing indicators and use them in the model alongside imputed variables. This practice can result in improved outcomes, even in cases where the variables are normally distributed and have few missing values.
Manage Variables	The Manage Variables node enables you to make modifications (such as changing the role of a variable or adding new transformations) to the data while within a Model Studio pipeline. The options available to you are a subset of the options available under the Data tab.
Replacement	The Replacement node enables you to replace outliers and unknown class levels with specified values. Much like with imputation, simple replacement of outliers and unknown class level is not always effective. Care should be taken to use replacement effectively.
Transformations	The Transformations node enables you to alter your data by replacing an input variable with some function of that variable. Transformations have many use cases. Transformations can be used to stabilize variances, remove nonlinearity, and correct non-normality.

Dimension reduction decreases the number of variables under consideration. In many applications, the raw data have very high-dimensional features, and some features are redundant or irrelevant to the task. Reducing the dimensionality helps find the true, latent relationship. Model Studio provides three nodes in SAS Visual Data Mining and Machine Learning for dimension reduction.

Model Studio: Data Preprocessing

Table 2.2: Model Studio Data Dimension Reduction Nodes

Node Name	Node Description
Feature Extraction	The Feature Extraction node transforms the existing features (variables) into a lower-dimensional space. Feature extraction in Model Studio is done using various techniques, including principal component analysis (PCA), robust PCA, singular value decomposition (SVD), and autoencoders. This is done by generating new features that are composites of the existing features. One drawback to feature extraction is that the composite variables are no longer meaningful with respect to the original problem.
Variable Clustering	The Variable Clustering node divides numeric variables into disjoint clusters and chooses a variable that represents each cluster. Variable clustering removes collinearity, decreases redundancy, and helps reveal the underlying structure of the data set.
Variable Selection	The Variable Selection node uses several unsupervised and supervised methods to determine which variables have the most impact on the model. Supervised variable selection techniques include variable selection based on linear models and tree-based models (such as decision tree, forest, and gradient boosting). This tool enables you to specify more than one selection technique, and there are several options for selection criteria. Because there can be disagreements on selected variables when different techniques are used, this functionality enables you to select variables that are consistently selected. Variables that fail to meet the selection criteria are marked as rejected and not used in successor modeling nodes.

When performing *unsupervised learning*, the machine is presented with unlabeled data (unlabeled data have no target). Unsupervised learning algorithms seek to discover intrinsic patterns that underlie the data, such as a clustering or a redundant parameter (dimension) that can be reduced.

Model Studio: Data Preprocessing

Model Studio provides the Clustering node to perform observation clustering based on distances that are computed from quantitative variables or qualitative variables (or both). The node uses the following algorithms:

- the *k*-means algorithm for clustering interval (quantitative) input variables

- the *k*-modes algorithm for clustering nominal (qualitative) input variables

- the *k*-prototypes algorithm for clustering mixed input that contains both interval and nominal variables

Clustering is often used to segment a large data set into several groups. Analysis can be performed in each group to help users find intrinsic patterns.

Demo 2.1: Exploring Source Data

In this demonstration, you use the Data Exploration node in Model Studio to assay and explore the **commsdata** data source. You will frequently find it useful to profile a data set before continuing your analysis. Here you select a subset of variables to provide a representative snapshot of the data. Variables can be selected to show the most important inputs, or to indicate suspicious variables (that is, variables with anomalous statistics).

1. From the Model Studio Projects page, open the **Demo** project from the available existing projects.
2. Click the **Pipelines** tab. (You should be looking at the pipeline called **Pipeline 1,** but if you are not, click on its tab.)
3. Right-click the **Data** node and select **Add child node   Miscellaneous ▶ Data Exploration**.

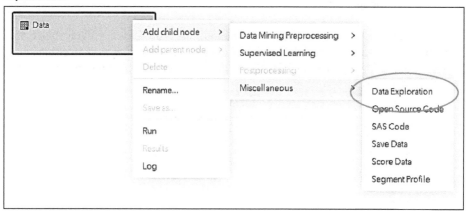

Note: You can also drag the node from the left pane, after clicking the **Nodes** button

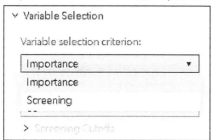 , to the top of the Data node, and the node is added below.

The Data Exploration node selects a subset of variables to provide a representative snapshot of the data. You can specify which data partition (or all input data) to analyze.

4. Keep the default setting for **Variable selection criterion**, which is **Importance**. The variable selection criterion specifies whether to display the most important inputs or suspicious variables. The other possible value is **Screening**.

Variables can be selected to show the most important inputs or to indicate anomalous statistics. By default, a maximum of 50 variables will be selected with the Importance criterion.

You can control the selection of suspicious variables by specifying screening criteria such as cutoff for flagging variables with a high percentage of missing values, high-cardinality class variables, class variables with dominant levels, class variables with rare modes, skewed interval variables, peaky (leptokurtic) interval variables, and interval variables with thick tails (that is, platykurtic distributions).

5. Right-click the **Data Exploration** node and select **Run** (or click **Run Pipeline** in the upper right corner).

The Data Exploration node gives you a statistical summary of the input data. This node can be a useful first step in analysis because it enables you to profile your data set. The Data Exploration node can be placed most anywhere in a pipeline except after the Model Comparison node.

6. When the pipeline finishes running, right-click the **Data Exploration** node and select **Results**.

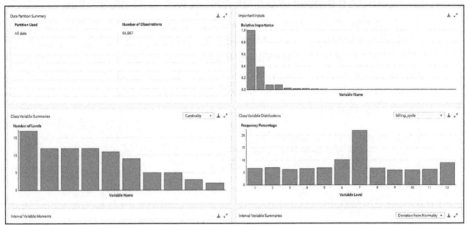

7. Click the **Expand** button on the **Important Inputs** bar chart and examine the relative importance of the ranked variables. This bar chart is available only if **Variable selection criterion** is set to **Importance**.

   Relative importance is calculated based on a decision tree, and is covered in more detail later in the feature selection section.

8. Exit the maximized view.

9. Expand the **Interval Variable Moments** table.

Variable Name	Minimum	Maximum	Mean	Standard Deviation	Skewness	Kurtosis	Relative Variability	Mean plus 2 SD	Mean minus 2 SD
MB_Data_Usg_M06	0	29.676	230.5686	718.7864	15.2432	360.4407	3.1127	1,668.1214	-1,207.0242
MB_Data_Usg_M07	0	13.672	96.2740	269.8391	17.6346	499.6026	2.7562	613.9521	-425.4041
MB_Data_Usg_M08	0	16.297	109.6912	348.7336	16.9031	467.9011	3.1821	807.0505	-587.8760
avg_days_suso	0	62	3.4714	3.8313	1.5937	5.0681	1.1037	11.1339	4.1912
bill_data_usg_m03	-13.678	67.1000	1,864.9142	1.634.5099	1.3974	13.7684	0.8765	5,133.9339	-1,404.1056
bill_data_usg_mt	17	82	44.6696	11.0640	0.4848	-0.1327	0.3478	66.7915	22.5276
calls_care_ltd	0	266	91.2472	49.2820	1.1421	0.3660	0.5406	190.1117	-7.4161
calls_in_offpk	-1,410.3900	40.2433	388.6469	406.1405	1.8186	5.6826	1.0460	1,200.9279	-423.6342
curr_days_susp	0	43	2.6708	4.0652	2.4918	8.2810	1.5221	10.8013	-5.4596
ever_days_over_plan	0	142	13.7507	16.8382	1.6871	4.1334	1.1519	46.4270	-17.9257
ever_times_over_plan	0	26	2.6003	2.4628	1.0692	1.6823	0.9693	7.4359	-2.3762
mb_data_ndist_mo6m	-92.4717	87.7572	0.0627	4.1431	0.1290	18.7767	66.1244	8.3408	-8.2235
mou_onnet_pet_MOM	-45	124.7273	-0.2595	3.8854	2.8060	91.5615	14.9703	7.6112	-8.0303
seconds_of_data_log	0	11.2083	8.4619	1.8860	-2.4949	7.6802	0.2236	12.2220	4.6819

This table displays the interval variables with their associated statistics, which include minimum, maximum, mean, standard deviation, skewness, kurtosis, relative variability, and the mean plus or minus two standard deviations. Note that some of the input variables have negative values.

10. Exit the maximized view of this window.

11. Scroll down in the Data Exploration Results window to examine the Interval Variable Summaries scatter plot. Observe that several variables have deviation from normality— that is, high kurtosis on the Y axis and high skewness on the X axis.

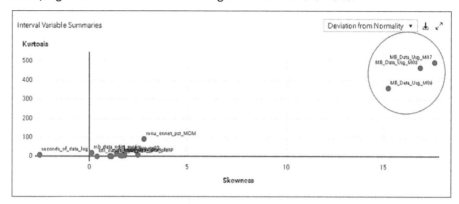

12. Use the drop-down menu in the upper right corner to examine a bar chart of the relative variability for each interval variable.

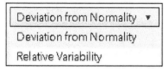

Note: Relative variability is useful for comparing variables with similar scales, such as several income variables. Relative variability is the coefficient of variation, which is a measure of variance relative to the mean, $CV=\sigma/\mu$.

13. Scroll down in the Data Exploration Results window to examine the Missing Values bar chart and validate that quite a few variables have missing values.

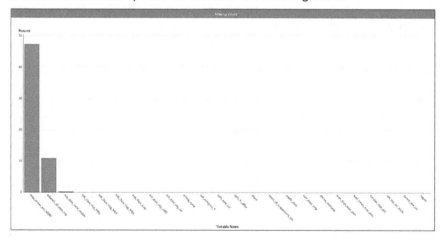

This is an important finding that you will address in the next demonstration.

14. Click **Close**.

15. Double-click the **Pipeline 1** tab and rename it **Data Exploration**. Press the Enter key.

End of Demonstration

Divide the Data

As discussed in Chapter 1, supervised learning starts with a training data set. The observations in a training data set are known as *training cases*. The variables are called *inputs* and *targets*.

In order to train a model, the data must be split into two non-overlapping data sets, *training* and *validation,* some data for training the model and some data for evaluating the model. This is known as *data partitioning*. The split is usually 70:30 but you could use 50:50. Generally, it is best to use more data to train the model than to validate, to prevent under fitting.

Figure 2.3: Partitioning the Input Data Set

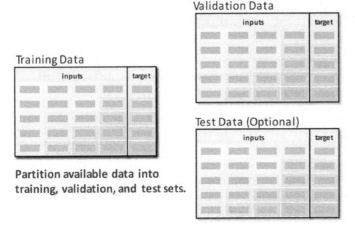

Sometimes a third data set is held out for the final test. This can be important if your testing needs to be completely unbiased. The validation data is used to fine-tune and ultimately choose the best or champion model, so the model developed using this has some bias. The *test* data has not been used to validate or build the model, so this provides completely unbiased results.

For each modeling algorithms, a series of models is constructed, and the models increase in complexity. Some of these models will be too simple (underfit), and others will be too complex (overfit). Each of these models are assessed using the validation data to optimize the complexity of the model and find the balance or sweet spot between being underfit and being overfit.

Honest Assessment

Honest assessment is the technique that uses the validation data set to select the model that performs best. It is important to remember that the validation set is held out and is not used to train, or fit, the model.

> The best model is the simplest model with the highest validation performance.

It is critical that all transformations that are used to prepare the training data are applied to any validation, test, or other holdout data. It is critical that information from test data or holdout data does not leak into the training data. Information leakage can occur in many ways and can potentially lead to overfitting or overly optimistic error measurements. For example, think of taking a mean or median across your data before partitioning and then later using this mean or median to impute missing values across all partitions of your data. In this case, your training data would be aware of information from your validation, test, or holdout partitions. To avoid this type of leakage, values for imputation and other basic transformations should be generated from only the training data or within each partition independently.

Address Rare Events

Rare events are characterized as a rare event relative to your total number of samples; for example, if the proportion of events (desired outcome) is very low. Applications such as detecting fraudulent activity must take special steps to ensure that the data used to train the model include a representative number of fraudulent samples in to capture the event sufficiently. (For example, 1 out of every 1,000 credit card transactions is fraudulent.) Fitting a model to such data without accounting for the extreme imbalance in the occurrence of the event gives you a model that is extremely accurate at telling you absolutely nothing of value! The event in the training data was so rare that a good prediction would be for it not to occur—ever—regardless of the other variables.

Special sampling methods that modify an imbalanced data set, such as *event-based sampling,* are commonly used to provide a more balanced distribution when modeling rare events. Such techniques enable you to build models from a sample with a primary outcome (desired outcome) proportion greater than from the true population proportion. For example, in the data below the primary outcome (yellow dots) is much rarer that the secondary outcome or non-event (blue dots).

Figure 2.4: The Modeling Sample—Secondary and Primary Outcomes

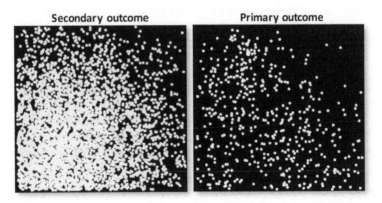

The target-based samples are created by considering primary outcomes cases separately from the secondary outcome cases. All the primary outcome cases (desired outcome) are selected but only some, randomly selected secondary cases (non-events) are included in the sample.

Thus, event-based sampling draws samples separately based on the target events (desired outcomes) and non-events. In the case of a rare event, usually all events are selected. Then each outcome is matched by one or (optimally) more non-event outcomes.

Figure 2.5: Event-Based Sampling – Each Event Outcome is Matched by One or More Non-Event Outcomes.

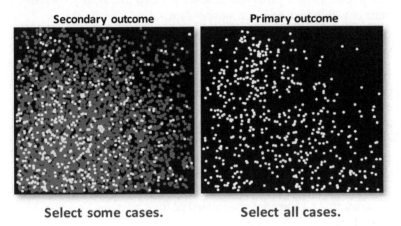

The advantage of event-based sampling is that you can obtain (on the average) a model of similar predictive power with a smaller overall case count. This is in concordance with the idea that the amount of information in a data set with a categorical outcome is determined not by the total number of cases in the data set itself, but instead by the number of cases in the rarest outcome category. For binary target data sets, this is usually the event outcome (Harrell 2006).

This advantage might seem of minimal importance in the age of extremely fast computers. However, the model-fitting process occurs only after the completion of long, tedious, and error-prone data preprocessing. Smaller sample sizes for data preprocessing are usually welcome.

Although it reduces analysis time, event-based sampling also introduces some analysis complications:

- Most model fit statistics (especially those related to prediction decisions) and most of the assessment plots are closely tied to the outcome proportions in the training samples. If the outcome proportion in the training and validation samples do not match the outcome proportions in the scoring population, model performance can be greatly misestimated. To overcome this, you must adjust assessment measures and graphics.

- If the outcome proportions in the training sample and scoring populations do not match, model prediction estimates are biased.

Model Studio

Model Studio automatically adjusts assessment measures, assessment graphs, and prediction estimates for bias. After running the pipeline, which executes an automated sequence of steps to build models, you can examine the score code. The score code contains a section titled **Adjust Posterior Probabilities**. This code block modifies the posterior probability by multiplying it by the ratio of the actual probability to the event-based sampling values specified previously.

Demo 2.2: Modifying the Data Partition

In this demonstration, you modify metadata roles of some variables, explore the advanced project settings, and change the data partition properties.

1. Ensure that the **Demo** project is open and that the variable **churn** is not selected on the Data tab. Reopen the project if you have closed it and deselect **churn** if it is selected by clicking the check box next to the variable's name.

   Note: Here is a caution about selecting variables! Because selecting a variable using the check box **does not** deselect other variables, it is easy for new users to inadvertently re-assign variable roles. Taking a few minutes to get comfortable with the variable selection functionality is considered a best practice for using the software. Here are some tips:

   o Individual variables can be selected for role assignment by either clicking the variable name or by selecting their corresponding check box.

   o Individual variables are deselected after their role is assigned by either clearing their check box or by selecting another variable's name.

   o All variables can be selected or deselected by using the check box at the top of the Variable Name column.

   o More than one variable can be selected at the same time using the check boxes or by holding down the shift key and clicking to select a list of variables.

2. Modify the following properties of the specified variables:

   a. To specify properties of a variable on the Data tab, first select the desired variable. (You can select the check boxes of several variables at the same time.)

b. In the right pane, select the new role or level of the variables.

Note: Variable metadata include the role and measurement level of the variable. Common variable roles are Input, Target, Rejected, Text, and ID, and their meaning is straightforward. Common variable measurement levels are Interval, Binary, Nominal, and Ordinal. See the appropriate drop-down menus in Model Studio for the full list of variable roles and measurement levels.

For the following 11 variables, change the role to **Rejected**:

- **city**
- **city_lat**
- **city_long**
- **data_usage_amt**
- **mou_onnet_6m_normal**
- **mou_roam_6m_normal**
- **region_lat**
- **region_long**
- **state_lat**
- **state_long**
- **tweedie_adjusted**

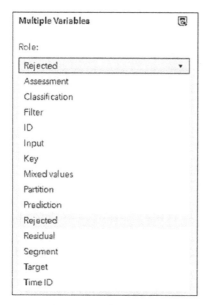

Below are the descriptions of some other variable roles:

○ Assessment: Supports decision processing. Role is currently not used, available for future use.

○ Classification: Model classification for class target. For example, with CHURN as the target, it is the **I_CHURN** variable that has the 0/1 prediction based on predicted probabilities and cutoff used. Note that the classification cutoff is applied only to the binary target.

○ Filter: Used for filtering. The variable with this role has entries filtered out when value=1 and entries kept when value=0. It is used by the Filtering node and the Anomaly Detection node.

○ Key: Observation identifier. This variable must be unique for all observations. This variable is used by the Text Mining node and in the generation of observation-based Model Interpretability reports.

○ Offset: Numeric variable. This variable is used by the GLM node. An offset variable is typically used for a covariate with "known" slope. The parameter for this variable is not estimated, and the variable is simply added to the model.

○ Prediction: Model prediction variables—that is, the prediction for interval target or posterior probabilities for class target. It is used during model assessment.

○ Residual: Error residual, used for informational purposes only.

○ Segment: Segment variable. It is created by the Clustering node for cluster ID that is created. This variable is used when there is a Segment Profiler node or when segmentation modeling is supported.

○ Time ID: Time variable, used for informational purposes only.

- ○ Change the default partition by clicking (**Settings**) in the upper right corner of the window.

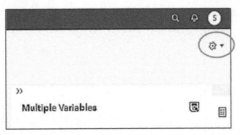

Note: When you create a new project in Model Studio, by default, partitioning is performed. If you want to see or modify the partition settings before creating the project, you can do this from the user settings. In the user settings, the Partition tab enables you to specify the method for partitioning as well as associated percentages. Any settings at this level are global and are applied to any new project created.

3. Select **Project settings**. With **Partition Data** selected in the Project Settings window, change the Training percentage to **70** and the Test percentage to **0**.

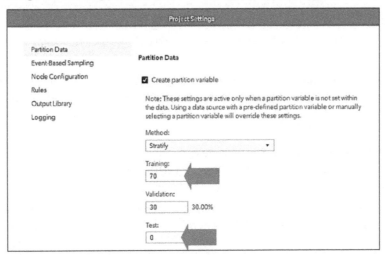

These settings can be edited only if no pipelines in the project have been run. After the first pipeline has been run, the partition tables are created for the project, and partition settings cannot be changed.

Note: Recall that it was shown in the last demonstration that the Partition Data options could also be accessed and changed while the project is being created, under the Advanced settings.

Note: The partition will be stratified based on the target levels. This can be a little confusing because you can specify the partition when you create the project (before you specify a target), but the partition is not created until you run the Data node for the first time, so Model Studio still requires you to specify a target before it creates the partition. Thus, the partition can be stratified based on the target.

4. Select **Event-Based Sampling**.

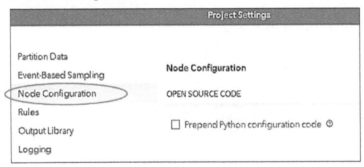

When event-based sampling is turned on (it is off by default), the desired proportion of event and non-event cases can be set after the sampling is done. When they are turned on, the default proportions for both events and non-events after sampling is 50% for each. The sum of both must be 100%. *After a pipeline has been run in the project, the Event-Based Sampling settings cannot be changed.*

Note: Recall that it was shown in the last demonstration that the Event-Based Sampling options could also be accessed and changed while the project is being created, under the Advanced settings.

Keep the Event-Based Sampling options at their default settings.

5. Select **Node Configuration**.

The Node Configuration setting enables code to be prepended to user-written code when the Open Source Code node is used. When the check box is selected, a code editor appears. You can add open-source code in the Python language to the editor. This code is automatically prepended to every Open Source Code node when the **Language** property is set to **Python**. You learn more about the Open Source Code node in a later chapter. Keep the check box deselected.

6. Select **Rules**.

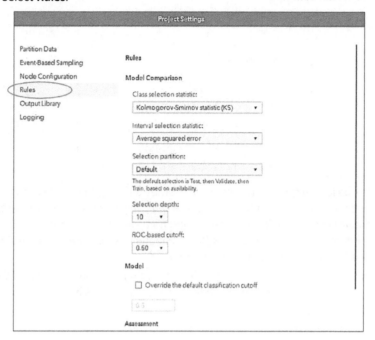

The Rules options can be used to change the selection statistic and partitioned data set that determine the champion model during model comparison. Statistics can be selected for class and interval targets.

Keep the Rules options at their default settings.

7. Be sure to click **Save** because the partition options were changed.

8. Until now, you worked on the Data tab. Click the **Pipelines** tab in the Demo project.

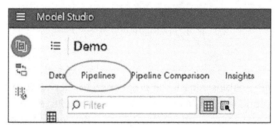

On the Pipelines tab, you can create, modify, and run pipelines. Each pipeline has a unique name and optional description.

Other tabs include the Pipeline Comparison tab and the Insights tab. The Insights tab contains summary reports about the project, champion models, and challenger models. No information is available on the Insights tab unless a pipeline containing a model node has successfully run.

9. The Pipeline Comparison tab and the Insight tab are discussed later in this book. Right-click the **Data** node and select **Run**.

The green check mark in the node indicates that it ran without error. The partition is successfully created.

Note: After you run the Data node, you cannot change the partitioning, event-based sampling, project metadata, project properties, or the target variable. However, you can change variable metadata with the Manage Variables node.

10. The log file for this partitioning action can be viewed. Click **Settings** in the upper right corner.

11. Select **Project logs**.

12. From the Available Logs window, select **Log for Project Partition** and then click **Open**.

The log file can be viewed and even downloaded.

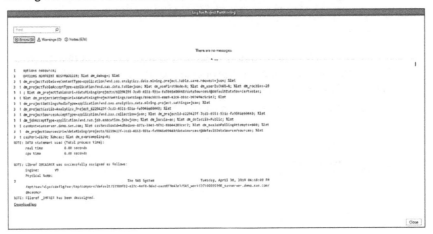

13. Click **Close ▶ Cancel** to return to the pipeline.

End of Demonstration

Data Preparation Best Practices

Data preprocessing covers a range of processes that are different for raw, structured, and unstructured data (from one or multiple sources). Data preprocessing processes focus on improving the quality of data and their completeness, standardizing how it is defined and structured, collecting and consolidating it, and taking transformation steps to make it useful, particularly for machine learning analysis. The selection and type of preparation processes can differ depending on your purpose, your data expertise, how you plan to interact with the data, and what type of question you want to answer.

Table 2.3 summarizes some challenges that you might encounter in preparing your data. It also includes suggestions for how to handle the challenge by using the Data Mining Preprocessing pipeline nodes in Model Studio.

Table 2.3: Data Preparation Challenges

Data Problem	Common Challenges	Suggested Best Practice
Data collection	Incomplete data	Enrich the data
	High-dimensional data	Dimension reduction (Feature Extraction, Variable Clustering, and Variable Selection nodes)
	Sparsity	Change representation of data (Transformations node)
	Biased data	Take time to understand the business problem and its context
"Untidy" data	Value ranges as columns Multiple variables in the same column Variables in both rows and columns	Transform the data with SAS code (Code node)
Outliers	Out-of-range numeric values and unknown categorical values in score data	Discretization (Transformations node) Winsorizing (Imputation node)
Sparse target variables	Low primary event occurrence rate Overwhelming preponderance of zero or missing values in target	Proportional oversampling
Variables of disparate magnitudes	Misleading variable importance Distance measure imbalance Gradient dominance	Standardization (Transformations node)

Data Problem	Common Challenges	Suggested Best Practice
High-cardinality variables	Overfitting Unknown categorical values in holdout data	Binning (Transformations node) Replacement (Replacement node)
Missing data	Information loss Bias	Binning (Transformations node) Imputation (Imputation node)
Strong multicollinearity	Unstable parameter estimates	Dimension reduction (Feature Extraction, Variable Clustering, and Variable Selection nodes)

Some of these challenges can also be handled in the modeling stage, such as using tree-based methods for handling missing data automatically, which is discussed in subsequent chapters.

Building and extracting good features requires experience and domain knowledge about the problem and the data that you are working with. Here are the four groups used to classify feature engineering techniques:

- Constructing new features from a combination of one or more existing features
- Selecting key features using supervised or unsupervised techniques
- Clustering features into groups
- Extracting new features from existing features

There are various feature engineering techniques (PROCs and corresponding nodes in Model Studio) available in SAS Viya. Some of them you have already dealt with in previous sections.

For more details, see "4 ways to classify feature engineering in SAS Viya."
(https://communities.sas.com/t5/SAS-Communities-Library/4-ways-to-classify-feature-engineering-in-SAS-Viya/ta-p/508855)

Model Studio: Feature Engineering Template

Figure 2.6 shows the feature engineering pipeline template in Model Studio. Whether you perform feature selection or feature extraction, your goal is to include the subset of features that describe most, but not all, of the variance and to reduce the signal-to-noise ratio in your data. Although intuition would tell you that elimination of features equates to a loss of information, in the end, this loss is compensated for by the ability of the model to more accurately map the remaining features to the target in a lower-dimensional space. The result is simpler models, shorter training times, improved generalization, and a greater ability to visualize the feature space.

Figure 2.6: Feature Engineering template

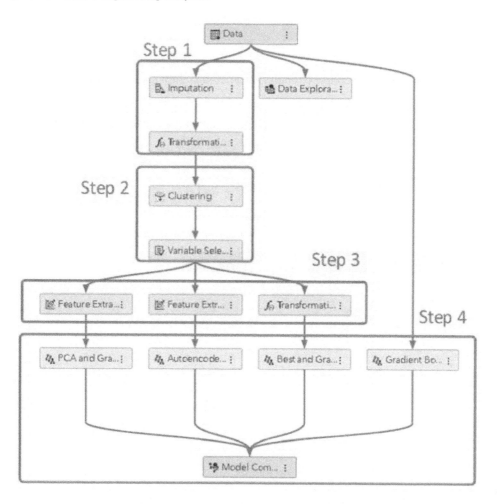

Model Studio: Feature Engineering Template

In Figure 2.6, the Imputation node imputes missing values in interval inputs with their respective medians and creates missing indicators that are subsequently used as inputs.

More effective transformations for high-cardinality variables include target-based transformations such as creating a feature that captures the frequency of the occurrence of each level of the nominal variable. For high cardinality, this helps a lot! You might use ratio or percentage of a level to all the levels present. Similarly, you can encode a high-cardinality variable by using another numeric input variable by choosing the max, min, or median value of that variable for each level of the high-cardinality nominal variable. WOE (weight of evidence) encoding is another powerful target-based transformation.

Demo 2.3: Running the Feature Engineering Pipeline Template

In this demonstration, you run the automated feature engineering pipeline template on **commsdata**.

1. Click the plus sign next to the current pipeline tab in the upper left corner of the canvas.

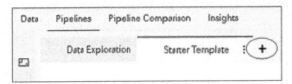

2. In the New Pipeline window, for **Template**, select **Browse templates**.

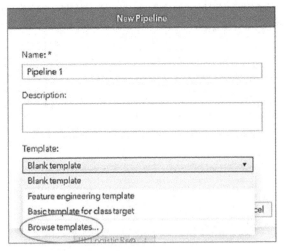

Note: Some of the options on the Template menu might be different on your computer.

3. In the Browse Templates window, select **Feature engineering template**. Click **OK**.

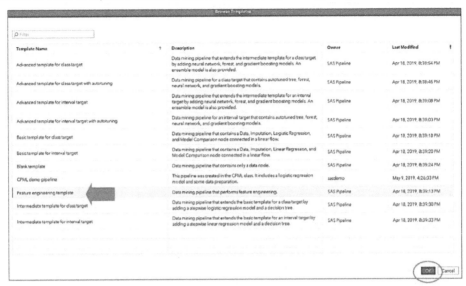

4. In the New Pipeline window, enter the name **Feature Engineering**.

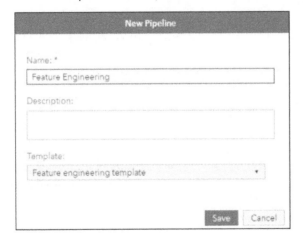

5. Click **Save**.

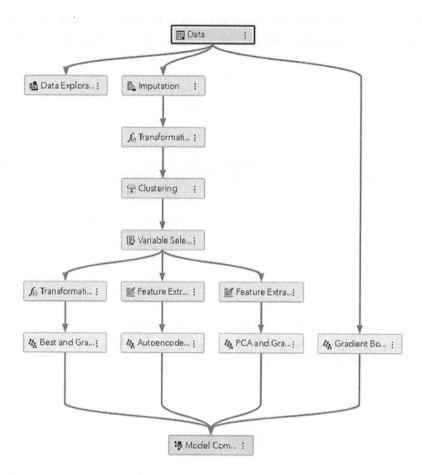

The template automatically creates engineered features by using popular feature transformation and extraction techniques. The idea is to automatically learn a set of features (from potentially noisy, raw data) that can be useful in supervised learning tasks without manually creating engineered features.

6. Right-click the **Data Exploration** node and select **Run.**

7. Open the results. Expand the **Class Variables Summaries** bar chart and observe that the data does not contain high-cardinality variables.

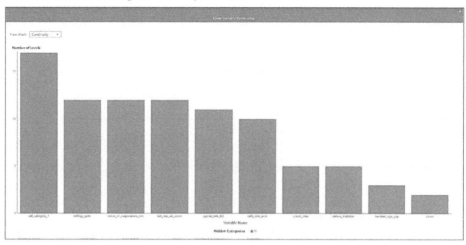

8. Exit the maximized view and close the results.
9. Expand the **Nodes** pane on the left side of the canvas. Expand **Data Mining Preprocessing**.

10. Click and drag the **Manage Variables** node and drop it between the Data node and the Imputation node.

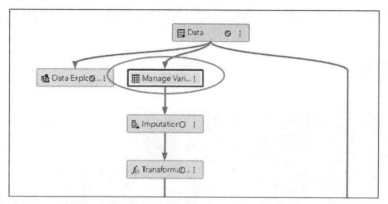

11. Run the **Manage Variables** node.
12. After the node runs, right-click the node again and select the **Manage Variables** option.
13. In the Manage Variables window, click the **Comments** column heading twice to sort by this column. Notice that the variables that exceed the maximum number of levels cutoff are grouped together.
14. Select **issue_level1**. This variable has 55 categories.

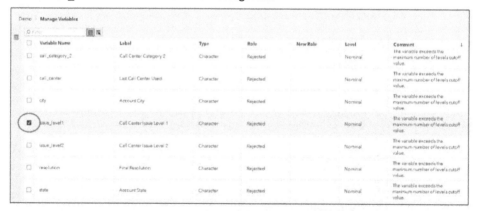

call_category_2, call_center, city, issue_level1, issue_level2, resolution, and **state** are all high-cardinality nominal input variables that were rejected earlier due to the default cutoff of 20 categories. You can select all of them if you want them to be included in the analysis. To reduce the processing time, we select only one of them.

15. Change its role from Rejected to **Input**.

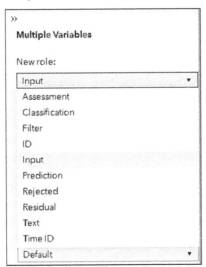

16. After altering the metadata, ensure that you have deselected these variables.
17. Select **Close** to exit the Manage Variables window. Click **Save** when asked if you want to save the changes. The attribute alterations are applied.
18. Run the Variable Selection node.

    Resulting output variables from the Clustering node such as cluster label (**_CLUSTER_ID_**) and distance to centroid (**_DISTANCE_**) were used as inputs in the Variable Selection node.
19. From here on, select each node one-by-one, right-click, and select **Run**. Do *not* click the Run pipeline icon.

    Note: Running this template can substantially increase the run time. Remember that limited resources are available in your class environment. Automatic hyperparameter tuning (autotuning) is turned on to find the optimal hyperparameter settings of the gradient boosting algorithm, so the comparison between feature sets is fairer and not dependent on the hyperparameters. However, keep in mind that autotuning comes with an additional computing cost. If this step takes too long to run, you can change the autotuning settings, or simply turn it off and use the default hyperparameter settings. With the default settings in the template, we recommend running this pipeline node-by-node. You might encounter an error of insufficient resources if you run the entire pipeline.
20. After the entire pipeline has successfully run, right-click the **Model Comparison** node and select **Results**.

21. Examine the Model Comparison table. Unless specified, the default fit statistic (KS) is used for selecting a champion model with a class target.

	Champion	Name	Algorithm Name	KS (Youden)	Misclassification Rate
Model Comparison					
	⊠	Best and Gradient Boosting	Gradient Boosting	0.5843	0.0589
		Gradient Boosting	Gradient Boosting	0.5775	0.0590
		Autoencoder and Gradient Boosting	Gradient Boosting	0.5715	0.0590
		PCA and Gradient Boosting	Gradient Boosting	0.5767	0.0592

Explore the results.

Compare the performance of the four different feature sets (three automatically engineered sets and the original set without target encoding).

It is important to remember that using this template does not guarantee that one of the automatically created feature sets performs better than the original features for your data because every data set is unique, and this template uses only a few techniques. Instead, the goal of this is to show an example of how you can create different automatically engineered feature sets by using many other tools provided in Model Studio and test their performance in a similar way with minimal effort.

22. Click **Close** to close the Model Comparison Results window.

End of Demonstration

Quiz

1. The Data Exploration node in Model Studio enables you to do which of the following? (Select all that apply.)

   a. Profile a data set.

   b. Observe the most important inputs or suspicious variables.

   c. Drop variables that have deviation from normality.

   d. Select variables with a high percentage of nonmissing values as inputs.

2. Which of the following statements is **true** while defining metadata in Model Studio?

   a. The Data tab enables you to edit variable values by changing the lower limit or the upper limit (or both).

   b. The Replacement node cannot replace outliers and unknown class levels unless you specify the metadata prior to this node.

   c. Metadata properties can be defined either on the Data tab or in the Manage Variables node and then can be invoked by using an appropriate node.

   d. None of the above.

Chapter 3: Preparing Your Data: Missing and Unstructured Data

Introduction

In this chapter, we look at dealing with missing data and then focus and how to handle unstructured data such as textual data. By *unstructured,* we mean data that is not provided in a traditional row-column database. It is the opposite of *structured* data—the data stored in fields in database. Unstructured data is typically text-heavy, but can also contain dates, numbers, and facts.

Dealing with Missing Data

Missing values can be theoretically and practically problematic for many machine learning tasks, especially when missing values are present in the target variable. This section addresses only the more common scenario of missing values in input variables. The issue of missing values in data is (nearly) always present and always a concern. When faced with missing values in input variables, you must consider whether missing values are distributed randomly or whether missingness is somehow predictive of the target. If missing values appear at random in the input data, the input rows that contain missing values can be dropped from the analysis without introducing bias into the model. However, such a *complete case analysis* can remove a tremendous amount of information from the training data and reduce the predictive accuracy of the model. Many modeling algorithms in SAS Visual Data Mining and Machine Learning operate under complete case analysis (for example, linear and logistic regression, neural networks and support vector machines).

Complete case analysis assumes that data are missing completely at random and so does the mean imputation. Imputation can be a more complicated issue, when missingness is nonrandom, dependent on inputs, or canonical. In this book, we use a simple approach that is often useful, but you should be aware that it is not always the best thing to do.

Missing values affect both model construction and model deployment.

Figure 3.1: Missing Values—Problem 1

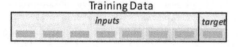

Consequence: Missing values can significantly reduce your amount of training data for regression modeling.

Even a smattering of missing values can cause an enormous loss of data in high dimensions. For example, suppose that each of the k input variables is missing at random with probability α. In this situation, the expected proportion of complete cases is as follows:

$$(1-\alpha)^k$$

Therefore, a 1% probability of missing (α=.01) for 100 inputs retains only 37% of the data for analysis, 200 keeps 13%, and 400 preserves 2%. If the "missingness" were increased to 5% (α=.05), then less than 1% of the data would be available with 100 inputs.

The second missing value problem relates to model deployment or using the prediction formula. How would a model built on the complete cases score a new case if it had a missing value? If there is missingness in your training data, it is very likely that your scoring data or the new data would also have, ideally, a similar type of missingness, but in amount.

Figure 3.2: Missing Values—Problem 2

$$\text{logit}(\hat{p}) = -0.81 + 0.92 \cdot x_1 + 1.11 \cdot x_2$$

Predict: $(x_1, x_2) = (0.3, ?)$

Problem: What if the scoring data also have missing values?

$$\text{logit}(\hat{p}) = -0.81 + 0.92 \cdot x_1 + 1.11 \cdot ?$$

Predict: $(x_1, x_2) = (0.3, ?)$

$$\text{logit}(p) = ?$$

Consequence: Prediction formulas cannot score cases with missing values.

The following section describes some common techniques to deal with the two problems of missing values. We will see that the appropriate remedy depends on the reason for the missing values.

Managing Missing Values

Missingness can be predictive. Retaining information that is associated with missing values, including the missing values themselves, can increase the predictive accuracy of a model.

The following table describes practices for accounting for missingness in training a machine learning model and describes how missing values must also be handled when scoring new data.

Table 3.1: Missing Values

Practice Name	Practice Description
Naïve Bayes	Naïve Bayes models elegantly handle missing values for training and scoring by computing the likelihood based on the observed features. Because of conditional independence between the features, naïve Bayes ignores a feature only when its value is missing. Thus, you do not need to handle missing values before fitting a naïve Bayes model unless you believe that the missingness is not at random. For efficiency reasons, some implementations of naïve Bayes remove entire rows from the training process whenever a missing value is encountered. When missing is treated as a categorical level, infrequent missing values in new data can be problematic when they are not present in training data because the missing level will have had no probability associated with it during training. You can solve this problem by ignoring the offending feature in the likelihood computation when scoring.
Decision trees	In general, imputation, missing markers, binning, and special scoring considerations are not required for missing values when you use a decision tree. Decision trees allow for the elegant and direct use of missing values in two common ways.
	When a splitting rule is determined, missing can be a valid input value, and missing values can either be placed on the side of the splitting rule that makes the best training prediction or be assigned to a separate branch in a split.
	Surrogate rules can be defined to allow the tree to split on a surrogate variable when a missing value is encountered. For example, a surrogate rule could be defined that allows a decision tree to split on the state variable when the ZIP code variable is missing.
Missing markers	Missing markers are binary variables that record whether the value of another variable is missing. They are used to preserve information about missingness so that missingness can be modeled. Missing markers can be used in a model to replace the original corresponding variable with missing values, or they can be used in a model alongside an imputed version of the original variable.

Practice Name	Practice Description
Imputation	Imputation refers to replacing a missing value with information that is derived from nonmissing values in the training data. Simple imputation schemes include replacing a missing value in an input variable with the mean or mode of that variable's nonmissing values. For nonnormally distributed variables or variables that have a high proportion of missing values, simple mean or mode imputation can drastically alter a variable's distribution and negatively impact predictive accuracy. Even when variables are normally distributed and contain a low proportion of missing values, creating missing markers and using them in the model alongside the new, imputed variables is a suggested practice. Decision trees can also be used to derive imputed values. A decision tree can be trained using a variable that has missing values as its target and all the other variables in the data set as inputs. In this way, the decision tree can learn plausible replacement values for the missing values in the temporary target variable. This approach requires one decision tree for every input variable that has missing values, so it can become computationally expensive for large, dirty training sets. More sophisticated imputation approaches, including multiple imputation (MI), should be considered for small data sets (Rubin 1987).
Binning	Interval input variables that have missing values can be discretized into many bins according to their original numeric values to create new categorical, nominal variables. Missing values in the original variable can simply be added to an additional bin in the new variable. Categorical input variables that have missing values can be assigned to new categorical nominal variables that have the same categorical levels as the corresponding original variables plus one new level for missing values. Because binning introduces additional nonlinearity into a predictive model and can be less damaging to an input variable's original distribution than imputation, binning is generally considered acceptable, if not beneficial, until the binning process begins to contribute to overfitting. However, you might not want to use binning if the ordering of the values in an input variable is important, because the ordering information is changed or erased by introducing a missing bin into the otherwise ordered values.

Practice Name	Practice Description
Scoring missing data	If a decision tree or decision tree ensemble is used in training, missing values in new data will probably be scored automatically according to the splitting rules or the surrogate rules of the trained tree (or trees). If another type of algorithm was trained, then missing values in new data must be processed in the exact way that they were processed in the training data before the model was trained.

Source: *Best Practices for Machine Learning Applications* (Wujek, Hall, and Güneş 2016), SAS Institute Inc.

Model Studio: Handling Missing Values

In Model Studio, you can use a one-size-fits-all approach to handle missing values. In any case, with a missing input measurement, the missing value is replaced with a fixed value. The net effect is to modify an input's distribution to include a point mass at the selected fixed number. The location of the point mass in synthetic distribution methods is not arbitrary. Ideally, it should be chosen to have minimal impact on the magnitude of an input's association with the target. With many modeling methods, this can be achieved by locating the point mass at the input's mean value.

Model Studio supports the following imputation methods for interval inputs:

- **Cluster Mean** specifies that missing values are replaced with the arithmetic average of the observation's cluster. In order to use this method of imputation, you must have a Clustering node in the pipeline immediately preceding the Imputation node.

- **Constant Value** specifies that missing values are replaced with the value that is specified in the **Constant number value** field. The default value is 0.

- **Maximum** specifies that missing values are replaced with the maximum value for the variable found in training.

- **Mean** specifies that missing values are replaced with the arithmetic average.

- **Median** specifies that missing values are replaced with the midpoint of a frequency distribution of the observed values.

- **Midrange** specifies that missing values are replaced with the maximum value plus the minimum value divided by 2.

Model Studio: Handling Missing Values

- **Minimum** specifies that missing values are replaced with the minimum value for the variable found in training.

- **None** specifies that only the imputations specified in the Data pane are performed.

The default value is **Mean**.

Model Studio supports the following imputation methods for class inputs:

- **Cluster Count** specifies that missing values are replaced with the variable's most frequent nonmissing value in the observation's cluster. In order to use this method of imputation, you must have a Clustering node in the pipeline immediately preceding the Imputation node.

- **Constant Value** specifies that missing values are replaced with a character specified in the Constant character value field.

- **Count** specifies that missing values are replaced with the variable's most frequent value. There are no other configurations to set.

- **Distribution** specifies that missing values are replaced with randomly assigned values from an empirical distribution of the nonmissing values of the variable. As a result, the Distribution imputation typically does not significantly change the distribution of the data. The initial seed value for randomization is specified in the **Distribution method random seed** field. The default value is 12345.

- **None** specifies that only the imputations specified in the Data pane are performed.

The default value is **Count**.

Note: The default method specifies the default transformation method for all class/interval input variables. Any transformation specified in the metadata takes precedence over the method specified here.

Demo 3.1: Modifying and Correcting Source Data

In this demonstration, you use the Data tab and Replacement node to modify a data source.

1. Click the **Data** tab.

2. Right-click the **Role** column and select **Sort ▶ Sort (ascending)**.

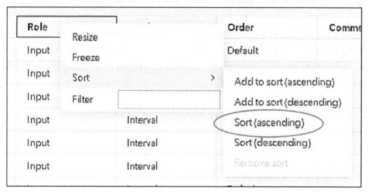

All the Input variables are grouped together after the ID variable (or variables) and before the Rejected variables.

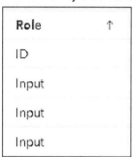

3. Scroll to the right. Right-click the **Minimum** column and select **Sort ▶ Add to sort (ascending)**.

   Variables with negative minimum values are grouped together.

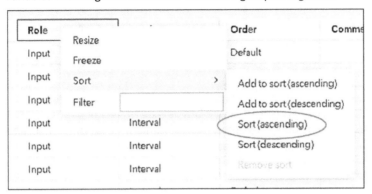

   Note: Add to sort means that the initial sorting done by role still holds, so the sort on minimum values takes place within each sorted role group.

4. Select the following ***interval*** input variables:

   (Scroll back to the left to find the Variable Name column. You select 22 interval input variables.)

   ○ **tot_mb_data_roam_curr**

   ○ **seconds_of_data_norm**

   ○ **lifetime_value**

   ○ **bill_data_usg_m03**

   ○ **bill_data_usg_m06**

   ○ **voice_tot_bill_mou_curr**

   ○ **tot_mb_data_curr**

   ○ **mb_data_usg_roamm01** through **mb_data_usg_roamm03**

   ○ **mb_data_usg_m01** through **mb_data_usg_m03**

   ○ **calls_total**

   ○ **call_in_pk**

   ○ **calls_out_pk**

   ○ **call_in_offpk**

   ○ **calls_out_offpk**

   ○ **mb_data_ndist_mo6m**

   ○ **data_device_age**

   ○ **mou_onnet_pct_MOM**

   ○ **mou_total_pct_MOM**

Note: Selecting the check box of a variable and then selecting another variable while holding down the Shift key selects those two variables and all the variables between them.

Note: You can drag and drop the Minimum column to the left, closer to the Variable Name column so that you can see the Minimum column along with the variable names.

5. In the right pane, enter **0.0** in the **Lower Limit** field in the Multiple Variables window. This specifies the lower limit to be used in the Filtering and Replacement nodes with the Metadata limits method.

Note: This is customer billing data, and negative values often imply that there is a credit applied to the customer's account, so it is not outside the realm of possibility that there are negative numbers in these columns. However, there is a general practice to convert negative values to zeros in telecom data.

Note that you did not edit any variable values. Instead, you have just set a metadata property that can be invoked.

6. Click the **Pipelines** tab.

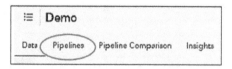

7. Select the **Basic Template** pipeline.

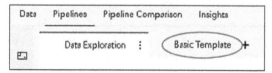

Notice that because of the change in metadata, the green check marks in the nodes in the pipeline have been changed to gray circles. This indicates that the nodes need to be rerun to reflect the change in metadata. The nodes will show the green check marks again when the pipeline is rerun.

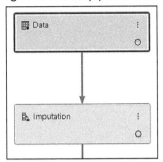

8. Expand the **Nodes** pane on the left side of the canvas.
9. Expand Data Mining Preprocessing.

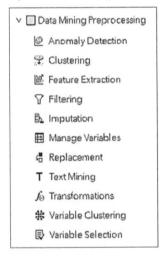

10. Click and drag the **Replacement** node and drop it *between* the Data node and the Imputation node.

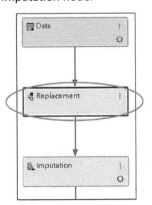

The Replacement node can be used to replace outliers and unknown class levels with specified values. This is where you invoke the metadata property of the lower limit that you set before.

11. In the options panel on the right side, complete the following for the Interval Variables section:

 a. Set **Default limits method** to **Metadata limits**.

 b. Change **Alternate limits method** to **(none)**. This property specifies the alternate method by which the lower and upper limits are derived for interval variables when Metadata limits is the default limits method and the metadata limits are missing.

 c. Leave **Replacement value** as the default, **Computed limits**. Another option is Missing value.

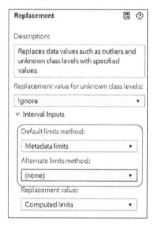

12. Right-click the **Replacement** node and select **Run**. Negative values are replaced with zeros in the training partition of the data.

13. View the results of the Replacement node. The Interval Variables table shows which variables now have a lower limit of 0.

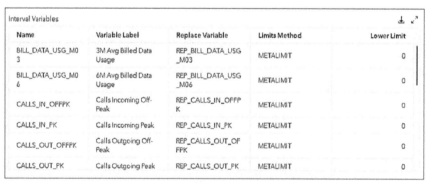

Name	Variable Label	Replace Variable	Limits Method	Lower Limit
BILL_DATA_USG_M03	3M Avg Billed Data Usage	REP_BILL_DATA_USG_M03	METALIMIT	0
BILL_DATA_USG_M06	6M Avg Billed Data Usage	REP_BILL_DATA_USG_M06	METALIMIT	0
CALLS_IN_OFFPK	Calls Incoming Off-Peak	REP_CALLS_IN_OFFPK	METALIMIT	0
CALLS_IN_PK	Calls Incoming Peak	REP_CALLS_IN_PK	METALIMIT	0
CALLS_OUT_OFFPK	Calls Outgoing Off-Peak	REP_CALLS_OUT_OFFPK	METALIMIT	0
CALLS_OUT_PK	Calls Outgoing Peak	REP_CALLS_OUT_PK	METALIMIT	0

14. Close the results window of the Replacement node.

15. To update the remainder of the results of the pipeline, click **Run Pipeline**.

16. Right-click the **Model Comparison** node and select **Results**.

 Model performance can be seen in the Model Comparison table.

Model Comparison				
Champion	Name	Algorithm Name	KS (Youden)	Misclassification Rate
☑	Logistic Regression	Logistic Regression	0.5480	0.0662

17. Select **Close** to return to the pipeline.

End of Demonstration

 Demo 3.2: Alternate Method for Modifying and Correcting Source Data Using the Manage Variables Node

In addition to using the Data tab, the Manage Variables node is another powerful tool that can be used to modify and correct data. The Manage Variables node is used directly within a pipeline.

Note: The Data tab should be used to modify and correct source data as described in the previous demonstration. This demonstration provides another means of assigning metadata rules to data. **One drawback to the method shown in this demonstration is that rules defined in the Manage Variables node are not saved if the pipeline is saved to the Exchange.**

1. Select the **Basic Template** pipeline.
2. Expand the **Nodes** pane on the left side of the canvas.
3. Expand **Data Mining Preprocessing**.

4. Click and drag the **Manage Variables** node and drop it *between* the Data node and the Imputation node.

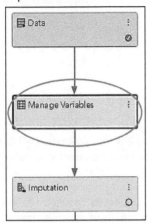

Note: Notice that after the Manage Variables node is placed in the pipeline, any nodes beneath it in the same path change in appearance from showing a green check mark to showing a gray circle. This indicates that they require a rerun.

The Manage Variables node is a preprocessing node that enables you to make modifications to the metadata while it is within a Model Studio pipeline.

You see a window indicating that the node must be run before it can be opened.

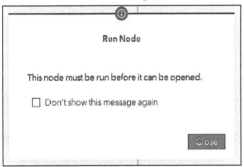

5. Click **Close** in the Run Node window.

6. Right-click the **Manage Variables** node and select **Run**.

   This reads the observations and variables and sets up the incoming variables before modifying their metadata.

7. After the node runs, right-click the node again and select the **Manage Variables** option.

8. In the Manage Variables window, right-click the **Role** column and select **Sort** ▶ **Sort (ascending)**.

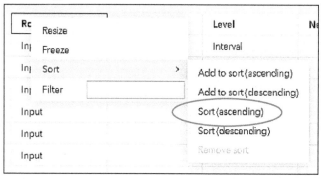

9. Scroll to the right. Right-click the **Minimum** column and select **Sort** ▶ **Add to sort (ascending)**.

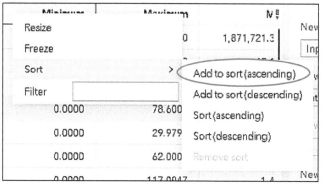

10. Modify the following properties of the variables specified:

    a. To modify the metadata of a variable in the Manage Variables window, first select the desired variable. (You might want to select several variables at one time.)

       Select the following *interval* input variables:

       - **tot_mb_data_roam_curr**
       - **seconds_of_data_norm**
       - **lifetime_value**
       - **bill_data_usg_m03**
       - **bill_data_usg_m06**
       - **voice_tot_bill_mou_curr**
       - **tot_mb_data_curr**
       - **mb_data_usg_roamm01** through **mb_data_usg_roamm03**
       - **mb_data_usg_m01** through **mb_data_usg_m03**
       - **calls_total**
       - **call_in_pk**

- **calls_out_pk**
- **call_in_offpk**
- **calls_out_offpk**
- **mb_data_ndist_mo6m**
- **data_device_age**
- **mou_onnet_pct_MOM**
- **mou_total_pct_MOM**

(Scroll back to the left to find the Variable Name column. You select 22 interval input variables.)

Note: Selecting the check box of a variable and then selecting another variable while holding down the Shift key selects those two variables and all the variables between them.

a. In the right pane, enter **0.0** in the **New lower limit** field in the Multiple Variables window.

No variable values were edited. Instead, a metadata property has been defined that can be invoked by using an appropriate node.

11. Select **Close** to exit the Manage Variables window. Click **Save** when asked if you want to save the changes. The attribute alterations are applied.

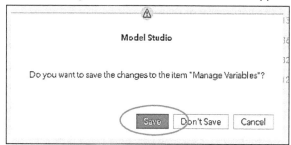

12. Click and drag the **Replacement** node and drop it *between* the Manage Variables node and the Imputation node.

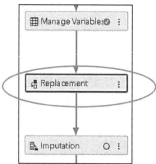

13. In the options panel on the right side, complete the following for Interval Variables:

    a.   Set **Default limits method** to **Metadata limits**.

    b.   Change **Alternate limits method** to **None**.

    c.   Leave **Replacement value** as the default, **Computed limits**.

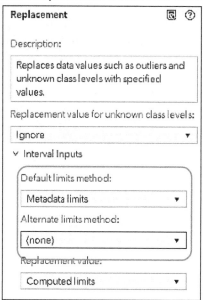

14. Right-click the **Replacement** node and select **Run**. Negative values are replaced with zeros in the training partition of the data.

15. Close the results window of the Replacement node.

End of Demonstration

Add Unstructured Data

Unstructured, free-form text data are commonly available in business. For example, survey results, call center logs, product reviews, social media feeds, blogs, customer feedback, and other text data contain information useful for predictive modeling outcomes that is not readily available in structured data. It is therefore extremely informative to analyze these combined text data sources and use them along with the structured data.

> Organizations today are generating and storing tremendous amounts of data. IDC has estimated that up to 80% of that is *unstructured*—that is, information that either does not have a predefined data model or is not organized in a predefined way. Unstructured data includes formats such as audio, images, video, and textual content. Although this type of information is often rich with insights, unlocking the full potential within these complex data sources can be tricky. Much of the big data explosion is due to the rapid growth of unstructured data!
>
> *Source: IDC Digital Universe Study, sponsored by EMC, May 2010.*

Often, you might be able to improve the predictive ability of your models that use only numerical data if you add selected text mining results (clusters or SVD values) to the numerical data. Data are processed in two phases: text parsing and transformation. Text parsing processes textual data into a term-by-document frequency matrix. Transformations such as singular value decomposition (SVD) alter this matrix into a data set that is suitable for data mining purposes. A document collection with thousands of documents and terms can be represented in a compact and efficient form.

Figure 3.3: Text Mining Feature Extraction

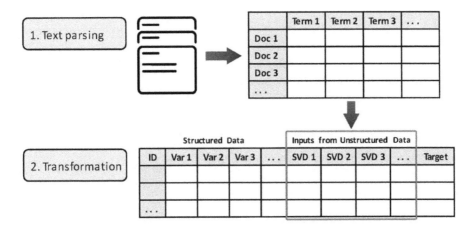

Single Value Decomposition (SVD)

SVD projects the high-dimensional document and term spaces into a lower-dimensional space. It decomposes a matrix into three other low-ranking matrices. The singular values can be thought of as providing a measure of importance used to decide how many dimensions to keep.

$$\mathbf{A} = U\,S\,V^T \text{ where}$$

- **A** is the matrix that we want to decompose, with m terms and n documents.
- U is an orthogonal $m \times r$ matrix.
- S is a diagonal $r \times r$ matrix consisting of r positive 'singular values' $s_1 \geq s_2 \geq \ldots \geq s_r > 0$.
- V is an orthogonal $r \times n$ matrix and V^T represents a matrix transpose.
- r is the rank of matrix **A**. As discussed previously, a document collection with thousands of documents and terms can be represented in a compact and efficient form using SVD transformation.

Using SVD for Dimensionality Reduction

As discussed previously, a document collection with thousands of documents and terms can be represented in compact and efficient form using SVD transformation, resulting in a matrix with a lower rank that is said to approximate the original matrix.

To do this, we perform an SVD operation on the original data and select the top k largest singular values in Σ. These columns can be selected from Σ and the rows selected from V^T.

An approximate **B** of the original matrix **A** can then be reconstructed.

$$B = U\Sigma_k V_k^T$$

In text processing, this approach can be used on matrices of word occurrences or word frequencies in documents and is called *latent semantic analysis* or *latent semantic indexing*.

Understanding SVD Pictorially

SVD decomposition allows us to express our *original matrix as a linear combination of low-rank matrices*. Rank is a measure of how much unique information is stored in a matrix. So we are able to represent our large matrix A by three smaller matrices U, S and V. In other words, we reduce a matrix to its constituent parts in order to make certain subsequent matrix calculation.

So how does this help in dimensionality reduction? To help answer this it is helpful to look at an alternate representation of the decomposition. See the figure below.

Figure 3.4: Matrix Decomposition

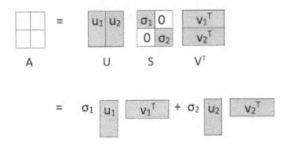

The SVD dimensions are ordered by the size of their singular values (their *importance*). In a practical application, you will observe that only the first few, say k, singular values are large. The rest of the singular values approach zero. As a result, terms except the first few can be ignored without losing much of the information. See how the matrices are truncated in the figure below.

Figure 3.5: Truncating Matrices

We can obtain a *k-rank approximation* of A by selecting the first k singular values and truncating the 3 matrices accordingly.

For example, consider three documents:

Doc 1: Error: invalid message file format

Doc 2: Error: unable to open message file using message path

Doc 3: Error: unable to format variable

These three documents generate the following 11 x 3 term-document matrix **A**.

		doc 1	doc 2	doc 3
Term 1	error	1	1	1
Term 2	invalid	1	0	0
Term 3	message	1	2	0
Term 4	file	1	1	0
Term 5	format	1	0	1
Term 6	unable	0	1	1
Term 7	to	0	1	1
Term 8	open	0	1	0
Term 9	using	0	1	0
Term 10	path	0	1	0
Term 11	variable	0	0	1

We compute the SVD decomposition and obtain the separate matrices, U, S, and V.

The product $\mathbf{U}^T\mathbf{A}$ produces the SVD projections of the original document vectors. These are the document SVD input values (COL columns) that you will see in the next demonstration produced by the Text Mining node (except that they are normalized for each document as explained later).

This amounts to forming linear combinations of the original (possibly weighted) term frequencies for each document.

First, project the first document vector $d1$ into a three-dimensional SVD space by the matrix multiplication.

$$U^T d_1 =$$

$$
\begin{vmatrix}
0.43 & 0.11 & 0.55 & 0.33 & 0.21 & 0.31 & 0.31 & 0.22 & 0.22 & 0.22 & 0.09 \\
0.30 & 0.13 & -0.37 & -0.12 & 0.55 & 0.18 & 0.18 & -0.25 & -0.25 & -0.25 & 0.43 \\
0.11 & 0.52 & 0.2 & 0.36 & 0.27 & -0.41 & -0.41 & -0.16 & -0.16 & -0.16 & -0.25
\end{vmatrix}
\ast\
\begin{vmatrix}
1 \\ 1 \\ 1 \\ 1 \\ 1 \\ 0 \\ 0 \\ 0 \\ 0 \\ 0 \\ 0
\end{vmatrix}
$$

U^T was obtained using the SVD matrix function in PROC IML applied to matrix **A**.

d_1 is the term-frequency vector for document 1.

The product of the 3 x 11 U^T matrix with the 11 x 1 term-frequency vector d_1 for doc 1 gives the following:

$$U^T d_1 = \hat{d}_1 = \begin{vmatrix} 1.63 \\ 0.49 \\ 1.45 \end{vmatrix}$$

And then, write this in transposed form with column labels.

$$\hat{d}_1^{\,T} = \begin{vmatrix} \text{SVD1} & \text{SVD2} & \text{SVD3} \\ 1.63 & 0.49 & 1.45 \end{vmatrix}$$

The SVD dimensions are ordered by the size of their singular values (their *importance*). Therefore, the document vector can simply be truncated to obtain a lower-dimensional projection.

The 2-D representation for doc 1 is $\begin{vmatrix} \text{SVD1} & \text{SVD2} \\ 1.63 & 0.49 \end{vmatrix}$.

As a final step, these coordinate values are normalized so that the sums of squares for each document are 1.0.

Using this document's 2-D representation, $1.63^2 + 0.49^2 = 2.847$ and $\sqrt{2.897} = 1.70$.

Therefore, the final 2-D representation for doc 1 would be $\begin{vmatrix} \text{SVD1} & \text{SVD2} \\ 0.96 & 0.29 \end{vmatrix}$.

These are the SVD1 and SVD2 values that you would see for this document. A similar calculation is performed for the other two documents.

This brief discussion is based on the very helpful paper "Taming Text with the SVD" by Dr. Russ Albright of SAS R&D (recommended reading and readily available to download from the internet).

Demo 3.3: Adding Text Mining Features

In this demonstration, you create new features using the Text Mining node. The **commsdata** data has five text variables. You use the text variable **verbatims**, which represents free-form, unstructured data from a customer survey.

Of the four text variables not used in this demonstration, two are already rejected and two require a metadata change to be rejected. The variables **call_center** and **issue_level1** already have roles of Rejected, but the roles for **issue_level2** and **resolution** need to be changed to **Rejected**.

1. Click the **Data** tab. Verify that previously selected variables are deselected.
2. Right-click the **Role** column and select **Sort ᵭ Sort (ascending)**.

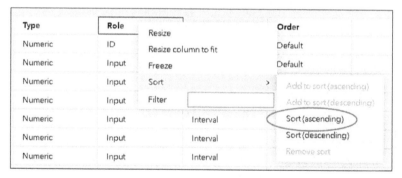

3. Scroll until the end of the list. All the unrejected Text variables are listed together. Select **issue_level2** and **resolution**.

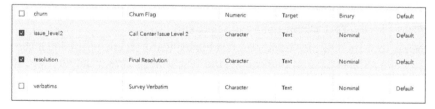

In the pane on the right, change the role from Text to **Rejected**.

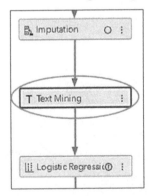

Multiple Variables

Role:

Text ▾

Assessment
Classification
Filter
ID
Input
Prediction
Rejected ←
Residual
Text
Time ID

This ensures that only the **verbatims** variable is used as an input for the Text Mining node.

4. Return to the Starter Template pipeline. (Click the **Pipelines** tab and then select **Starter Template**.)

5. From the pane on the left, drag and drop a **Text Mining** node *between* the Imputation node and the Logistic Regression node.

6. Right-click the **Text Mining** node and select **Run**.

Note: To score new data using your text mining features, you might find it useful to save the ASTORE binaries that contain the Text Mining score code. After you save the ASTORE file, you can use it to score new text data in SAS Studio.

7. Open the results of the Text Mining node. Many windows are available, including the Kept Terms and Dropped Terms tables. These tables include terms used and ignored, respectively, during the text analysis.

Kept Terms					Dropped Terms				
Term	Role	Attribute	Freq	Number of Docum...	Term	Role	Attribute	Freq	Number of Docum...
very	ADV	Alpha	12,160	12,481	+ be	V	Alpha	47,246	28,046
+ service	N	Alpha	9,188	7,992	+ have	V	Alpha	14,782	10,197
not	ADV	Alpha	7,830	6,139	+ do	V	Alpha	6,438	4,571
mtt	PN	Alpha	7,073	6,034	+ get	V	Alpha	6,300	4,487
+ phone	N	Alpha	6,280	4,963	+ will	V	Alpha	6,095	4,240
helpful	A	Alpha	6,023	4,946	t	N	Alpha	4,907	4,054
+ customer	N	Alpha	5,577	4,899	+ can	V	Alpha	3,698	3,252
+ call	V	Alpha	4,097	3,500	i	N	Alpha	2,992	1,976

Stop lists are automatically included and applied for all languages in the Text Mining node.

Note: The plus sign next to a word indicates stemming (for example, *+service* might represent *service*, *services*, *serviced*, and so on).

8. Expand the **Topics** table. This table shows topics created by the Text Mining node.

   Topics are created based on groups of terms that occur together in several documents. Each term-document pair is assigned a score for every topic. Thresholds are then used to determine whether the association is strong enough to consider whether that document or term belongs in the topic. Because of this, terms and documents can belong to multiple topics.

Topics		
Topic ID	**Topic**	**Term Cutoff**
1	helpful, very, +great service, pleasant, +great	0.0120
2	very, professional, +happy, pleasant, +well	0.0120
3	ok, +thank	0.0120
4	+great, always, mtt	0.0120
5	+thank, no, +speak	0.0120
6	+good, +keep, +job, +good service, very	0.0120
7	+good, all	0.0120
8	mtt, +love, +happy, +love, +call	0.0120
9	+rep, pleasant, mtt, +understand, helpful	0.0120
10	+customer, +customer service, mtt, +service, +great	0.0120
11	+friendly, very, helpful, +customer, professional	0.0120
12	+satisfy, very, mtt, +customer, +speak	0.0120
13	+year, many, best, don, ever	0.0130
14	+speak, +understand, english, best, don	0.0130
15	+great service, +great, +job, +service, +great experience	0.0120

Because 15 topics were discovered, 15 new columns of inputs are created. The output columns contain SVD scores that can be used as inputs for the downstream nodes.

9. Click the **Output Data** tab.

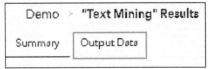

10. Click **View Output Data**.

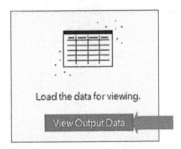

11. Click **View Output Data** again. In this step, you can choose to create a sample of the data to be viewed.

12. Scroll to the right until you see column headings for variables that begin **Score for....** These columns represent the topics created by the Text Mining node.

The SVD coefficients (scores) are shown for the 15 topics discovered, for each observation in the data set. Those columns are passed along for the following nodes.

Score for "helpf...	Score for "very,...	Score for "ok, +...	Score for "+gre...	Score for "+tha...	Score for "+go...	Score for "+go...	Score for "mtt, ...	Score for "+rep,...	Score for "+cust.. !
-0.002056447	-0.012370016	0	0.0012028397	-0.002806626	0.1844404499	0	0.092730021	0.0026061926	0.0110224974
0	0	0.000163191	0	0.0107379701	0	0	0.0002719861	0	0
0.4824671704	0.1958948819	0	0	-0.001236844	0.0141169866	0	-0.031987513	0.0142063274	0.2303599196
0	-0.001565641	0	0	0	-0.004302061	0	-0.004181295	0.0067701497	0.154946912
0	0	0	0	0	0	0	0	0	0
0.0024391397	0.0020326164	0	0.0016260932	-0.003794217	0.0035232018	0	0.1317136469	0.0035232018	0.0065043726
0.6695098207	0.2970202295	0	0	0	0.027505688	0	-0.024348163	0.0325159149	0
0	0.0097767583	0	0	0	-0.000856495	0	0	0.0007821407	0
0	0.0080967216	0	0	0	0	0	0.0041950834	0	0.0011166844
0	0	0	0	0	0	0	0	0	0
0	0	0	0	0	0	0	0	0	0
0.0014324038	0.0155816758	0	0	-0.002203698	-0.009948495	0	-0.01556091	0.006893689	0.4164435026
0	0	0	0	0	0	0	0	0	0
0	0	0	0	0	0	0.9984492492	-0.011993384	0	0
0.4775695173	0.0466180452	0	0	0	0.0064450231	0	-0.016792191	-0.015398586	-0.030506024
0	0	1	0	-0.016	0	0	0	0	0
0.0007682511	0.0006587075	0	0.0004381747	-0.00119316	0.0009493786	0	0.036537542	0.0009493786	0.0019204922
0	0	0	0	0	0	0	0	0	0
0.086988272	0.4483927305	0	0	0	0.7969911793	0	-0.04314167	0	0.0197729274

13. Close the Results window.
14. Alternatively, use the Manage Variables node to see that 15 new interval input columns were added to the data. Right-click the **Text Mining** node and select **Add child node ▶ Data Mining Preprocessing ▶ Manage Variables**.

    Click **Close** in the Run Node window when it appears.

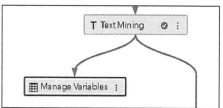

15. Run the **Manage Variables** node and view the results when the run is complete. Expand the **Incoming Variables** table. At the top of the Incoming Variables table are the 15 new columns representing the dimensions of the SVD calculations based on the 15 topics discovered by the Text Mining node.

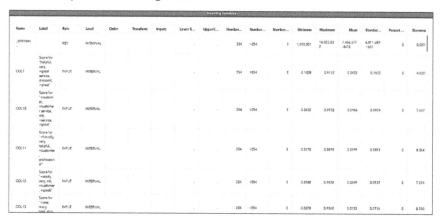

    These 15 columns (**COL1** through **COL15**) serve as new interval inputs for subsequent models.
16. Restore the view of the Incoming Variables table and close the results.
17. To run the entire pipeline, click **Run pipeline**.
18. Open the results of the Model Comparison node.

    The model does not necessarily improve. Explore the results of the final regression model and see whether it contains one of the text variables.
19. Close the results of the Model Comparison node.
20. Open the results of the Logistic Regression model.
21. Scroll down in the results until you see the Output window. Expand the window.
22. Scroll down in the Output window until you see the Selection Summary table. This table shows that one of the columns created by the Text Mining node (**COL12**) did enter the model during the stepwise selection process but was ultimately removed from the

model after optimization of complexity on the holdout sample. This variable entered in step 22, but the final model is from step 19, based on minimum SBC.

		Selection Summary		
Step	Effect Entered		Number Effects In	SBC
0	Intercept		1	29271.0671
1	curr_days_susp		2	23553.3794
2	handset_age_grp		3	22286.7881
3	ever_days_over_plan		4	21192.8397
4	avg_days_susp		5	20812.9567
5	pymts_late_ltd		6	20429.1444
6	REP_SECONDS_OF_DATA_NORM		7	20179.6624
7	ever_times_over_plan		8	19909.0189
8	times_susp		9	19720.0654
9	wrk_orders		10	19592.9676
10	calls_care_ltd		11	19496.8731
11	delinq_indicator		12	19409.5158
12	MB_Data_Usg_M08		13	19360.3752
13	IMP_REP_MB_DATA_NDIST_MO6M		14	19314.8376
14	IMP_REP_MOU_ONNET_PCT_MOM		15	19301.0003
15	bill_data_usg_m09		16	19301.0688
16	open_tsupcomplnts		17	19293.0994
17	REP_BILL_DATA_USG_M03		18	19296.3256
18	REP_MB_DATA_USG_M03		19	19285.4108
19	IMP_MB_Data_Usg_M09		20	19277.6165*
20	MB_Data_Usg_M07		21	19277.7978
21	rfm_score		22	19279.9577
22	COL12		23	19283.7038
	* Optimal Value Of Criterion			

Selection stopped at a local minimum of the SBC criterion.

The model at step 19 is selected where SBC is 19277.62.

23. Restore the view of the Output window and close the Results window.

End of Demonstration

Quiz

1. Which of the following statements is **true** about the Text Mining node?

   a. It enables you to process audio/video data in a media collection.

   b. It does not allow terms and documents to belong to multiple topics.

   c. It transforms term-by-document frequency matrix using singular value decomposition (SVD) to provide binary values.

   d. It creates topics based on groups of terms that occur together in several documents. Each term-document pair is assigned a score for every topic.

Chapter 4: Preparing Your Data: Extract Features

Introduction

Often, the initial (structured) data set of raw features might be too large and unwieldy to be effectively managed, requiring an unreasonable amount of computing resources. Alternatively, the data set might be too robust, causing a classification algorithm to overfit, and providing poor extrapolation in the event of new observations. In this chapter, we discuss how to extract useful information while limiting the number of features or reducing the dimensionality of the input data.

Extract Features

Feature extraction is the process of transforming the existing features into a lower-dimensional space, typically generating new features that are composites of the existing features. SVD is such a technique we have already discussed. There are many other techniques that reduce dimensionality through such a transformation process, including those discussed in this chapter.

Model Studio: The Feature Extraction Node

In Model Studio, the Feature Extraction node can be used to provide a more manageable, representative subset of input variables. The Feature Extraction node creates new features from the initial set of data. These features encapsulate the central properties of a data set and represent it in a low-dimensional space.

The node offers four methods:

- singular value decomposition (SVD)
- principal component analysis (PCA)
- robust principal component analysis (RPCA)
- autoencoder

Principal Component Analysis (PCA)

You can deploy a variety of techniques to correct for (or perhaps more accurately, take advantage of) the distribution flattening. One of the most common statistical approaches is that of *principal component analysis (PCA)*. PCA attempts to find a series of orthogonal vectors that better describe the directions of variation in the data than the original inputs do. (A geometric interpretation of orthogonal is that the vectors are perpendicular. A statistical interpretation is that the vectors are uncorrelated.) The goal is to be able to characterize most of the variation in the data with as few vectors as possible.

PCA starts by searching the data's standardized joint distribution for the direction of maximum variance. It rotates the data set in a way such that the rotated features are statistically uncorrelated. When found, this direction (or vector) is labeled the *first principal component*, or *first eigenvector*. This is the direction that contains most of the information, or in other words, the direction along which the features are most correlated with each other.

The effect of the first principal component can be removed by projecting the data to a lower dimensional subspace perpendicular to the first principal component. The difference between the dimension of the original distribution (that is, the number of inputs) and the effective dimension of the projected points is called the *first eigenvalue*.

Then the algorithm finds the direction that contains the most information while being orthogonal (at a right angle) to the first direction. In two dimensions, there is only one possible orientation that is at a right angle, but in higher-dimensional spaces there would be (infinitely) many more. In other words, the data, projected to remove variation in the direction of the first principal component, are again searched for the direction of maximum variation. When identified, this direction is labeled the *second principal component.* The corresponding second eigenvalue can be calculated by again projecting (the data already projected in the first step) along the direction of the second principal component and determining the difference in dimension between the once and twice projected data.

> PCA is an unsupervised method and does not use class information when finding the rotation. It simply looks at correlations in the data.

The directions found using this process are called *principal components,* as they are the main directions of variance in the data. In general, there as many principal components as original features.

Figure 4.1: Principal Component Analysis (PCA)

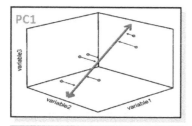

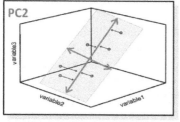

- Principal components are constructed as linear transformations of the input variables.

- The first principal component (PC1) is constructed in such a way that it captures as much of the variation in the input variables set as possible.

- The second principal component (PC2) is orthogonal to PC1 and captures as much as possible of the variation in the input data not captured by PC1.

- And so on ...

The process of identifying directions of variability, projecting, and calculating eigenvalues continues until the sum of the eigenvalues calculated at each step is close to the dimension of the original input space. This is a common stopping rule: **How many unique components exist in the data?** There are as many components as it takes to ensure that the sum of the eigenvalues is greater than 80% or 90% of the input count.

In the presence of redundant inputs, most of the data variability can be described by a few independent principal component vectors. We can reduce the dimensionality by only retaining some of the principal components. For example, in the figure above, we could choose only to keep the first principal component, thus reducing the data from a two-dimensional data set to a one-dimensional data set. Instead of keeping only one of the original features, we found the most interesting direction and this, the first principal component.

By default, the PCA node in Model Manager only rotates (and shifts) the data, but it keeps all principal components. To reduce the dimensionality of the data, you need to specify how many components you want to keep.

In summary, PCA is a powerful technique used to reduce dimensionality of the input data. In the presence of redundant features or inputs, most of the data variability can be described by a few independent principal component vectors. The downside is that the two axes in the plot are not always easy to interpret as the principal components correspond to directions in the original data, so they are *complex combinations* of the original features.

Robust Principal Analysis

Robust principal component analysis (RPCA) decomposes an input matrix into a sum of two matrices: a *low-rank matrix* and a *sparse matrix*.

$$M = L_0 + S_0$$

Where L_0 is a low-rank matrix used for *feature extraction* and S_0 is a sparse matrix used for *anomaly detection*.

A *sparse matrix* is a matrix in which most of the elements are zero. By contrast, if most of the elements are nonzero, then the matrix is considered dense.

This decomposition is obtained by solving a convex programming problem called *principal component pursuit (PCP)*. The aim in the robust principal component analysis is to recover a low-rank matrix L_0 from highly corrupted measurements M. Unlike the small noise term N_0 in classical PCA, the entries in S_0 can have arbitrarily large magnitude, and their support is assumed to be sparse but unknown. You can use the low-rank matrix L_0 to do feature extraction and use the sparse matrix S_0 to detect anomalies. Robustness in RPCA comes from the property that the principal components are computed from observations after removing the outliers—that is, from the low-rank matrix.

There are many applications of RPCA focused on the low-rank matrix, including image processing, latent semantic indexing, ranking, and matrix completion (Candès et al. 2011). Similarly, there are many applications of RPCA focused on the sparse matrix. One example is the extraction of moving objects from the background in surveillance videos.

Autoencoders

An autoencoder is a neural network that is used for efficient codings and widely used for feature extraction and nonlinear principal component analysis. It is a neural network that used inputs to predict the inputs. We will cover neural networks in more detail in Chapter 9. Architecturally, an autoencoder is like a multilayer perceptron neural network because it has an input layer, hidden layers (encoding layers), and an output layer (decoding layer). However, it differs in that the output layer is duplicated from the input layer. Therefore, autoencoders are unsupervised learning models. The network is trained to reconstruct its inputs, which forces the hidden layer to try to learn good representations of the inputs.

Figure 4.2: Autoencoder: Single Hidden Layer

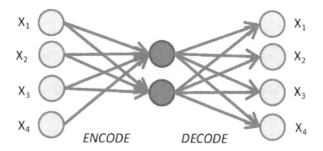

- An autoencoder is a neural network that uses inputs to predict the inputs.
- Autoencoders extract a highly representative set of nonlinear features from the bottleneck layer of a specialized network.

Autoencoders are like PCA but are much more flexible than PCA. Autoencoders can represent both linear and nonlinear transformation in encoding, but PCA can perform only linear transformation. Autoencoders can be layered to form a deep learning network due to its network representation.

For greater network flexibility, we often use more hidden layers with many nodes, like the one in Figure 4.3.

Figure 4.3: Autoencoder: Many Hidden Layers

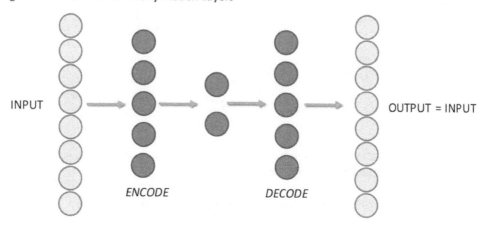

Each layer of the deep network is trained separately by using the output of the previous layer, or by using the training inputs in the case of the first layer. The weights of the individually trained layers are then used to initialize the entire deep network, and all layers are trained again simultaneously on the original training examples. When many inputs are used in conjunction with a much smaller number of hidden units, the features that are extracted as outputs of the hidden units are a nonlinear projection of the training examples onto a lower-dimensional space. Such features can be highly predictive of a training example's class label.

> An obvious drawback to feature extraction is that the actual inputs to the model are no longer meaningful with respect to the business problem. However, you can simply consider this another transformation of the original inputs to be provided to the model, something that must be accounted for as part of the scoring process when the model is deployed.

Handling Extreme or Unusual Values

Transformations can be done to change the shape of the distribution of a variable by stretching or compressing it to reduce the effect of outliers or heavy tails, or to standardize inputs to be on the same range and scale. Another major reason that transformations of inputs are done is to reduce the bias in model predictions.

Figure 4.4: Input Transformations

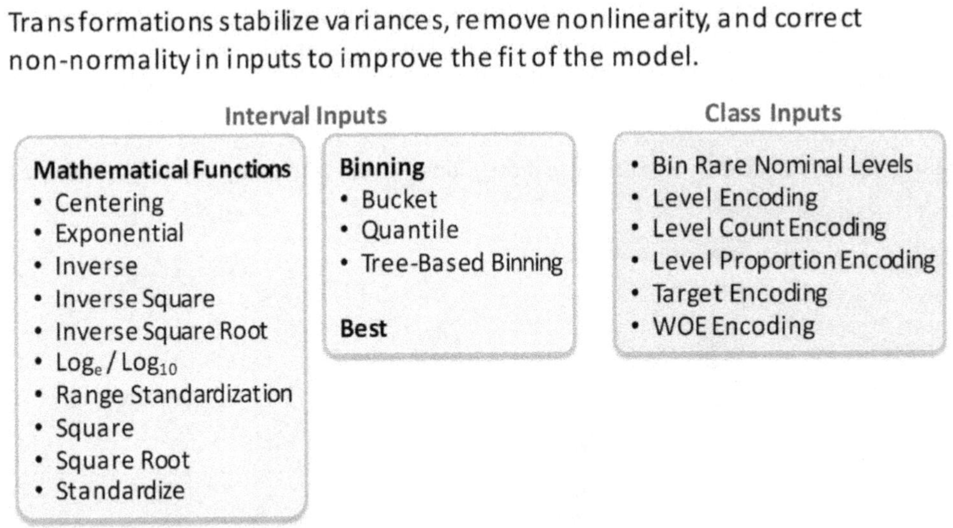

Transformations stabilize variances, remove nonlinearity, and correct non-normality in inputs to improve the fit of the model.

Interval Inputs

Class Inputs

Mathematical Functions
- Centering
- Exponential
- Inverse
- Inverse Square
- Inverse Square Root
- Log_e / Log_{10}
- Range Standardization
- Square
- Square Root
- Standardize

Binning
- Bucket
- Quantile
- Tree-Based Binning

Best

- Bin Rare Nominal Levels
- Level Encoding
- Level Count Encoding
- Level Proportion Encoding
- Target Encoding
- WOE Encoding

Transformation of input variables is a common data preprocessing task. In machine learning, two types of variable transformations are commonly used:

- mathematical transformations such as square, square root, log, or inverse
- binning such as bucket, quantile, or tree-based binning

> Log, Log10, Square root, and Inverse square root add an offset to variables to ensure positive values. Inverse and Inverse square add an offset to variables to ensure nonzero values. This prevents creating missing values during the transformation when input variable values are zero.

Transforming Inputs: Mathematical Functions

The simple illustration in the figure below shows a variable distribution, which is positively skewed.

Figure 4.5: Transforming Inputs: Mathematical Functions

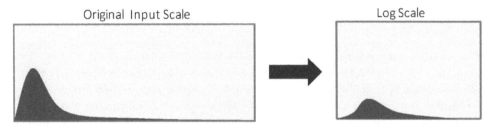

The log transformation reduces skewness in it. A distribution that is symmetric or nearly so is often easier to handle and interpret than a skewed distribution. Extreme input distributions are often problematic in predictive modeling. A simpler and, arguably, more effective approach transforms or regularizes offending inputs to eliminate extreme values. Then, a predictive model can be accurately fit using the transformed input in place of the original input. This not only mitigates the influence of extreme cases but also creates the desired asymptotic association between input and target on the original input scale.

Transforming Inputs: Binning

The simple illustration below shows a variable, **Age**, that ranges from 0 to infinity. (In practice, **Age** would not identically equal zero nor approach infinity, but the example is to illustrate how a continuous variable with a large range could be converted to bins.) The **Age** variable is converted into a new variable that takes on only four values, represented by the bins 1 through 4. When the original **Age** variable falls into a certain age range, the binned version of **Age** simply takes the value of the bin that it falls into.

Figure 4.6: Transforming Inputs: Binning

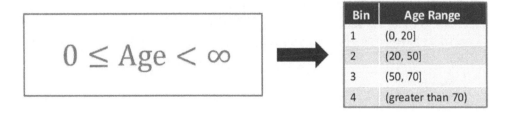

Bin	Age Range
1	(0, 20]
2	(20, 50]
3	(50, 70]
4	(greater than 70)

There are many ways that binning can be done. In one case, the bins themselves are of equal width, but the frequency count within each bin can then be varied. (This type of binning is known as *bucketing*.) Another approach is to make the width of the bins different but the frequency count of observations in each bin consistent. (This type of binning is known as *quantile binning*.)

Binning can be done for several reasons. It can be used to classify missing values of a variable, reduce the effect that outliers might have on a model, or illustrate nonlinear relationships between variables. A binned version of a variable also has less variance than the original numeric variable.

Model Studio: The "Best" Transformation

"Best" is not really a transformation, but a method or process to select the best transformation for an interval input. In the Transformations node (shown in Demo 4.1), this method is accessed by selecting "Best" via the **Default interval inputs method** property. When specified, the Best method is applied to all interval inputs coming into the node, unless overridden by specific variable transformations identified in metadata via the Data tab or Manage Variables node.

For more information, see "Best transformation – a new feature in SAS Model Studio 8.3" at https://communities.sas.com/t5/SAS-Communities-Library/Best-transformation-a-new-feature-in-SAS-Model-Studio-8-3/ta-p/489604.

Demo 4.1: Transforming Inputs

In this demonstration, you use the Transformations node to apply a numerical transformation to input variables.

1. Open the **Data Exploration** pipeline by clicking on its tab.

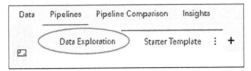

2. Run the **Data Exploration** node. (The pipeline requires a rerun because metadata rules have been applied on the Data tab.)
3. Right-click the **Data Exploration** node and select **Results**.
4. Expand the **Interval Variable Moments** table. Note that three of the **MB_Data_Usg_M** variables have a high degree of skewness. Why are only three listed? There is a total of six in the data set.

Variable Name	Minimum	Maximum	Mean	Standard Deviation	Skewness
MB_Data_Usg_M06	0	29,676	230.5486	718.7864	15.2432
MB_Data_Usg_M07	0	13,672	94.2740	259.8391	17.6346
MB_Data_Usg_M08	0	16,297	109.5912	348.7336	16.9031
avg_days_susp	0	62	3.4714	3.8313	1.5937
bill_data_usg_m03	-13,678	40,767.1000	1,864.9142	1,634.5099	1.3974
bill_data_usg_tot	17	82	44.6595	11.0660	0.4048

5. Restore the view of the Interval Variable Moments table.

6. Expand the **Important Inputs** chart. Notice that the same **MB_Data_Usg_M** variables have been selected as being important variables. Only three of the six **MB_Data_Usg_M** variables are listed in the Interval Variable Moments table because, by default, only the variables found to be important are summarized in the results of the Data Exploration node. Importance is defined by a decision tree using PROC TREESPLIT. You should transform these three inputs.

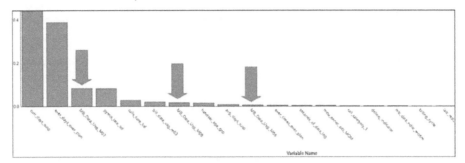

Note: The entire chart is not shown above.

7. Restore the view of the Important Variables table.

8. Close the Results window. Transformation rules are assigned on the Data tab. (Alternatively, transformation rules could be assigned using a Manage Variables node. In the Manage Variables window, the New Transform column is hidden by default but can be displayed and used. Click the **Manage Columns** button in the upper right corner of the Manage Variables table. From the Manage Columns window, the column for New Transform can be moved from the Hidden columns list to the Displayed columns list. However, recall that rules established in the Manage Variables node are not saved if the pipeline is saved to the Exchange.)

9. Click the **Data** tab. Make sure that any selected variables are deselected. It might help to sort by the Variable Name column if that column is currently not sorted.

10. Scroll down until you see the **MB_Data_Usg_M** variables. Although only three were deemed as important in the Data Exploration node, we will apply a Log transformation to all six of them.

11. Select all six **MB_Data_Usg_M** variables by selecting the check boxes next to their names.

     Note: Be sure to select the correct variable names, which use uppercase letters. Very similar variable names exist in lowercase letters. Do *not* select the variable names with lowercase letters.

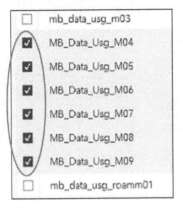

12. In the Multiple Variables window, in the right pane, select the **Transform** menu and select **Log**.

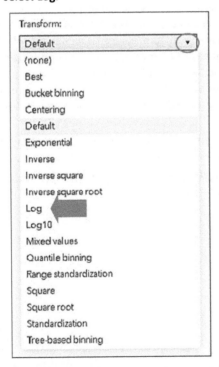

Note: Metadata always overrules transformations that are defined within the Transformation node. Metadata can be set using the Manage Variable node or on the Data tab.

The Transform column does not appear by default in the table on the Data tab, but it can be added.

13. Click the **Manage columns** button in the upper right corner of the data table.

Order	Comment	Number
Default		5
Default		>254

14. In the Manage Columns window, under **Hidden columns,** select **Transform,** and then click the single right arrow that has a plus sign on it.

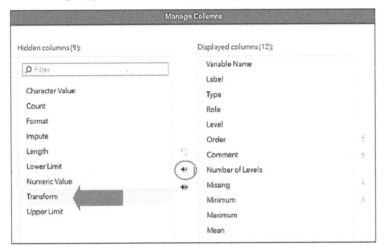

15. Click **OK**. On the Data tab, the Transform column can be seen by scrolling to the right. All six **MB_Data_Usg_M** variables show Log as the transformation rule.

Maximum	Mean	Transform
40,761.3406	1,698.6531	Default
40,784.2343	1,696.2538	Default
14,606.0000	159.3069	Log
24,707.0000	142.7953	Log
29,676.0000	230.5486	Log
13,672.0000	94.2740	Log
16,297.0000	109.5912	Log
8,869.0000	95.9824	Log
11,400.0000	133.8720	Default
18,727.0000	125.7288	Default

16. Return to the Starter Template pipeline.

17. Expand the left pane on **Nodes** if it is not opened. Under Data Mining Preprocessing, select the **Transformations** node and place it *between* the Replacement node and the Imputation node.

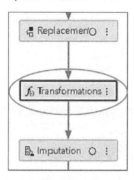

Note: The idea is that you first change metadata in the Data tab or using the Manage Variables node to specify what you want to do with the variables. (So far, you have seen Replacement and Transformation.) Then you need to add a node (in our example, Replacement or Transformation) to make those changes to the data. The subsequent node (Replacement or Transformation) actually performs the changes that you encoded in metadata.

18. Do *not* make changes to the properties of the Transformations node. Although the **Default interval inputs method** property indicates **(none)**, the metadata rules assigned to the variables under the Data tab override this default setting.

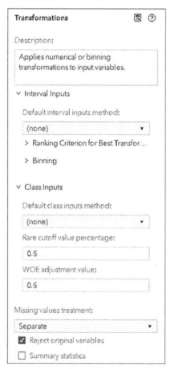

19. Right-click the **Transformations** node and select **Run**.

20. When the run is finished, open the results. Expand the **Transformed Variables Summary** table. This table displays information about the transformed variables, including how they were transformed, the corresponding input variable, the formula applied, the variable level, type, and variable label.

    Notice that a Log transformation has been applied to all six **MB_Data_Usg_M** variables and that the term **LOG_** now appears at the beginning of the names of those variables.

Transformed Variable	Method	Input Variable	Formula	Variable Level	Type	Variable Label
LOG_MB_Data_Usg_M04	LOG	MB_Data_Usg_M04	log(MB_Data_Usg_M04'n + 1)	INTERVAL	N	Transformed MB of Data Usage Month 4
LOG_MB_Data_Usg_M05	LOG	MB_Data_Usg_M05	log(MB_Data_Usg_M05'n + 1)	INTERVAL	N	Transformed MB of Data Usage Month 5
LOG_MB_Data_Usg_M06	LOG	MB_Data_Usg_M06	log(MB_Data_Usg_M06'n + 1)	INTERVAL	N	Transformed MB of Data Usage Month 6
LOG_MB_Data_Usg_M07	LOG	MB_Data_Usg_M07	log(MB_Data_Usg_M07'n + 1)	INTERVAL	N	Transformed MB of Data Usage Month 7
LOG_MB_Data_Usg_M08	LOG	MB_Data_Usg_M08	log(MB_Data_Usg_M08'n + 1)	INTERVAL	N	Transformed MB of Data Usage Month 8
LOG_MB_Data_Usg_M09	LOG	MB_Data_Usg_M09	log(MB_Data_Usg_M09'n + 1)	INTERVAL	N	Transformed MB of Data Usage Month 9

Note: In the Formula column, notice that the formula for the Log transformations includes an offset of 1 to avoid the case of **Log(0)**.

21. Restore the Transformed Variables Summary window and close the results.

22. Run the entire pipeline.

23. Open the results of the Model Comparison node.

	Champion	Name	Algorithm Name	KS (Youden)	Misclassification Rate
Model Comparison					
	☑	Logistic Regression	Logistic Regression	0.5689	0.0642

24. Close the Results window.

End of Demonstration

Feature Selection

When a model is fit using all available inputs, it typically results in a model that does not generalize well. The purpose of all predictive models is that they are eventually applied to new data. When a model is overfit to one data source, it might be very accurate at making predictions for that same data source, but it might lose a significant amount of accuracy when applied to new data. A model using all available inputs will likely be overfit to the data set used to construct the model. One way to avoid this is to use only a subset of all inputs in the final model.

Figure 4.7: Feature Selection

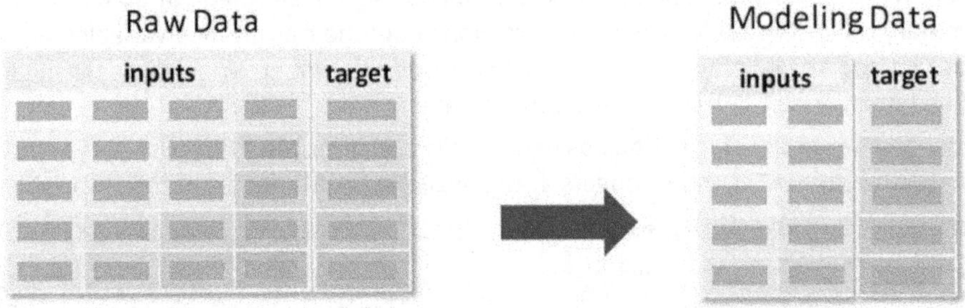

Details: The Curse of Dimensionality

The *dimension* of a problem refers to the number of input variables (more accurately, *degrees of freedom*) that are available for creating a prediction. Data mining problems are often massive in dimension.

The *curse of dimensionality* refers to the exponential increase in data required to densely populate space as the dimension increases. For example, the eight points fill the one-dimensional space but become more separated as the dimension increases. In a 100-dimensional space, they would be like distant galaxies.

The curse of dimensionality limits your practical ability to fit a flexible model to noisy data (real data) when there are many input variables. A densely populated input space is required to fit highly complex models. When you assess how much data is available for data mining, you must consider the dimension of the problem.

There are many techniques available for selecting inputs for a model. Some of these methods might be supervised, where the target variable is used in the process. Other techniques are unsupervised and ignore the target. Further, some modeling algorithms themselves might reduce the number of inputs during the model building process (for example, decision trees) but others might not (for example, neural networks), where some external method is used to select inputs.

Feature Selection Strategies

Input selection (that is, reducing the number of inputs) is the obvious way to thwart the curse of dimensionality. Unfortunately, reducing the dimension is also an easy way to disregard important information.

The two principal reasons for eliminating a variable are redundancy and irrelevancy.

Figure 4.8: Feature Selection Strategies

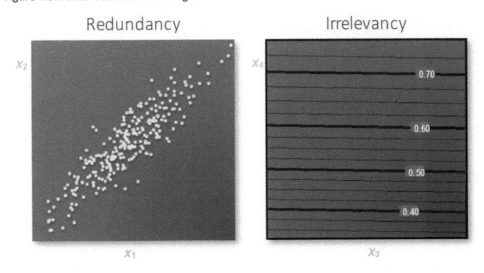

A *redundant* input does not give any new information that was not already explained by other inputs. In the example above, knowing the value of input $x1$ gives you a good idea of the value of $x2$.

For decision tree models, the modeling algorithm makes input redundancy a relatively minor issue. For other modeling tools, input redundancy requires more elaborate methods to mitigate the problem. An *irrelevant* input does not provide information about the target. In the example above, predictions change with input $x3$, but not with input $x3$.

Figure 4.9: Supervised Selection

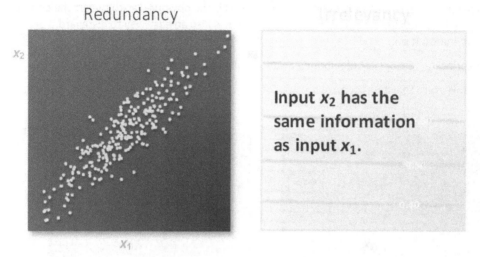

Example: x_1 is household income and x_2 is home value.

For decision tree models, the modeling algorithm automatically ignores irrelevant inputs. Other modeling methods must be modified or rely on additional tools to properly deal with irrelevant inputs.

Figure 4.10: Supervised Selection

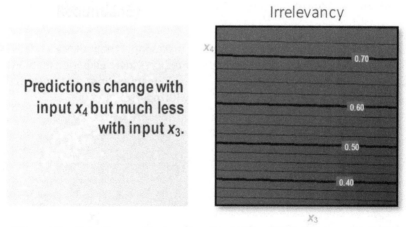

Example: Target is the response to direct mail solicitation, x_3 is religious affiliation, and x_4 is the response to previous solicitations.

When presented with many variables to predict an outcome, you might want to reduce the number of variables in some way to make the prediction problem easier to tackle. Many of these variables are redundant.

Including redundant inputs can degrade the analysis by:

- destabilizing the parameter estimates
- increasing the risk of overfitting
- confounding interpretation
- increasing computation time
- increasing scoring effort
- increasing the cost of data collection and augmentation

Model Studio: Feature Selection

Many data mining databases have hundreds of potential model inputs (independent or explanatory variables) that can be used to predict the target (dependent or response variable). The Variable Selection node assists you in reducing the number of inputs by rejecting input variables based on the selection results. This node finds and selects the best variables for analysis by using unsupervised and supervised selection methods. You can choose among one or more of the available selection methods in the variable selection process.

Figure 4.11: Feature Selection in Model Studio

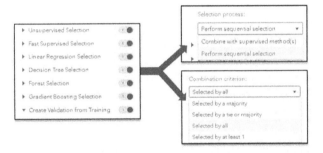

If you choose the unsupervised selection method, you can specify in the **Selection process** property whether this method is run prior to the supervised methods (sequential selection). If you choose to perform a sequential selection, which is the default, any variable rejected by the unsupervised method is not used by the subsequent supervised methods. If you are not performing a sequential selection, the results from the unsupervised method are combined with the chosen supervised methods.

Model Studio: Feature Selection

If you choose multiple methods, the results from the individual methods are combined to generate the final selection result. This is done with *combination criterion*. This is a "voting" method such that each selection method gets a vote on whether a variable is selected. As an option, you choose at what voting level (combination criterion) a variable is selected. Voting levels range from the least restrictive option (at least one chosen method selects the variable) to the most restrictive option (all chosen methods select the variable). Any variable that is not selected in the final outcome is rejected, and subsequent nodes in the pipeline do not use that variable.

You also have the option to accomplish *pre-screening* of the input variables before running the chosen variable selection methods. In pre-screening, if a variable exceeds the maximum number of class levels threshold or the maximum missing percent threshold, that variable is rejected and not processed by the subsequent variable selection methods.

The Advisor options also accomplish variable pre-screening when the project is created, so this option can be used to increase the level of pre-screening over what is done at the project level.

Details: Variable Selection Methods

The following variable selection methods are available in the Variable Selection node:

- **Unsupervised Selection:** Identifies the set of input variables that jointly explains the maximum amount of data variance. The target variable is not considered with this method. Unsupervised Selection specifies the VARREDUCE procedure to perform unsupervised variable selection by identifying a set of variables that jointly explain the maximum amount of data variance. Variable selection is based on covariance analysis.

- **Fast Supervised Selection:** Identifies the set of input variables that jointly explain the maximum amount of variance contained in the target. Fast Supervised Selection specifies the VARREDUCE procedure to perform supervised variable selection by identifying a set of variables that jointly explain the maximum amount of variance contained in the response variables. Supervised selection is essentially based on AIC, AICC, and BIC stop criterion.

Model Studio: Feature Selection

- **Linear Regression Selection:** Fits and performs variable selection on an ordinary least squares regression predictive model. This is valid for an interval target and a binary target. In the case of a character binary target (or a binary target with a user-defined format), a temporary numeric variable with values of 0 or 1 is created, which is then substituted for the target. Linear Regression Selection specifies the REGSELECT procedure to perform linear regression selection based on ordinary least square regression. It offers many effect-selection methods, including Backward, Forward, Forward-swap, Stepwise methods, and modern LASSO and Adaptive LASSO methods. It also offers extensive capabilities for customizing the model selection by using a wide variety of selection and stopping criteria, from computationally efficient significance level-based criteria to modern, computationally intensive validation-based criteria.

- **Decision Tree Selection:** Trains a decision tree predictive model. The residual sum of squares variable importance is calculated for each predictor variable, and the relative variable importance threshold that you specify is used to select the most useful predictor variables. Decision Tree Selection specifies the TREESPLIT procedure to perform decision tree selection based on CHAID, Chi-square, Entropy, Gini, Information gain ratio, F test, and Variance target criterion. It produces a classification tree, which models a categorical response, or a regression tree, which models a continuous response. Both types of trees are called decision trees because the model is expressed as a series of IF-THEN statements.

- **Forest Selection:** Trains a forest predictive model by fitting multiple decision trees. The residual sum of squares variable importance is calculated for each predictor variable, averaged across all the trees, and the relative variable importance threshold that you specify is used to select the most useful predictor variables. Forest Selection specifies the FOREST procedure to create a predictive model that consists of multiple decision trees.

- **Gradient Boosting Selection:** Trains a gradient boosting predictive model by fitting a set of additive decision trees. The residual sum of squares variable importance is calculated for each predictor variable, averaged across all the trees, and the relative variable importance threshold that you specify is used to select the most useful predictor variables. Gradient Boosting Selection specifies the GRADBOOST procedure to create a predictive model that consists of multiple decision trees.

- **Create Validation Sample from Training Data:** Specifies whether a validation sample should be created from the incoming training data. This is recommended even if the data have already been partitioned so that only the training partition is used for variable selection, and the validation partition can be used for modeling.

Demo 4.2: Selecting Features

In this demonstration, you use the Variable Selection node to reduce the number of inputs for modeling.

1. In the Starter Template, place a Variable Selection node ***between*** the Text Mining node and the Logistic Regression node.

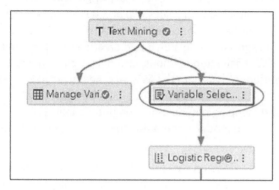

2. Select the Variable Selection node.

    In the properties, varying combinations of criteria can be used to select inputs. Keep **Combination Criterion** at **Selected by at least 1**. This means that any input selected by at least one of the selection criteria chosen is passed on to subsequent nodes as inputs. The **Fast Supervised Selection** method is selected by default. The **Create Validation from Training** property is also selected by default, but its button is initially disabled.

3. In addition, turn on the **Unsupervised Selection** and **Linear Regression Selection** methods by clicking the button slider next to each property name. When a property is turned on, additional options appear. The display capture below shows the additional options of the **Unsupervised Selection** method after it is selected. You can hide the new options by selecting the down arrow next to the property name.

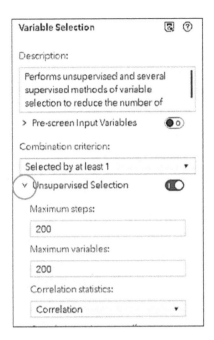

Keep the default settings for all the new options that appear for the Unsupervised Selection and Linear Regression Selection methods.

After the **Unsupervised Selection** and **Linear Regression Selection** methods are selected and the options for each are hidden, the properties panel resembles the following:

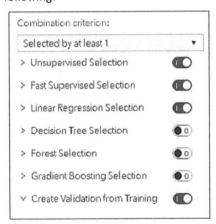

Note: The **Create Validation from Training** property was initially selected by default, but the slider button did not become active until another method was selected. This property specifies whether a validation sample should be created from the incoming training data. It is recommended to create this validation set even if the data have already been partitioned so that only the training partition is used for variable selection and the original validation partition can be used for modeling.

4. Run the **Variable Selection** node and view the results when it is complete.

5. Expand the **Variable Selection** table. This table contains the output role for each variable. At the top of the table are the input variables selected by the node. These variables have a blank cell in the Reason column.

Name	Variable Label	Variable Level	Role	Reason
CHURN	Churn Flag	BINARY	TARGET	
AVG_DAYS_SUSP	Days Suspended Last 6M	INTERVAL	INPUT	
DELINQ_INDICATOR	Delinquent Indicator	NOMINAL	INPUT	
EVER_DAYS_OVER_PLAN	Total Days Over Plan	INTERVAL	INPUT	
HANDSET_AGE_GRP	Handset Age Group	NOMINAL	INPUT	
IMP_REP_MB_DATA_NDIST_MO6M	Imputed Replacement: 6M Avg Billed Data Usage Normally Distributed	INTERVAL	INPUT	
IMP_REP_MOU_ONNET_PCT_MOM	Imputed Replacement: Minutes On Network Pct Change Month over Month	INTERVAL	INPUT	
LOG_MB_DATA_USG_M6s	Transformed MB of Data Usage Month 6	INTERVAL	INPUT	
PYMTS_LATE_LTD	Total Late Payments Lifetime	NOMINAL	INPUT	
REP_CALLS_TOTAL	Replacement: Total Calls Curr	INTERVAL	INPUT	
TIMES_DELINQ	Consecutive Mths Delinquent	NOMINAL	INPUT	
TIMES_SUSP	Number of Times Suspended	NOMINAL	INPUT	
WRK_ORDERS	Open Work Orders	NOMINAL	INPUT	
CUSTOMER_ID	Primary Key	INTERVAL	ID	
DMINDEX		NOMINAL	KEY	

6. Scroll down in the Variable Selection table. It shows which variables have been rejected by the node. The reason for rejection is shown in the Reason column. Only a subset of the rejected variables is shown below.

Name	Variable Label	Variable Level	Role	Reason
DMINDEX		NOMINAL	KEY	
PARTIND	Partition Indicator	NOMINAL	PARTITION	
ACCT_AGE	Account Tenure	INTERVAL	REJECTED	Variance Explained (Unsupervised)
BILLING_CYCLE	Billing Cycle	NOMINAL	REJECTED	Combination Criterion
BILL_DATA_USG_M09	9M Avg Billed Data Usage	INTERVAL	REJECTED	Variance Explained (Unsupervised)
BILL_DATA_USG_TOT	Total Billed Data Usage	INTERVAL	REJECTED	Combination Criterion
CALLS_CARE_3MAVG_ACCT	Number Calls Care Center 3 Month Avg	INTERVAL	REJECTED	Combination Criterion
CALLS_CARE_6MAVG_ACCT	Number Calls Care Center 6 Month Avg	INTERVAL	REJECTED	Variance Explained (Unsupervised)
CALLS_CARE_ACCT	Number Calls Care Center	NOMINAL	REJECTED	Combination Criterion
CALLS_CARE_LTD	Total Calls to Care Lifetime	INTERVAL	REJECTED	Variance Explained (Unsupervised)
CALLS_FE_ACCT	Number Calls Tech Support	INTERVAL	REJECTED	Combination Criterion
CALL_CATEGORY_1	Call Center Category 1	NOMINAL	REJECTED	Combination Criterion

The Variable Selection table shows the variables that are rejected because of the variable selection and pre-screening process (turned off in this case), as well as the reason for the rejection. This is in addition to other variables not processed by the Variable Selection node.

Recall that sequential selection (default) is performed, and any variable rejected by the unsupervised method is not used by the subsequent supervised methods. The variables that are rejected by supervised methods are represented by *combination criterion* (at least one in this case) in the Reason column. If you want to see whether they were selected or rejected by each method, look the Variable Selection Combination Summary table.

7. Restore the view of the Variable Selection table.

8. Expand the Variable Selection Combination Summary table. For each variable, the table includes the result (Input or Rejected) for each method that was used, the total count of each result, and the final output role (Input or Rejected). Finally, specific output for each selection method is also available in the results. Only a subset of the variables is shown below.

Name	Variable Label	Fast	Linear Regression	Input	Rejected	Output Role
AVG_DAYS_SUSP	Days Suspended Last 6M	INPUT	INPUT	2	0	INPUT
BILLING_CYCLE	Billing Cycle	REJECTED	REJECTED	0	2	REJECTED
BILL_DATA_USG_TOT	Total Billed Data Usage	REJECTED	REJECTED	0	2	REJECTED
CALLS_CARE_3MAVG_ACCT	Number Calls Care Center 3 Month Avg	REJECTED	REJECTED	0	2	REJECTED
CALLS_CARE_ACCT	Number Calls Care Center	REJECTED	REJECTED	0	2	REJECTED
CALLS_TS_ACCT	Number Calls Tech Support	REJECTED	REJECTED	0	2	REJECTED
CALL_CATEGORY_1	Call Center Category 1	REJECTED	REJECTED	0	2	REJECTED
COL1	Score for "helpful, very, +great service, classes, agree"	REJECTED	REJECTED	0	2	REJECTED

The first variable in the table is selected by both fast-supervised selection and linear regression, so it is selected as an input (shown above). For any variable rejected by both methods, the output role of the variable is Rejected. If a variable is selected by only one of the selection methods, but not the other, the output role of the variable is Input. This is because of the property **Combination criterion** being set to **Selected by at least 1**.

9. Restore the view of the Variable Selection Combination Summary table and close the results.

10. Run the pipeline by clicking the **Run pipeline** button.

11. Open the results of the Model Comparison node.

	Champion	Name	Algorithm Name	KS (Youden)	Misclassification Rate
	☒	Logistic Regression	Logistic Regression	0.5329	0.0800

12. Close the results of the Model Comparison node.

End of Demonstration

Demo 4.3: Saving a Pipeline to the Exchange

The current Starter Template pipeline is in multiple demonstrations of machine learning algorithms. In this demonstration, you save the Starter Template pipeline to the Exchange, where it will be available for other users.

1. Click the **Options** button next to the name **Starter Template**. Select **Save to The Exchange**.

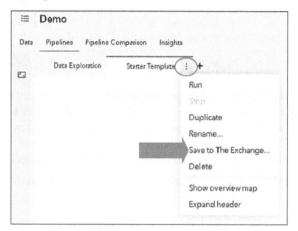

2. Change the name of the pipeline to CPML demo pipeline, and for the description, enter **This pipeline was created in the CPML class**. It includes a logistic regression model and some data preparation. Click **Save**.

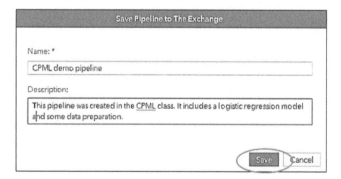

3. To see the saved pipeline in The Exchange, click the shortcut button, which is located next to the Data tab.

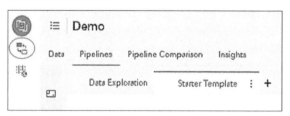

4.   In the left pane, expand **Pipelines** and select **Data Mining and Machine Learning**.

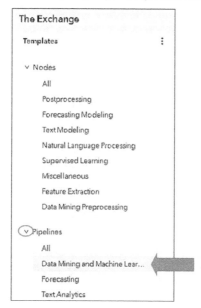

The newly saved CPML demo pipeline is added to the list of pipeline templates.

To open a pipeline, right-click its name and select **Open**. Alternatively, you can double-click the name of the pipeline to open it.

Note: When you save a pipeline to the Exchange, you in fact create a new template from a pipeline. Therefore, it will also be available in the pipeline templates list.

5.   To exit the Exchange and return to the **Demo** project, click the **Projects** shortcut button next to the name **The Exchange**.

End of Demonstration

Variable Clustering

Another approach to variable reduction is variable clustering. Clustering is the task of partitioning the data set into groups called *clusters*, where data points within a single cluster are very similar and points in different clusters different. Variable clustering divides numeric variables (by default) into disjoint or hierarchical clusters. Variables in different clusters are conditionally independent given their own clusters. For each cluster that contains more than one variable, the variable that contributes the most to the variation in that cluster is chosen as the representative variable. All other variables are rejected.

Figure 4.12: Variable Clustering

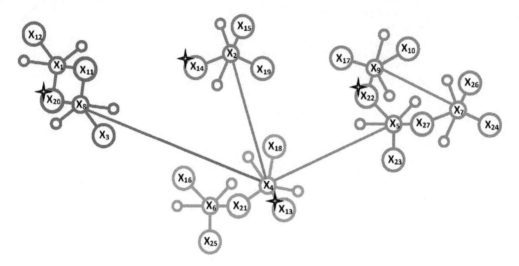

By default, variable clustering is performed only on numeric input variables. In order for variable clustering to include categorical input variables, the property **Include Class Inputs** must be turned on.

Variable clustering is a useful technique for data reduction because it finds the best variables for analysis. It removes collinearity, decreases variable redundancy, and helps reveal the underlying structure of the input variables in a data set in the sense that the groups of variables reveal the main dimensionalities of the data.

Demo 4.4: Clustering Inputs for Data Reduction

In this demonstration, you use the Variable Clustering node to reduce the number of inputs for modeling.

1. Return to the **Demo** project and open the **Data Exploration** pipeline by clicking its tab.

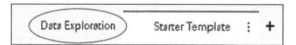

2. In the Data Exploration pipeline, right-click the **Data** node and select **Add child node >
Data Mining Preprocessing ð Variable Clustering**. Your pipeline should resemble the
following:

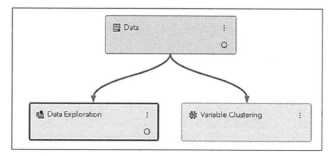

3. Select the **Variable Clustering** node. In the properties, you have an option of including
categorical variables in the analysis. Turn the option on by selecting the **Include class
inputs** box. This means that class variables are also used in variable clustering.

Also, clear the box for **Export class level indicators**. This specifies to not export the class
level indicators to replace the original class variables.

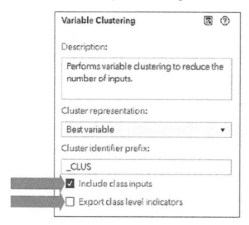

You can use the **Cluster identifier prefix** property to specify the prefix used to name the
variable cluster identifiers and to name the cluster component variables when **Cluster
representation** is set to **Cluster component**.

Note: Class variables are handled in a different way in Model Studio. Individual binary
class level variables are used in the clustering process, but the original class variables
are kept or dropped in the selection process. This selection depends on the variables
that are included in a cluster and the variable or variable level that is selected from each
cluster.

Note: Also note that you have a **Cluster representation** property where you can choose
to export the first principal component for each cluster (property value **Cluster
component**). With the **Cluster component** option, the first principal component is
extracted from all variables in a cluster and output as the new variable **_CLUS***n* (for
example, **_CLUS1**, **_CLUS2**, **_CLUS3**, and so on), and the original cluster variables are
rejected. The total number of generated component variables corresponds to the

number of identified clusters. For more information, see "Three new Variable Clustering features in SAS Model Studio 8.3" at https://communities.sas.com/t5/SAS-Communities-Library/Three-new-Variable-Clustering-features-in-SAS-Model-Studio-8-3/ta-p/489430.

4. Observe that the default value of the regularization parameter Rho (r) is 0.8. You do not need to change its value.

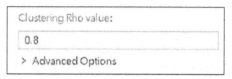

Note: You use Rho to control the sparsity of connections among variables. Tuning the regularization parameter from low to high increases the number of disconnected components and splits larger clusters into smaller ones. Those divided clusters naturally form a hierarchical structure during this process.

5. Run the **Variable Clustering** node and view the results when it is complete.

Expand the **Clustered Variables** table. This table contains all the clustered variables, a list of their cluster IDs, variable labels, first principal components, and whether they were selected. Only a subset of the selected variables is shown below.

Note: For class variables, the principal component might be blank. This is valid and expected.

Cluster ID	Variable	Variable Label	Principal Component 1	Variable Selected
_CLUS1	cs_ttl_rural	Census Area Total Rural	0.7071	YES
_CLUS1	cs_ttl_urban	Census Area Total Urban	-0.7071	NO
_CLUS2	forecast_region	Forecasted Region Key	0.6637	YES
_CLUS2	region_Pacific	Account Region=Pacific	0.5401	NO
_CLUS2	region_Mid Atlantic	Account Region=Mid Atlantic	-0.5174	NO
_CLUS3	count_of_suspensions_6m_3	Times Suspended Last 6M= 3	0.3808	YES
_CLUS3	count_of_suspensions_6m_0	Times Suspended Last 6M=0	-0.2683	YES
_CLUS3	billing_cycle_7	Billing Cycle=7	0.3469	NO
_CLUS3	product_plan_desc_Lotta Minutes	Plan Name=Lotta Minutes Classic FT	0.3275	NO
_CLUS3	rp_pooled_ind_Y	Pooled Rate Plan=Y	0.3138	NO
_CLUS3	rp_pooled_ind_N	Pooled Rate Plan=N	-0.3138	NO
_CLUS3	handset_Apple	Handset Mfg=Apple	0.2700	NO
_CLUS3	sales_channel_Retail	Acquisition Channel=Retail	0.2470	NO
_CLUS3	product_plan_desc2_Lotta Minutes	Plan Name=Lotta Minutes Classic SL	-0.2230	NO
_CLUS3	credit_class_prime	Credit Class=prime	0.2162	NO

The first column has cluster membership against each variable. Scrolling down in the Clustered Variables table shows that there are nearly 13 clusters created. Each cluster has a different number of inputs. The last column has information about the input variables selected (YES) or not selected (NO) within each cluster by the node. You can verify that the original class variables are kept or dropped in the selection process and not the dummy variables.

Graphical LASSO based on Friedman, Hastie, and Tibshirani (2008) is performed. It estimates the inverse covariance matrix at a specified regularization parameter (r=0.8 in this case). The inverse covariance matrix interprets the partial correlation between variables given other variables. Conditional dependency among variables is interpreted by estimating the inverse covariance matrix. The off-diagonal elements of an inverse covariance matrix correspond to partial correlations, so the zero elements imply conditional independence between the pair of variables. The conditional independence provides a better model for understanding the direct link between variables than does simple correlation analysis, which models each pair of variables without considering other variables.

6. Restore the view of the Clustered Variables table.

7. Expand the Clustered Variables Network.

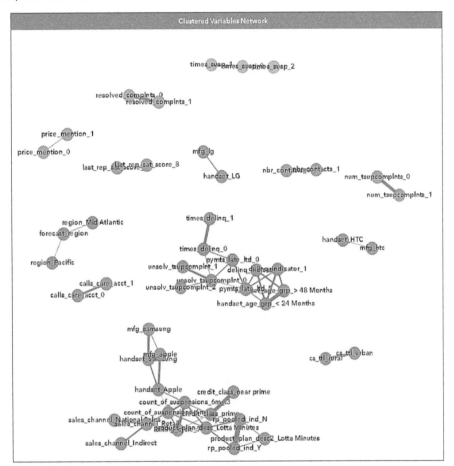

The Clustered Variables Network is a spatial map that gives the orientation and relative distance of clusters and cluster members. Cluster members with a stronger link are connected by a thicker line. There are clearly **13** clusters standing out in different color shades. Many of them seem to be closer and consequently similar. Thus, you might want to try decreasing the number of clusters.

8. Restore the view of the Clustered Variables Network.

9. Close the results.

End of Demonstration

Quiz

Why bin an input?

a. It can reduce the effects of an outlier.

b. It can classify missing values (into a category or bin).

c. It can generate multiple effects.

d. All of the above.

Chapter 5: Discovery: Selecting an Algorithm

Introduction

Now that you have ensured that you have enough appropriate data, massaged the data into a form suitable for modeling, identified key features to include in your model, and established how the model is to be used, you are ready to use powerful machine learning algorithms to build predictive models or discover patterns in your data. This is really the phase where you should allow yourself more freedom to experiment with different approaches to identify the algorithms (and configuration of options for those algorithms) that produce the best model for your specific application.

The success of your machine learning application comes down to the effectiveness of the actual model that you build. In choosing the best model or champion, you should consider the following essential discovery tasks:

- Select an algorithm

- Improve the model

- Optimize complexity of the model

- Regularize and tune

- Build ensemble models

Select an Algorithm

There is no one answer or recipe in choosing the perfect algorithm. The advice is to try many different models and compare the results. The popular "no free lunch" theorem (Wolpert 1996) states that no one model works best for every problem.

You can, however, use the following questions to guide your decision (Wujek, Hall, and Günes 2016):

- What is the size and nature of your data?
- What are you trying to achieve with your model?
- How accurate does your model need to be?
- How much time do you have to train your model?
- How interpretable or understandable does your model need to be?
- Does your model have automatic hyperparameter tuning capability?

Beginners often tend to choose algorithms that are easy to implement and can obtain results quickly. This approach is acceptable if it is the first step of the process. After you obtain some results and become more familiar with the data, you can spend more time experimenting with more sophisticated algorithms. This might strengthen your understanding of the data and potentially further improve the results.

Even in this stage, the best algorithms might not be the methods that have achieved the highest reported accuracy. Most algorithms usually require careful tuning and extensive training to obtain the best achievable performance. Selecting the modeling algorithm for your machine learning application can sometimes be the most difficult part. Before deciding which algorithms to use, consider the questions posed in the sections that follow.

What Is the Size and Nature of Your Data?

If you expect a linear relationship between your features and your target, linear or logistic regression or a linear kernel support vector machine might be sufficient. Linear models are also a good choice for large data sets due to their training efficiency and due to the curse of dimensionality. As the number of features increase, the distance between points grows and observations are more likely to be linearly separable. To an extent, nonlinearity and interaction effects can be captured by adding higher-order polynomial and interaction terms in a regression model. More complex relationships can be modeled through the power of the more sophisticated machine learning algorithms such as decision trees, random forests, neural networks, and nonlinear kernel support vector machines. Of course, these more sophisticated algorithms can require more training time and might be unsuitable for very large data sets.

What Are You Trying to Achieve with Your Model?

Are you creating a model to classify observations, predict a value for an interval target, detect patterns or anomalies, or provide recommendations? Answering this question directs you to a subset of machine learning algorithms that specialize in the problem.

What Is the Required Accuracy?

Although you always want your model to be as accurate as possible when applied to new data, it is still always good to strive for simplicity. Simpler models train faster and are easier to understand, making it easier to explain how and why the results were achieved. Simpler models are also easier to deploy. Start with a regression model as a benchmark, and then train a more complex model such as a neural net, random forest, or gradient boosted model. If your regression model is much less accurate than the more complex model, you have probably missed some important predictor or interaction of predictors. An additional benefit of a simpler model is that it is less prone to overfitting the training data.

What Is the Time Available to Train Your Model?

This ties in with how accurate your model needs to be. If you need to train a model in a short amount of time, linear or logistic regression and decision trees are probably your best options. If training time is not an issue, take advantage of the powerful algorithms (neural networks, support vector machines, gradient boosting, and so on) that iteratively refine the model to better represent complex relationships between features and the target of interest.

What Level of Interpretability Do You Need?

It is very important to establish the expectations of your model's consumers about how explainable your model must be. If an uninterpretable prediction is acceptable, you should use as sophisticated an algorithm as you can afford in terms of time and computational resources. Train a neural network, a support vector machine, or any flavor of ensemble model to achieve a highly accurate and generalizable model. If interpretability or explainable documentation is important, use decision trees or a regression technique, and consider using penalized regression techniques, generalized additive models, quantile regression, or model averaging to refine your model.

Do You Have Automatic Hypertuning Capability?

Does your model have any automatic hypertuning capability that you can leverage? Optimal hyperparameter settings are extremely data dependent. Therefore, it is difficult to offer a general rule about how to identify a subset of important hyperparameters for a learning algorithm or how to find optimal values of each hyperparameter that would work for all data sets. Controlling hyperparameters of a learning algorithm is very important because proper control can increase accuracy and prevent overfitting.

Table 5.1 presents some best practices for selecting SAS Visual Data Mining and Machine Learning supervised learning algorithms.

Table 5.1: Selecting Supervised Learning Algorithms

Target Type	Usage	Scale	Interpret ability	Auto- tuning	Common Concerns
Regression (Linear, Logistic, GLM)					
· Linear regression and GLM for interval target. · Logistic regression for nominal and binary target.	· Modeling linear or linearly separable phenomena. · Manually specifying nonlinear and explicit interaction. · LASSO regression includes a regularization term for linear and logistic regression to deal with multicollinearity and overfitting issues.	Small to large data sets	High	No	· Missing values · Outliers · Standardization · Parameter tuning
SVM					
Binary	Modeling linear or linearly separable phenomena by using linear kernels or polynomial kernels up to degree three	Small to large data sets	Low	Yes	· Missing values · Overfitting · Outliers · Standardization · Parameter tuning

Target Type	Usage	Scale	Interpretability	Auto-tuning	Common Concerns

Tree-based Modeling (Decision Tree, Forest, Gradient Boosting)

Target Type	Usage	Scale	Interpretability	Auto-tuning	Common Concerns
· Interval · Binary · Nominal	· Modeling nonlinear and nonlinear separable phenomena in large data sets · Interactions considered automatically, but implicitly · Missing values and outliers in input variables handled automatically in many implementations · Tree ensembles (forests, gradient boosting) can increase prediction accuracy and decrease overfitting, but also decrease scalability and interpretability	Mid-size to large data sets	Moderate	Yes	· Instability with small training sets · Gradient boosting can be unstable with noise or outliers · Overfitting · Parameter tuning

Neural Network

Target Type	Usage	Scale	Interpretability	Auto-tuning	Common Concerns
· Interval · Binary · Nominal	· Modeling nonlinear and nonlinearly separable phenomena. · All interactions considered in fully connected, multilayer topologies.	Mid-size to large data sets	Low	Yes	· Missing values · Overfitting · Outliers · Standardization · Parameter tuning

Target Type	Usage	Scale	Interpret ability	Auto- tuning	Common Concerns

Bayesian Network

Target Type	Usage	Scale	Interpret ability	Auto- tuning	Common Concerns
· Binary · Nominal	· Modeling linearly separable phenomena in large data sets. · Well suited for extremely large data sets where complex methods are intractable.	Small to very large data sets	Moderate	Yes	· Linear independence assumption · Infrequent categorical levels

The following section and later chapters discuss the most commonly used algorithms. We start with one that you might already be familiar with, classification and regression.

Classification and Regression

Two major types of supervised machine learning problems are *classification* and *regression*. In classification, the goal is to predict a *class label* or group where the outcome or target is more similar to others in that particular group or class, than it is to the other targets in other groups; for example, classifying an animal into one species. In regression, the goal is to predict a continuous number; for example, house price or income.

K-Nearest Neighbors

The K-Nearest Neighbors (*k*-NN) is one of the simplest machine learning algorithms. It makes predictions by finding the closest data points in the training data set—in other words, its nearest neighbors.

In its simplest form, the *k*-NN algorithm considers exactly one nearest neighbor, which is the closest training point to the point that we want to predict the class label for that new point. The prediction is then simply the same class as the closest training point.

Figure 5.1: Prediction Made by the Nearest Neighbor Model on the New Data Point

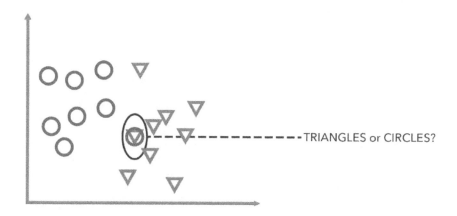

Instead of considering only the closest neighbor, we can also consider any number, k, of neighbors. Let's say $k = 5$, and the new data point is classified by the majority of votes from its five neighbors. The new point would be classified as a triangle since four out of five neighbors are a triangle. We are effectively voting to assign a class label, where each neighbor has one vote. Thus, for each point in the data set we count how many k neighbors belong to class 0 and how many neighbors belong to class 1. We then assign the class that is more frequent, the majority class among the k-nearest neighbors.

Figure 5.2: Predictions Made by the Five Nearest Neighbors Model on the New Data Point

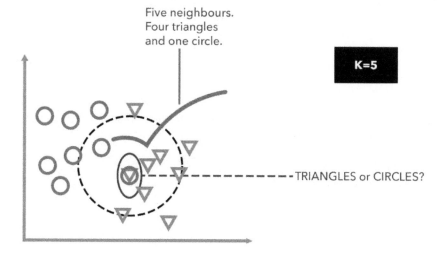

The above example illustrates a binary classification problem, but this method can be used on data sets with any number of classes. In the case of multiple classes, we count how many neighbors belong to each class and again predict the most frequent class.

But how do we choose the value of *k*? There is no set way to determine the best value for *k*, so we have to try out a few values before settling on one. Here are some pointers:

- Small values for *k* can be noisy and subject to the effects of outliers.

- Larger values of *k* have smoother decision boundaries, which mean lower variance but increased bias.

- Use odd values of *k* to avoid confusion between two classes of data.

Another common technique of choosing *k* is *cross-validation*. One way to select the cross-validation data set from the training data set is to take a small portion from the training data set and call it a validation data set, and then use the same to evaluate different possible values of *k*. This way we are going to predict the label for every instance in the validation set using with *k* equals 1, *k* equals 2, *k* equals 3, and so on. Then, we look at which value of *k* gives us the best performance on the validation set. We then choose that value of *k* to minimize the validation error.

Another general practice to choose the value of k is $k = sqrt(N)$ where N stands for the number of samples in your training data set.

The *k*-NN Algorithm

In the classification setting, the *k*-nearest neighbor algorithm calculates a majority vote between the *k* most similar instances to a given "unseen" observation. Similarity is defined according to a distance metric between two data points. A popular one is the Euclidean distance method.

$$\sqrt{\sum_{i=1}^{k} (x_i - y_1)^2}$$

Other methods are Manhattan, Minkowski, and Hamming distance methods. For categorical variables, the hamming distance must be used.

A more detailed example of K-NN can be found in this SAS communities post: https://communities.sas.com/t5/SAS-Communities-Library/A-Simple-Introduction-to-K-Nearest-Neighbors-Algorithm/ta-p/565402

Model Studio: The Clustering Node

In Model Studio, the **Clustering** node is a Data Mining Preprocessing node. Use the Clustering node to perform observation clustering based on distances that are computed from quantitative or qualitative variables (or both). The observations are divided into clusters such that every observation belongs to exactly one cluster. Clustering places observations into groups or clusters suggested by the data, such that observations within a cluster are similar and observations from different clusters are dissimilar.

This node uses the following algorithms:

- the k-means algorithm for clustering interval (quantitative) input variables

- the k-modes algorithm for clustering nominal (qualitative) input variables

- the k-prototypes algorithm for clustering mixed input that contains both interval and nominal variables

Clustering is accomplished by updating the cluster centroids and the cluster membership of the data iteratively until the convergence criterion is satisfied or until the maximum number of iterations is reached. The aligned box criterion (ABC) technique is used to estimate the number of clusters needed when you do not specify the desired number of clusters.

Observations with missing input values are not used during training. Therefore, you might need to impute your data. It is recommended that you standardize interval variables because variables that have large variances tend to affect the distance measurements more than variables with small variances.

After clustering is performed, the characteristics of the clusters can be examined graphically using the Clustering Results. The consistency of clusters across variables is of particular interest. The multidimensional charts and plots enable you to graphically compare the clusters.

Note that the cluster identifier for each observation can be passed to subsequent nodes for use as an input, ID, or segment variable. The default is a segment variable.

General Properties

Cluster initialization specifies the method used to determine initial cluster membership. Here are the possible values:

Forgy assigns k data points as the k initial clusters.

Random randomly assigns each observation to a cluster.

Model Studio: The Clustering Node

Automatic gamma specifies whether to automatically compute the gamma coefficient in the mixed distance computation.

User-specified gamma specifies the value for the coefficient gamma in the mixed distance computation.

Random seed specifies a positive integer to be used to start the pseudo-random number generator. The default value is 12345.

Interval Inputs

Missing interval inputs specifies the imputation method for interval input variables. Possible values are **Exclude** or **Impute with mean**. The default setting is **Impute with mean**.

Standardization method specifies the method for standardizing interval input variables. Here are the possible values:

- (none)
- Range
- Z Score

Specify **Range** to standardize on the range of the input variable, or specify **Z Score** to standardize on the calculated Z Score. Select **(none)** to disable standardization. The default setting is **(none)**.

Similarity distance specifies the distance measure for similarity measurement for interval input variables. Possible values are **Euclidean distance** and **Manhattan distance**. **Euclidean distance** calculates the line segment distance between two clusters. **Manhattan distance**, or taxicab distance, calculates the distance between two clusters using only axis-aligned movements. The default setting is **Euclidean distance**.

Class Inputs

Missing class inputs specifies the imputation method for class input variables. Possible values are **Exclude** and **Impute with mode**. The default setting is **Exclude**.

Model Studio: The Clustering Node

Similarity distance specifies the distance measure for similarity measurement of class input variables. Here are the possible values:

- **Binary**

- **Global frequency**

- **Relative frequency**

Binary calculates a simple matching distance. **Global frequency** and **Relative frequency** calculate distances based on the frequency of class input variables in the input data table or in each cluster respectively. The default setting is **Binary**.

Number of Clusters Estimation

Number of clusters method specifies the method used to estimate the number of clusters. Possible values are **Aligned box criterion** and **User specify**. Select **User specify** to enter the number of clusters in the **Number of clusters** field.

Select the **Aligned box criterion** property to generate the number of clusters based on the following parameters:

- **Number of reference data sets** specifies the number of reference data sets to be created for each cluster candidate. The default value is 1.

- **Maximum number of clusters** specifies the maximum number of clusters. If the number of observations is less than the number specified, then the number of clusters will be set to the number of observations. If the number of observations in a cluster is zero, then this cluster will not be displayed in the results. The default value is 6.

- **Minimum number of clusters** specifies the minimum number of clusters. The default value is 2.

- **Estimation criterion** specifies the criterion to use to estimate the number of clusters that use the statistics obtained in the ABC method. Here are the possible values:

  ○ **All criteria** specifies that the number of clusters is determined by a combination of the other three available property settings.

  ○ **First peak value** specifies that the number of clusters is determined by the first peak among the peak values in gap statistics.

Model Studio: The Clustering Node

- o **First peak with one-standard-error** specifies that the number of clusters is determined by the smallest k such that the gap value for that k is greater than the one-standard-error adjusted gap value for $k+1$.

- o **Global peak value** specifies that the number of clusters is determined by the maximum value among all peak values in gap statistics.

  The default value is **Global peak value**.

Alignment method specifies the method for aligning the reference data set based on the input data. Possible values are **(none)** and **PCA**. If set to **(none)**, the node generates the reference data set from a uniform distribution over the range of values for each subset of the input data set. If set to **PCA**, the node generates the reference data set from a uniform distribution over a box aligned with the principal components of each subset of the input data set.

Stop Criterion

Stop method specifies the stop criterion method. The possible values are **Cluster change** and **Within cluster distance**. **Cluster change** is the default.

Cluster change parameter specifies the percentile of observations that do not change their cluster for the iteration. The range is between 0 and 100, and the default value is 20. If you select **Cluster change** as the **Stop method**, the cluster calculation will conclude when the number of observations that change clusters is smaller than the chosen parameter value.

Within cluster distance parameter specifies the difference of within-cluster distance change between iterations. If you select **Within cluster distance** for the **Stop method**, the cluster calculation will conclude if the cluster distance changes by less than the given parameter after an iteration.

Maximum number of iterations specifies the maximum number of iterations for the algorithm to perform. The default value of 10. In each iteration, each observation is assigned to the nearest cluster centroid, and the centroids are recomputed.

Model Studio: The Clustering Node

Scored Output Roles

Cluster variable role specifies the role that you want to assign to the cluster variable. By default, the cluster variable (segment identifier) is assigned a role of **Segment**. Here are the available roles:

- **ID**
- **Input**
- **Rejected**
- **Segment**

    The role of segment is useful for BY-group processing. Note that the segment identifier retains the selected variable role when it is passed to subsequent nodes in the pipeline.

Cluster distance role specifies the role that is assigned to the cluster distance variable. The default role is **Rejected**.

Regression

For this book, we are assuming that you have a basic understanding of linear and logistic regression. Below we provide a quick refresher.

Linear Regression is an example of a *linear model*. Linear models make predictions using a *linear function* of the input features. For regression the formula is written:

$$y = w_0 * x_0 + w_1 * x_1 + \ldots + w_p * x_p + b$$

where x_0 to x_p represent features of a single data point, w and b are parameters that the model learns, and y is the output or prediction. This formula provides a predictive line, where the prediction of new data points can be found by plotting its position on the line using the input features as coordinates. For simple models with two features, the model can be represented as a plane. For higher dimensions of multiple features, the model is represented by a hyperplane.

Classification regression is used for binary classification predictions. It is very similar to linear regression but instead of predicting a continuous outcome, its output is restricted to a value to the unit interval.

$$y = w_0 * x_0 + w_1 * x_1 + \ldots + w_p * x_p + b > 0$$

The formula looks very similar to the one for linear regression, but the threshold for the predicted value is zero. If the function is less than zero, we predict the class -1, and if the function is greater than zero, we predict the class +1.

Logistic Regression

In *logistic regression*, model predictions can be viewed as primary outcome probabilities. A linear combination of the inputs generates a *logit score* or log of the odds of primary outcome, in contrast to the linear regression's direct prediction of the target.

For binary prediction, any monotonic function that maps the unit interval to the real number line can be considered as a link. The *logit link function* is one of the most common. Its popularity is due in part to the interpretability of the model. But the logit function complicates the parameter estimation. Parameter estimates are obtained by maximum likelihood estimation. The likelihood function is the joint probability density of the data treated as a function of the parameters.

$$\sum log(\hat{p}_i) + \sum log(1 - \hat{p}_i)$$

The former quantity represents the primary outcome training cases, and the latter one represents the secondary outcome training cases, in the above expression.

The maximum likelihood estimates are the values of the parameters that maximize the probability of obtaining the training sample. These estimates can be used in the logit and logistic equations to obtain predictions. The plot on the right side of Figure 5.3 shows the prediction estimates from the logistic equation. One of the attractions of a standard logistic regression model is the simplicity of its predictions. The contours are simple straight lines commonly known as the *isoprobability lines*. (In higher dimensions, they would be hyperplanes.)

Figure 5.3: Logistic Regression Example

$$\text{logit}(\hat{p}) = -0.81 + 0.92 \cdot x_1 + 1.11 \cdot x_2$$

$$\hat{p} = \frac{1}{1 + e^{-\text{logit}(\hat{p})}}$$

Using the maximum likelihood estimates, the prediction formula assigns a logit score to each x_1 and x_2.

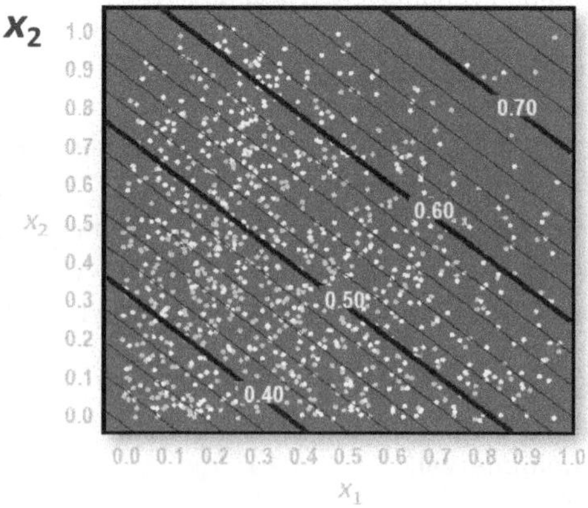

The predictions can be decisions, rankings, or estimates. The logit equation produces a ranking or logit score. To get a decision, you need a threshold. The easiest way to get a meaningful threshold is to convert the prediction ranking to a prediction estimate. You can obtain a prediction estimate using a straightforward transformation of the logit score, the logistic function. The *logistic function* is simply the inverse of the logit function. You can obtain the logistic function by solving the logit equation for *p*.

Quiz

1. What is the range of the logit function?
   a. $(-\infty, +\infty)$
   b. $[0, +\infty)$
   c. $[0,1]$
   d. $[1, +\infty)$

Chapter 6: Decision Trees: Introduction

Introduction

Decision trees and ensembles of trees are supervised learning algorithms that are widely used models for classification and regression tasks. In their simplest forms, *decision trees* learn a hierarchy of if/else questions, leading to a decision. Essentially, decision trees are statistical models designed for supervised prediction problems. Supervised prediction encompasses predictive modeling, pattern recognition, discriminant analysis, multivariate function estimation, and supervised machine learning.

But decision trees are unstable models - small changes in the training data can cause large changes in the topology of the tree. However, the overall performance of the tree remains stable (Breiman et al. 1984). You can combine many trees into "forests" to create an algorithm called a *decision tree ensemble* or *random forest* to overcome the instability that a single tree exhibits with minor perturbations of the training data.

Finally, we will discuss the dynamics and parameters to consider when building and combining decision trees.

Decision Tree Algorithm

A decision tree is so called because the predictive model can be represented by a tree-like structure. It builds up on iteratively asking questions to partition (split) the data. The questions get more specific as the tree gets deeper. The aim is to increase the predictiveness of the model as much as possible at each split, so the model keeps gaining information about the data set.

A decision tree is read from the top down starting at the *root node*. Each internal node represents a split based on the values of one of the inputs. The inputs can appear in any number of splits throughout the tree. Cases move down the branch that contains its input value. In a binary tree with interval inputs, each internal node is a simple inequality. A case moves left if the inequality is true and right otherwise. The terminal nodes of the tree are called *leaves*. The leaves represent the predicted target. All cases reaching a particular leaf are given the same predicted value.

> Decision trees can also have multi-way splits where the values of the inputs are partitioned into disjoint ranges. Multi-way splits request more evaluations for the candidate splits, considering all inputs in all n-way splits. For example, in 4-way splits, all possible candidates for 2-way splits, 3-way splits, and 4-way splits are evaluated.

Classification Tree

When the target is categorical, the model is a called a *classification tree*. The leaves give the predicted class as well as the probability of class membership. A *classification tree* can be thought of as defining several multivariate step functions.

Figure 6.1: Classification Tree

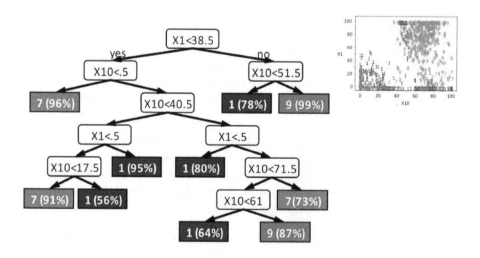

For classification trees, the most frequent response level of the training observations in a leaf is used to classify observations in that leaf.

Regression Tree

When the target is continuous, the model is a called a *regression tree*. The leaves give the predicted value of the target. All cases that reach a particular leaf are assigned the same predicted value.

The path to each leaf can be expressed as a Boolean rule. The rules take the following form:

If the inputs ∈ {*region of the input space*}, then the predicted value = *value*.

The regions of the input space are determined by the split values. For interval-scaled inputs, the boundaries of the regions are perpendicular to the split variables. Consequently, the regions are intersections of subspaces defined by a single splitting variable.

For regression trees, the average response of the training observations in a leaf is used to predict the response for observations in that leaf.

Figure 6.2: Regression Tree

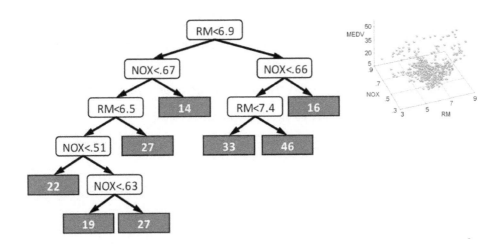

Building a Decision Tree

When building a decision tree, *learning* means learning the sequence of if/else questions that reach the true answer most quickly. In machine learning, these are called *tests* (not to be confused with the test data set). Often, data does not have binary yes/no features but is instead continuous. The tests that we would use on continuous data are in the following form:

Is feature *i* > value *d*

To build a tree, the algorithm searches over all possible tests and finds the one that is most informative about the target value. We want to split the data points in two groups at each step.

What you ask at each step is the most critical part and greatly influences the performance. The aim is to increase the predictiveness of the model at each partitioning (split) so that the model keeps gaining information about the data set. Randomly splitting the features does not usually give valuable insight, but splits that increase the purity of a node are more informative. The purity of a node is inversely proportional to the distribution of different classes in that node. Impurity increases with randomness. For example, if we have a box with ten counters in it, if all the counters are the same color then the impurity is zero, and we have no randomness. If, however, we have five red counters and five blue counters, then the impurity is one, and there is randomness.

> A node is 100% impure when a node is split evenly 50/50 and 100% pure when all of its data belongs to a single class. In order to optimize our model, we need to reach maximum purity and avoid impurity.

How Splits Are Chosen

As discussed above, splits are chosen to increase the purity of nodes and decrease the randomness. *Entropy* is a measure of uncertainty and randomness. The higher the entropy of the feature or input, the more the randomness is. The features with uniform distribution have the highest entropy. Choosing the split to give the most purity increases the information gain, which can be defined as follows:

Information gain = (Entropy before the split) - (Weighted entropy after the split)

When choosing the split, the decision tree algorithm tries to achieve:

- more predictiveness
- less impurity
- lower entropy

How Many Questions Are Asked?

How many splits are there? How many questions are chosen? When do you stop? Too many questions would give an overfitted model. The algorithm can keep splitting the data until the nodes are 100% pure but this model would not generalize well. In the following section we discuss how to limit the depth (number of splits) of a tree to prevent overfitting.

Details: Simple Prediction Illustration

Cases are scored using *prediction rules*. A *split-search* algorithm facilitates input selection. The process of building a decision tree begins with growing a large, full tree. To avoid potential overfitting, many predictive modeling procedures offer some mechanism for adjusting model complexity. For decision trees, this process is known as *pruning*. The process of pruning constructs a *subtree*. We will discuss optimization of model complexity in more detail in the following chapter.

The following simple prediction problem illustrates each of these model essentials.

Consider a data set with two inputs and a binary target. The inputs, x_1 and x_2, locate the case in the unit square. The target outcome is represented by a color: yellow is primary and blue is secondary. The analysis goal is to predict the outcome based on the location in the unit square.

Figure 6.3: Simple Prediction

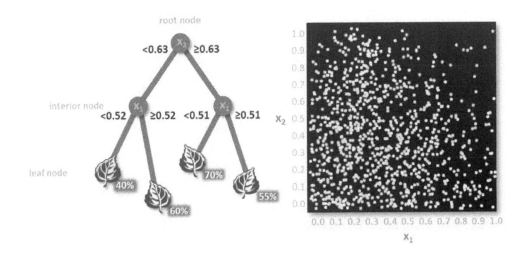

To predict cases, decision trees use rules that involve the values of the input variables.

The rules are arranged hierarchically in a tree-like structure with nodes connected by lines. The nodes represent decision rules, and the lines order the rules. The first rule, at the base (top) of the tree, is named the *root node*. Subsequent rules are named *interior nodes*. Nodes with only one connection are *leaf nodes*.

The *depth* of a tree specifies the number of generations of nodes. The root node is generation 0. The children of the root node are the first generation, and so on.

To score a new case, examine the input values and apply the rules defined by the decision tree.

Figure 6.4: Scoring a New Case

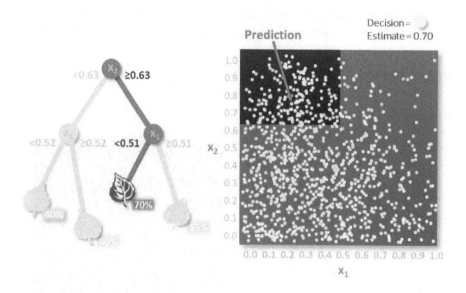

The input values of a new case eventually lead to a single leaf in the tree. A tree leaf provides a decision (for example, classify as yellow) and an estimate (for example, the primary-target proportion). Thus, a prediction on a new data point is made by checking which region of the partition of the feature space the point lies in, and then predicting the majority target (or the single target in the case of pure leaves) in that region. The region can be found by traversing the tree from the root and going left or right, depending on whether the test is fulfilled or not.

It is also possible to use trees for regression tasks, using exactly the same technique. To make a prediction, we traverse the tree based on the tests in each node and find the leaf the new data point falls into. The output for this data point is the mean target of the training points in this leaf.

Demo 6.1: Building a Decision Tree Model with Default Settings

In this demonstration, you use the CPML Demo Pipeline as a starting place in a new pipeline in the **Demo** project. You add a Decision Tree node and build a decision tree model using the default settings of the node.

1. Return to the **Demo** project and click the **Pipelines** tab. Click the plus sign (**+**) next to the Starter Template tab to add a new pipeline.

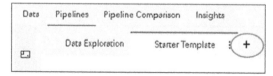

2. In the New Pipeline window, enter **Lesson 3** in the **Name** field. For **Template**, select **Browse templates**.

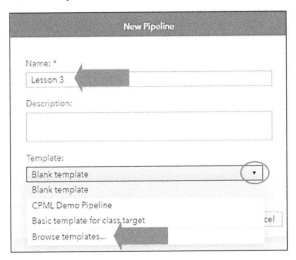

3. Scroll down as needed in the Browse Template window and select **CPML demo pipeline**. Click **OK**.

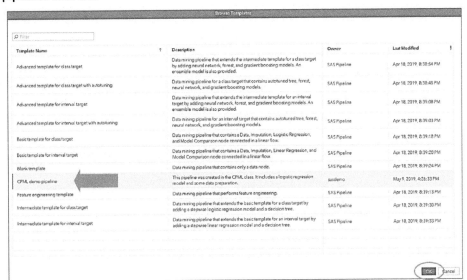

4. Click **Save** in the New Pipeline window.

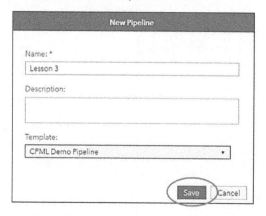

5. In the pipeline, right-click the **Variable Selection** node and select **Add child node** ▶ **Supervised Learning** ▶ **Decision Tree**.

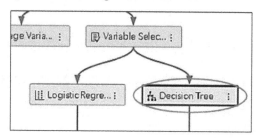

6. Keep all properties for the decision tree at their defaults. Run the Decision Tree node.

7. Open the results for the Decision Tree node.

There are several charts and plots to help you in evaluating the model's performance. The first plot is the *Tree Diagram*, which presents the final tree structure for this particular model, such as the depth of the tree and all end leaves.

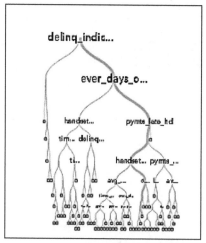

The *Pruning Error plot* shows the model's performance based on the misclassification rate—because the target is binary—throughout the recursive splitting process when new end leaves have been added to the final model.

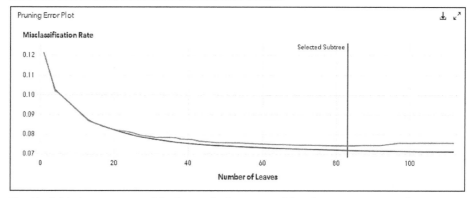

The *Variable Importance table* shows the input variables that are most significant to the final model. The most important input variable has its relative importance as 1 and all others are measured based on the most important input.

Variable Label	Variable Name	Validation Importa...	Importance Standa...	Relative Importance
Total Days Over Plan	ever_days_over_plan	850.1282	251.1943	1
Handset Age Group	handset_age_grp	578.8274	26.2636	0.6809
Delinquent Indicator	delinq_indicator	463.8066	133.8525	0.5456
Days Suspended Last 6M	avg_days_susp	463.7678	72.6183	0.5455
Total Late Payments Lifetime	pymts_late_ltd	309.8746	61.1060	0.3645
Number of Times Suspended	times_susp	273.5927	41.0806	0.3218

The Validation Importance column is the maximum RSS-based variable importance.

The Relative Importance column measures variable importance based on the change of residual sum of squares (RSS) when a split is found at a node. It is a number between 0 and 1, which is calculated as the RSS-based importance of this variable divided by the maximum RSS-based importance among all the variables. For example, 850.128/850.128=1, 578.827/850.128=0.6809, and so on. The RSS and relative importance are calculated from the validation data. If no validation data exist, they are calculated instead from the training data.

The Importance Standard Deviation column shows how much the variable importance differs from the mean importance value of that variable when that variable is used across multiple splits in the decision tree. That is the reason its value is 0 when the count value is 1.

The Count column (not shown in the display capture above) shows how many times a variable is used in splitting in the decision tree.

Model Studio gives three types of scoring codes. The *Node Score Code window* shows the individual score code for a specific node that can be deployed in production. You get this score code against every node in the Data Mining Preprocessing and the Supervised Learning groups that creates DATA step score code. The nodes that create ASTORE score file does not generate this output.

```
Node Score Code                                                              ↗
    1         length _strfmt_ $12; drop _strfmt_;                             |
    2         _strfmt_ = ' ';
    3
    4         array _tlevname_79837591_{2} $2 _temporary_ ( ' 1'
    5         ' 0');
    6
    7         array _dt_fi_79837591_{2} _temporary_;
    8
    9         _node_id_ = 0;
   10         _new_id_  = -1;
   11         nextnode_79837591:
   12         if _node_id_ eq 0 then do;
   13             _strfmt_ = left(trim(put(delinq_indicator,BEST2.)));
   14             if _strfmt_ in ('3',
   15             '?'
```

After you add a model in the pipeline (a Supervised Learning node), that node generates two additional score codes and a train code.

The *Path EP Score Code* is the "flow score code," which includes score code for all the nodes until and including that modeling node.

```
Path EP Score Code                                                           ↗
    1    ⊖ data sasep.out;                                                    |
    2         dcl double "REP_BILL_DATA_USG_M03" having label n'Replacement: 3M Avg Billed Data U
    3         dcl double "REP_BILL_DATA_USG_M06" having label n'Replacement: 6M Avg Billed Data U
    4         dcl double "REP_CALLS_IN_OFFPK" having label n'Replacement: Calls Incoming Off-Peak
    5         dcl double "REP_CALLS_IN_PK" having label n'Replacement: Calls Incoming Peak';
    6         dcl double "REP_CALLS_OUT_OFFPK" having label n'Replacement: Calls Outgoing Off-Pea
    7         dcl double "REP_CALLS_OUT_PK" having label n'Replacement: Calls Outgoing Peak';
    8         dcl double "REP_CALLS_TOTAL" having label n'Replacement: Total Calls Curr';
    9         dcl double "REP_DATA_DEVICE_AGE" having label n'Replacement: Avg Age of Devices on
   10         dcl double "REP_LIFETIME_VALUE" having label n'Replacement: Lifetime Value';
   11         dcl double "REP_MB_DATA_NDIST_MO6M" having label n'Replacement: 6M Avg Billed Data
   12         dcl double "REP_MB_DATA_USG_M01" having label n'Replacement: MB Data Usage 1 Mth Pr
   13         dcl double "REP_MB_DATA_USG_M02" having label n'Replacement: MB Data Usage 2 Mths P
   14         dcl double "REP_MB_DATA_USG_M03" having label n'Replacement: MB Data Usage 3 Mths P
   15
```

Typically, the Path Score Code or Path EP Score Code is the score code that would be used in other SAS environments (for example, SAS Studio) for scoring. EP stands for Embedded Process, and perhaps it is the underlying engine for in-database scoring (via scoring accelerators). The Path EP Score code that you get from any of the nodes in the process flow creates an ASTORE score file (here due to Text Mining node). Otherwise, you get Path Score Code. In addition, the *DS2 Package Code* (shown below) is score code packaged slightly differently. As a DS2 package, this score code can be used for MAS (SAS Micro Analytic Service). Note that both the Path EP Score Code and the DS2 Package Code are score codes written in DS2.

```
DS2 Package Code                                                                          ⤢
1       package MS_0cd884cf78784110be4361eef84ecfa3_31MAY2019022342719 / overwrite=yes;
2           dcl double "REP_BILL_DATA_USG_M03" having label n'Replacement: 3M Avg Billed Data U
3           dcl double "REP_BILL_DATA_USG_M06" having label n'Replacement: 6M Avg Billed Data U
4           dcl double "REP_CALLS_IN_OFFPK" having label n'Replacement: Calls Incoming Off-Peak
5           dcl double "REP_CALLS_IN_PK" having label n'Replacement: Calls Incoming Peak';
6           dcl double "REP_CALLS_OUT_OFFPK" having label n'Replacement: Calls Outgoing Off-Pea
7           dcl double "REP_CALLS_OUT_PK" having label n'Replacement: Calls Outgoing Peak';
8           dcl double "REP_CALLS_TOTAL" having label n'Replacement: Total Calls Curr';
9           dcl double "REP_DATA_DEVICE_AGE" having label n'Replacement: Avg Age of Devices on
10          dcl double "REP_LIFETIME_VALUE" having label n'Replacement: Lifetime Value';
11          dcl double "REP_MB_DATA_NDIST_M06M" having label n'Replacement: 6M Avg Billed Data
12          dcl double "REP_MB_DATA_USG_M01" having label n'Replacement: MB Data Usage 1 Mth Pr
13          dcl double "REP_MB_DATA_USG_M02" having label n'Replacement: MB Data Usage 2 Mths P
14          dcl double "REP_MB_DATA_USG_M03" having label n'Replacement: MB Data Usage 3 Mths P
15
```

On the other hand, the *Training Code window* shows the SAS training code that can be used to train the model based on different data sets or in different platforms. For example, when you scroll down in the Training Code window, you can see that the TREESPLIT procedure is used to train the decision tree model.

```
Training Code                                                                            ⤢
1       *----------------------------------------------------------------*;
2       * Macro Variables for input, output data and files;
3           %let dm_datalib =;
4           %let dm_lib      = WORK;
5           %let dm_folder   = %sysfunc(pathname(work));
6       *----------------------------------------------------------------*;
7       *----------------------------------------------------------------*;
8        * Training for tree;
9       *----------------------------------------------------------------*;
10      *----------------------------------------------------------------*;
11       * Initializing Variable Macros;
12      *----------------------------------------------------------------*;
13  ⊖ %macro dm_unary_input;
14      %mend dm_unary_input;
15      %global dm_num_unary_input;
```

Note: There is a new Score Data node in Model Studio that can be used to collect and accumulate score code at any point in the pipeline.

Finally, the Output window shows the final decision tree model parameters, the Variable Importance table, and the pruning iterations.

The SAS System

The TREESPLIT Procedure

Model Information	
Split Criterion	IGR
Pruning Method	Cost Complexity
Max Branches per Node	2
Max Tree Depth	10
Tree Depth Before Pruning	10
Tree Depth After Pruning	10
Number of Leaves Before Pruning	170
Number of Leaves After Pruning	83

8. Click the **Assessment** tab.

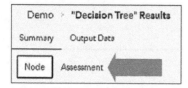

The first chart is the *Cumulative Lift*, showing the model's performance ordered by the percentage of the population. This chart is very useful for selecting the model based on a particular target of the customer base. It shows how much better the model is than the random events.

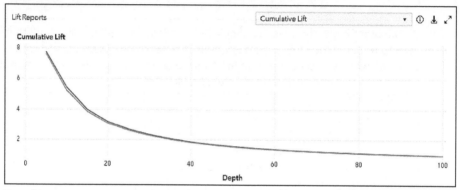

For a binary target, you also have the *ROC curve*, which shows the model's performance considering the true positive rate and the false positive rate. It is good to foresee the performance on a specific business events, when all positive cases are selected. It shows the model's performance based on the positive cases were predicted right and the positive cases were predicted wrong. ROC is very useful for deployment.

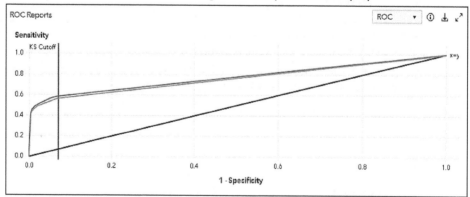

Finally, you have the *Fit Statistics output*, which shows the model's performance based on some assessment measures, such as average squared error.

Target...	Data Role	Partitio...	Formatt...	Sum of...	Averag...
churn	TRAIN	1	1	39,590	0.0638
churn	VALIDATE	0	0	16,967	0.0661

The Fit Statistics table shows an average squared error of 0.0661 on the VALIDATE partition.

9. Close the Results window.

End of Demonstration

Pros and Cons of Decision Trees

Decision trees ensembles are very useful predictive models. Here are some of the pros and cons:

Pros

- You do not usually need to normalize or scale features.
- Decision trees can work on a mixture of feature data types (continuous, categorical, binary).
- Easy interpretability.

Cons

- Prone to overfitting and need to be ensembled to generalize well.
- Unstable models.

Quiz

1. Which of the following statements is true regarding decision trees?
   a. To predict cases, decision trees use rules that involve the values or categories of the input variables.
   b. Decision trees can handle only categorical target.
   c. The predictor variables can appear only in a single split in the tree.
   d. The splits in decision trees can be only binary.

Chapter 7: Decision Trees: Improving the Model

Introduction

In this chapter we cover techniques to help optimize the model and how to regularize and tune parameters to further improve the model performance.

Improving a Decision Tree Model by Changing the Tree Structure Parameters

You can modify the tree structure parameters and then compare this new model performance to the models built earlier to find the best fit. Some properties that control the tree structure or topology include:

- **Maximum depth** specifies the maximum number of generations in nodes. The original node, generation 0, is called the root node. The children of the root node are the first generation. Possible values range from 1 to 50.

- **Minimum leaf size** specifies the smallest number of training observations that a leaf can have.

- **Number of interval bins** specifies the number of bins used for interval inputs. Bin size is (maximum value – minimum value) / interval bins. You often have many interval inputs in the form of continuous values. Many machine learning algorithms, including decision trees, operate only in discrete search or variable space. Decision trees typically bin the interval inputs to find the split points.

 Demo 7.1: Improving a Decision Tree Model by Changing the Tree Structure Parameters

In this demonstration, you change the default settings of the Decision Tree node that was just added in the Demo 6.1 pipeline. You modify the tree structure parameters and compare this model performance to the models built earlier.

1. To recall, the previous model, based on the default settings, achieved an average squared error of 0.0661 on the VALIDATE partition.

2. Try to improve the model's performance by modifying some of the settings of the decision tree model. Expand the **Splitting Options** properties in the properties pane of the Decision Tree node.

3. Increase **Maximum depth** from 10 to **14**.

   This specifies 14 as the maximum number of generations in nodes. The original node, generation 0, is called the root node. The children of the root node are the first generation. Possible values range from 1 to 50.

4. Increase **Minimum leaf size** from 5 to **15**.

   This specifies 15 as the smallest number of training observations that a leaf can have.

5. Increase Number of interval bins from 20 to 100.

   This specifies 100 as the number of bins used for interval inputs. Bin size is (maximum value – minimum value) / interval bins. You often have many interval inputs in the form of continuous values. Many machine learning algorithms, including decision trees, operate only in discrete search or variable space. Decision trees typically bin the interval inputs to find the split points.

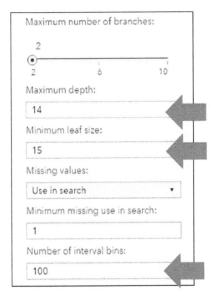

6. Quantile is the default interval bin method that bins interval input variables where the number of observations in each bin is approximately equal. Bucket is another method that bins interval input variables into fixed-width bins. Run the **Decision Tree** node.

7. Open the results for the Decision Tree node.

8. Click the **Assessment** tab and look at model performance using average squared error in the Fit Statistics table. (You might need to expand the Fit Statistics table.)

Target ...	Data Role	Partitio...	Formatt...	Sum of ...	Averag...
churn	TRAIN	1	1	39,590	0.0633
churn	VALIDATE	0	0	16,967	0.0650

The average squared error for the tuned decision tree model is 0.0650 on the VALIDATE partition. This fit statistic is slightly better (smaller) compared to that of the first model using the default settings.

9. Close the Results window.

End of Demonstration

Improving a Decision Tree Model by Changing the Recursive Partitioning Parameters

The most common method to improve decision tree models is to modify their growth by adjusting the **recursive partitioning parameters** that define the splits. The splits are basically driven by impurity. Impurity is a measure of the homogeneity of the labels on the node. There are three main techniques used:

- Gini Impurity
- Entropy
- Variance

To improve the model, try changing the partitioning parameter. Below is a brief discussion of how recursive partitioning works, followed by a quick discussion of the three most commonly used techniques and when best to use them. More detail can be found in the Appendix.

Details: Recursive Partitioning

Recursive partitioning is the standard method used to fit decision trees. Recursive partitioning is a top-down, greedy algorithm. A *greedy* algorithm is one that makes locally optimal choices at each step. Starting at the root node, a number of splits that involve a single input are examined. Finding the split point for the root node is the first step of recursive partitioning. For interval inputs, the splits are disjoint ranges of the input values. For nominal inputs, the splits are disjoint subsets of the input categories. Various split-search strategies can be used to determine the set of candidate splits. A splitting criterion is used to choose the split. The splitting criterion measures the reduction in variability of the target distribution in the child nodes. The goal is to reduce variability and thus increase purity in the child nodes. The cases in the root node are then partitioned according to the selected split.

Figure 7.1: Root-Node Split

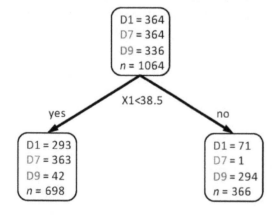

The root-node split corresponds to a partition of the input space where the boundary is perpendicular to one input dimension. The result is a tree that has a depth of 1 (hence the term *1-deep space*).

Figure 7.2: 1-Deep Space

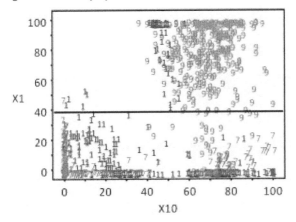

The process is repeated. The depth is governed by stopping rules, which are discussed later.

The Gini Impurity or Index

The Gini impurity is a measure of variability for categorical data (developed by the eminent Italian statistician Corrado Gini in 1912). In simple terms, Gini impurity is the *measure of impurity in a node*. Its formula is:

$$1 - \sum_{j=1}^{r} p_j^2 = 2 \sum_{j<k} p_j p_k$$

high diversity, low purity

$$\Pr(\text{interspecific encounter}) = 1 - 2(3/8)^2 - 2(1/8)^2 = .69$$

low diversity, high purity

$$\Pr(\text{interspecific encounter}) = 1 - (6/7)^2 - (1/7)^2 = .24$$

Where J is the number of classes present in the node and p is the distribution of the class in the node.

In reality, we evaluate a lot of different splits with different threshold values for a continuous variable and all the levels for categorical variables. And then choose the split that provides us with the lowest weighted impurity in the child nodes.

Entropy

Another popular way to split nodes in the decision tree is entropy. Entropy is the measure of randomness in the system. The formula for entropy is:

$$Entropy = \sum_{i=1}^{C} -p_i * log_2(p_1)$$

where C is the number of classes present in the node and p is the distribution of the class in the node.

Variance

Gini impurity and entropy work well for the classification scenario. But what about regression? In the case of regression, the most common split measure used is just the weighted variance of the nodes. It makes sense, too. We want minimum variation in the nodes after the split.

$$Variance = \frac{\Sigma(X - \overline{X})^2}{n}$$

In Figure 7.3, the target has an interval measurement level, and splitting criteria is based on reducing the variance of the target in child nodes.

Figure 7.3: Variance Reduction

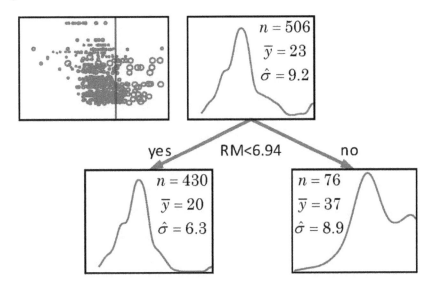

When the target has an interval measurement level, splitting criteris can be based on reducing variance of the target in child nodes. Other more robust measures of spread such as least absolute deviation (LAD) were proposed (Breiman et al. 1984). More detail of impurity reduction measures can be found in the appendix.

Model Studio: Split Criteria

In summary, these are the options in Model Studio to grow a decision tree.

For categorical responses, the available criteria are CHAID, CHISQUARE, ENTROPY, GINI, and IGR (information gain ratio). The default is IGR. For continuous responses, the available criteria are CHAID, FTEST, and VARIANCE. The default is VARIANCE.

- **CHAID** uses the value of a chi-square statistic for a classification tree or an *F* statistic for a regression tree. Based on the significance level, the value of the chi-square of *F* statistic is used to merge similar levels of the predictor variable until the number of children in the proposed split reaches the number specified as the maximum possible branches. The *p*-values for the final split determine the variable on which to split.

- Split criteria using the *p*-value (Chi-square, CHAID, or F test) can request a Bonferroni adjustment to the *p*-value for a variable after the split has been determined.

- **CHISQUARE** uses a chi-square statistic to split each variable and then uses the *p*-values that correspond to the resulting splits to determine the splitting variable.

Model Studio: Split Criteria

- **ENTROPY** uses the gain in information or the decrease in entropy to split each variable and then to determine the split. A minimum of decrease in entropy or increase in information gain ration can be specified.

- **GINI** uses the decrease in the Gini index to split each variable and then to determine the split.

- **IGR** uses the entropy metric to split each variable and then uses the information gain ratio to determine the split.

For continuous responses the available criteria are CHAID, FTEST, and VARIANCE.

- **CHAID** is described above.

- **FTEST** uses an *F* statistic to split each variable and then uses the resulting *p*-value to determine the split point.

- A Bonferroni adjustment can be applied to both CHAID and FTEST criteria.

- **VARIANCE** uses the change in response variance to split each variable and then to determine the split.

Decision Tree Split Search

To select useful inputs, trees use a *split-search* algorithm. Decision trees confront the curse of dimensionality by ignoring irrelevant inputs.

> Curiously, trees have no built-in method for ignoring redundant inputs. Because trees can be trained quickly and have a simple structure, this is usually not an issue for model creation. However, it can be an issue for model deployment, in that trees might somewhat arbitrarily select from a set of correlated inputs. To avoid this problem, you must use an algorithm that is external to the tree to manage input redundancy.

The details of the algorithm used for building trees can be found in the appendix and enables you to better use SAS Visual Data Mining and Machine Learning to build a tree and interpret your results.

Model Studio: Split Criteria

Handling Missing Values in Decision Trees

One of the key benefits of recursive partitioning is the treatment of missing input data. Parametric regression models require complete cases. One missing value on one input variable eliminates that case from analysis. Imputation methods are often used before model fitting to fill in the missing values.

If the value of the target variable is missing, the observation is excluded from training and evaluating the decision tree model.

Decision trees can use missing values in the calculation of the worth of a splitting rule. This consequently produces a splitting rule that assigns the missing values to the branch that maximizes the worth of the split. This is a desirable option when the existence of a missing value is predictive of a target value. Decision trees can use missing values in the split search as a new category or as an unknown numeric nonmissing value.

It treats missing input values as a separate level of the input variable. A nominal input with L levels and a missing value can be treated as an $L + 1$ level input. If a new case has a missing value on a splitting variable, then the case is sent to whatever branch contains the missing values.

For splits on a categorical variable, this amounts to treating a missing value as a separate category. For numerical variables, it amounts to treating missing values as having the same unknown nonmissing value.

One advantage of using missing data during the search is that the worth of the split is computed with the same number of observations for each input. Another advantage is that an association of the missing values with the target values can contribute to the predictive ability of the split.

The search for a split on an input uses observations whose values are missing on the input. All such observations are assigned to the same branch. The branch might or might not contain other observations. The resulting branch maximizes the worth of the split.

Another option is to not use missing values in the split search. In this case, decision trees assign the observations that contain missing values to a particular branch according to some criteria.

Surrogate rules are backup splitting rules that are used when the variable that corresponds to the primary splitting rule is missing.

Model Studio: Split Criteria

Figure 7.4: Surrogate Splits

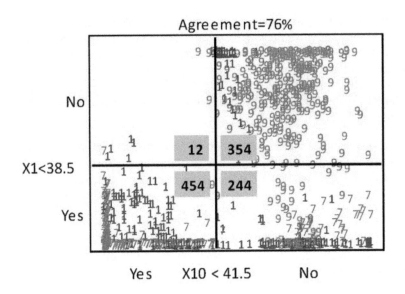

When a split is applied to an observation in which the required input value is missing, surrogate splitting rules can be considered before assigning the observation to the branch for missing values.

A surrogate splitting rule is a backup to the main splitting rule. For example, the main splitting rule might use **COUNTY** as input, and the surrogate might use **REGION**. If **COUNTY** is unknown and **REGION** is known, the surrogate is used.

If several surrogate rules exist, each surrogate is considered in sequence until one can be applied to the observation. If none can be applied, the main rule assigns the observation to the branch that is designated for missing values.

The surrogates are considered in the order of their agreement with the main splitting rule. The agreement is measured as the proportion of training observations that the surrogate rule and the main rule assign to the same branch. The measure excludes the observations to which the main rule cannot be applied. Among the remaining observations, those on which the surrogate rule cannot be applied count as observations that are not assigned to the same branch. Thus, an observation that has used a missing value on the input in the surrogate rule but not the input in the primary rule counts against the surrogate.

Model Studio: Split Criteria

The **Surrogate Rules** property determines the number of surrogates that are sought. A surrogate is discarded if its agreement is less than or equal to the largest proportion of observations in any branch. As a consequence, a node might have fewer surrogates specified than the number in the **Number of Surrogate Rules** property.

Surrogate splits can be used to handle missing values (Breiman et al. 1984). A surrogate split is a partition using a different input that mimics the selected split. A perfect surrogate maps all the cases that are in the same node of the primary split to the same node of the surrogate split. The agreement between two splits can be measured as the proportion of cases that are sent to the same branch. The split with the greatest agreement is taken as the best surrogate.

When surrogate rules are requested, if a new case has a missing value on the splitting variable, then the best surrogate is used to classify the case. If the surrogate variable is missing as well, then the second-best surrogate is used. If the new case has a missing value on all the surrogates, it is sent to the branch that contains the missing values of the training data.

Details: Variable Importance Based on Gini Reduction

Breiman et al. (1984) devised a measure of variable importance for trees. It can be particularly useful for tree interpretation.

Figure 7.5: Variable Importance Based on Gini Reduction

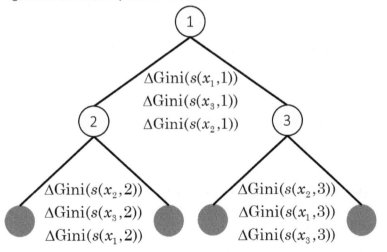

Model Studio: Split Criteria

Let $s(x_j, t)$ be a surrogate split (including the primary split) at the tth internal node using the jth input. Importance is a weighted average of the reduction in impurity for the surrogate splits using the jth input across all the internal nodes in the tree. The weights are the node sizes.

$$\text{Importance}(x_j) = \sum_{t=1}^{T} \frac{n_t}{n} \Delta(i)(s(x_j), t),$$

where $\Delta(i)$ represents impurity reduction. For interval targets, variance reduction is used. For categorical targets, variance reduction reduces to Gini reduction.

In the Decision Tree task, variable importance is calculated similarly to Breiman et al. (1984), although it takes the square root. Further, the Decision Tree node incorporates the agreement between the surrogate split and the primary split in the calculation. The variable importance measure is scaled to be between 0 and 1 by dividing by the maximum importance. Thus, larger values indicate greater importance. Variables that do not appear in any primary or saved surrogate splits have 0 importance.

One major difference between variable importance in the Decision Tree task and in Breiman et al. (1984) is that, by default, surrogates are not saved. Therefore, they are not included in the calculation. This practice disregards a fundamental purpose of variable importance: unmasking inputs that have splits that are correlated with primary splits.

If two variables are highly correlated and they are both used in primary splitting rules, they dilute each other's importance. Requesting surrogates remedies this, and also remedies the situation where one of the two variables happens not to appear in any primary splitting rule.

Demo 7.2: Improving a Decision Tree Model by Changing the Recursive Partitioning Parameters

In this demonstration, you change more settings of the Decision Tree node in the Demo 6.1 pipeline. You modify the recursive partitioning parameters and compare this model performance to the models built earlier in the course.

Recall that the previous model, based on changing the tree structure parameters, achieved an average squared error of 0.0650 on the VALIDATE partition. We will try to improve the model's performance by modifying some of the settings of the decision tree model.

1. Under the Grow Criterion properties, change **Class target criterion** from Information gain ratio to **Gini**.

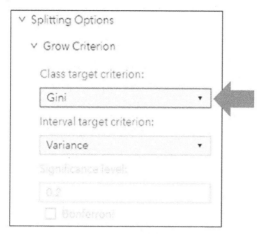

The Gini index is calculated by subtracting the sum of the squared probabilities of each class from one. It favors larger partitions.

Information gain multiplies the probability of the class times the log of that class probability. It favors smaller partitions with many distinct values.

In due course, you experiment with your data and the splitting criterion.

2. Run the **Decision Tree** node.
3. Open the results for the node.
4. Click the **Assessment** tab.

Target ...	Data Role	Partitio...	Formatt...	Sum of ...	Averag...
churn	TRAIN	1	1	39,590	0.0597
churn	VALIDATE	0	0	16,967	0.0605

The average squared error for the tuned decision tree model is 0.0605 on the VALIDATE partition. This fit statistic, again, is a slight improvement compared to that of the previous model by changing only the recursive partitioning parameters.

5. Close the Results window.

End of Demonstration

Optimizing the Complexity of the Model

Recall that a large decision tree can be grown until every node is as pure as possible. If at least two observations have the same values on the input variables but different target values, it is not possible to achieve perfect purity. The tree with the greatest possible purity on the training data is the *maximal classification* tree. The maximal tree is the result of overfitting. It adapts to both the systematic variation of the target (signal) and the random variation (noise). It usually does not generalize well on new (noisy) data. Conversely, a small tree with only a few branches might underfit the data. It might fail to adapt sufficiently to the signal. This usually results in poor generalization. There are two common strategies to prevent overfitting: stopping the creation of the tree early (also called *pre-pruning*) or building the tree but then removing or collapsing nodes that contain little information (also called *post-pruning* or just *pruning*). Possible criteria for pre-pruning include limiting the maximum depth of the tree, limiting the maximum number of leaves, or requiring a minimum number of points in a node to keep splitting it.

Figure 7.6: Model Complexity

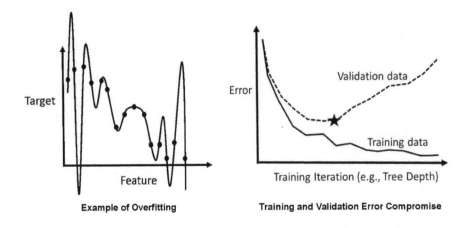

| Example of Overfitting | Training and Validation Error Compromise |

If we don't restrict the depth of a decision tree, the tree can become arbitrarily deep and complex. Evidently, a model that is complex enough to perfectly fit the existing data does not generalize well when used to score new observations. In the next section we look in detail at *pruning*.

Pruning

Honest assessment, which is highly related to the bias-variance tradeoff, involves calculating error metrics from scoring the model on data that were not used in any way during the training process. The distinctions between the validation data and the test data, and how to incorporate them as part of your model training, assessment, and selection process, were discussed briefly in Chapter 1 and are revisited in Chapter 12.

A large decision tree can be grown until every node is as pure as possible. If at least two observations have the same values on the input variables but different target values, it is not possible to achieve perfect purity. The tree with the greatest possible purity on the training data is the *maximal classification* tree.

Figure 7.7: Maximal Tree

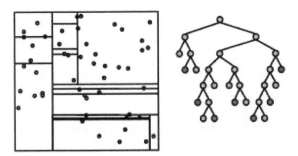

Two commonly applied approaches for finding the best subtree are cost-complexity pruning (Breiman et al. 1984) and C4.5 pruning (Quinlan 1993).

Tree complexity is a function of the number of leaves, the number of splits, and the depth of the tree. Determining complexity is crucial with flexible models like decision trees. A well-fit tree has low bias (adapts to the signal) and low variance (does not adapt to the noise). The determination of model complexity usually involves a tradeoff between bias and variance. An underfit tree that is not sufficiently complex has high bias and low variance. In contrast, an overfit tree has low bias and high variance. The maximal tree represents the most complicated model that you are willing to construct from a set of training data. To avoid potential overfitting, many predictive modeling procedures offer some mechanism for adjusting model complexity. For decision trees, this process is known as *pruning*.

There are two types of pruning:

- top down
- bottom up

Top-down pruning is usually faster but is considered less effective than bottom-up pruning. Breiman and Friedman, in their criticism of the FACT tree algorithm (Loh and Vanichsetakul 1988), discussed their experiments with stopping rules as part of the development of the CART methodology: "Each stopping rule was tested on hundreds of simulated data sets with different structures. Each new stopping rule failed on some data set. It was not until a very large tree was built and then pruned, using cross validation to govern the degree of pruning, that we observed something that worked consistently."

Bottom-Up Pruning

In bottom-up (post) pruning, a large tree is grown and then branches are lopped off in a backward fashion using some model selection criterion. The bottom-up strategy of intentionally creating more nodes than will be used is also called *retrospective pruning* and originated with cost-complexity pruning (Brieman et al. 1984).

Figure 7.8: Bottom-up Pruning

1. Grow a maximal tree:

2. Prune to create optimal sequence of subtrees:

For any subtree, T, in a tree grown from 1 to *n* leaves, define its complexity or size (number of leaves) as L, and define R(L) as the validation set misclassification cost. Other assessment measures can also be used.

In SAS Viya, the pruning process starts with the maximal tree T_{max} with L leaves. The maximal tree is denoted as T_L. Construct a series of smaller and smaller trees T_L, T_{L-1}, T_{L-2}, ..., T_1, such that the following holds: For every value of H*i*, where $1 \leq Hi \leq L$, consider the class T_{Hi} of all subtrees of size H*i*. Select the subtree in the series that minimizes $R(T_{Hi})$.

> The trees in the series of subtrees are not necessarily nested.

The subtree with the best performance on validation data is selected.

Figure 7.9: Bottom-up Pruning

3. Choose the best tree on validation data:

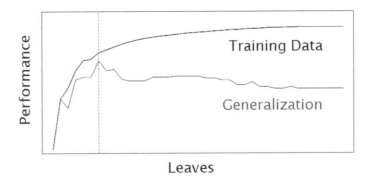

Bottom-up pruning has two requirements:

- **A method for honestly measuring performance.** The simplest remedy is to split the data into training and validation sets. The validation data are used for model comparison. Data splitting is inefficient when the data are small. Removing data from the training set can degrade the fit. Furthermore, evaluating performance on a single validation set can give imprecise results. A more efficient remedy—but more computationally expensive—is k-fold cross validation. In k-fold cross validation, performance measures are averaged over k models. Each model is fit with $(k\text{-}1)/k$ of the data and assessed on the remaining $1/k$ of the data. The average over the k holdout data sets is then used to honestly estimate the performance for the model fitted to the full data set. Cross validation is discussed later in this lesson.

- **A relevant model selection criterion.** For classification problems, the most appropriate measures of generalization depend on the number of correct and incorrect classifications and their consequences. For many purposes, including analyses with interval targets, average squared error has been found to work very well as a general method for selecting a subtree on the validation data. It is recommended for most practical situations and, in particular, in situations with rare target levels and in which the benefits or costs of correct or incorrect classification are not easy to specify.

Model Studio: Subtree Method

In Model Studio the *subtree method* specifies how to construct the subtree in terms of subtree methods. Here are the possible values:

- **C4.5**: The pruning is done with a C4.5 algorithm.
- **Cost complexity**: The subtree with a minimum leaf-penalized ASE is chosen.
- **Reduced error**: The smallest subtree with the best assessment value is chosen.

The C4.5 algorithm is available only for class targets.

With reduced error pruning, the assessment measure for class targets is misclassification rate, and the assessment measure for interval targets is ASE.

The *selection method* specifies how to construct the subtree in terms of selection methods. Here are the possible values:

- **Automatic**: specifies the appropriate subtree for the specified subtree pruning method.
- **Largest**: specifies the full tree.
- **N**: specifies the largest subtree with at most N leaves.
- **Cost-complexity alpha**: specifies the tree from cost-complexity pruning corresponding to the chosen alpha value.

The **Number of leaves** property specifies the number of leaves that are used in creating the subtree when the subtree selection method is set to N.

The **Confidence** property specifies the binomial distribution confidence level to use to determine the error rates of merged and split nodes. The default value is 0.25. This option is available only when C4.5 is the pruning method.

The **Cross validation folds** property specifies the number of cross validation folds to use for cost-complexity pruning when there is no validation data. Possible values range from 2 to 20.

The **1-SE rule** property specifies whether to perform the one standard error rule when performing cross validated cost complexity pruning.

Regularize and Tune Hyperparameters

As previously discussed, the objective of a machine learning algorithm is to find the model parameters that minimize the loss function over the independent samples. We have recently discussed some of these parameters, for example, maximum depth or split criteria in a decision tree. We have learned that to create a good statistical model, many choices must be made when deciding on algorithms and their parameters. The usual approach is to apply trial-and-error methods to find the optimal algorithms for the problem at hand. Often, you choose algorithms based on practical experience and personal preferences. This is reasonable, because usually there is no unique and relevant solution to create a machine learning model. Many algorithms have been developed to automate manual and tedious steps of the machine learning pipeline. Still, it requires a lot of time and effort to build a machine learning model with trustworthy results.

A large portion of this manual work relates to finding the optimal set of **hyperparameters** for a chosen modeling algorithm. Hyperparameters are the parameters that define the model applied to a data set for automated information extraction. There are several ways to support you in this cumbersome work of tuning machine learning model parameters. These approaches are called **hyperparameter optimization**.

The SAS Visual Data Mining and Machine Learning autotuning feature automatically decided on the following:

- Which modeling approaches to test
- Which data to choose to train the model
- Which data to test the results
- How to tune the parameters of the chosen model
- How to validate the results.

In general, there are three types:

- **Parameter sweep:** This is an exhaustive search through a predefined set of parameter values. The data scientist selects the candidates of values for each parameter to tune, trains a model with each possible combination, and selects the best-performing model. Here, the outcome very much depends on the experience and selection of the data scientist.

- **Random search:** This is a search through a set of randomly selected sets of values for the model parameters. This can provide a less biased approach to finding an optimal set of parameters for the selected model. Because this is a random search, it is possible to miss the optimal set unless enough experiments are conducted, which can be expensive.

- **Parameter optimization:** This is the approach that applies modern optimization techniques to find the optimal solution. It is the best way to find the most appropriate set of parameters for any predictive model, and any business problem, in the least expensive way.

Model Studio: Autotuning

SAS has conducted research in hyperparameter tuning. In SAS products, these capabilities are referred to as *autotuning*. Model Studio provides autotuning capabilities to SAS Visual Data Mining and Machine Learning users. This offering provides a hyperparameter autotuning capability that is built on local search optimization (LSO) in SAS.

Autotuning searches for the best combination of the decision tree parameters. ***Performing autotuning can substantially increase run time***. Autotuning runs based on some options, which limit the search of all possible combinations in terms of the decision tree parameters.

Maximum Depth specifies whether to autotune the maximum depth parameter. It ranges from 1 to 150. The default initial value for the maximum depth is 10. The default for the range is from 1 to 19.

Interval input bins specifies whether to autotune the number of interval input bins. It ranges from 2 to 500. The default initial value for the number of bins is 20. The default for the range is from 20 to 200.

Grow Criterion specifies whether to autotune the grow criterion. For class target, the options are Entropy, CHAID, Information gain ratio, Gini, and Chi-square. For interval target, the options are Variance, F test, and CHAID.

Search Options specifies the options for autotuning searching. The following options are available:

- **Bayesian** uses priors to seed the iterative optimization.

- **Genetic algorithm** uses an initial Latin hypercube sample that seeds a genetic algorithm. The genetic algorithm generates a new population of alternative configurations at each iteration.

- **Grid** uses the lower bound, upper bound, and midrange values for each autotuned parameter, with the initial value (or values) used as the baseline model.

- **Latin hypercube sample** performs an optimized grid search that is uniform in each tuning parameter, but random in combinations.

- **Random** generates a single sample of purely random configurations.

Number of evaluations per iteration specifies the number of tuning evaluations in one iteration. This option is available only if the search method is Genetic algorithm or Bayesian. The default value is 10. It ranges from 2 to 2,147,483,647.

Model Studio: Autotuning

Maximum number of evaluations specifies the maximum number of tuning evaluations. This option is available only if the Search method is Genetic algorithm or Bayesian. The default value is 50. It ranges from 3 to 2,147,483,647.

Maximum number of iterations specifies the maximum number of tuning iterations. This option is available only if the search method is Genetic algorithm or Bayesian. The default value is 5. It ranges from 1 to 2,147,483,647.

Sample size specifies the sample size. This option is available only if the search method is Random or Latin hypercube sample. The default value is 50. It ranges from 2 to 2,147,483,647.

There are some general options associated with the autotuning search.

Validation method specifies the validation method for finding the objective value. If your data are partitioned, then that partition is used. Validation method, validation data proportion, and cross validation number of folds are all ignored.

- **Partition** specifies using the partition validation method. With partition, you specify proportions to use for randomly assigning observations to each role.

  - **Validation data proportion** specifies the proportion of data to be used for the partition validation method. The default value is 0.3.

- **K-fold cross validation** specifies using the cross validation method. In cross validation, each model evaluation requires k training executions (on k-1 data folds) and k scoring executions (on one holdout fold). This increases the evaluation time by approximately a factor of k.

  - **Cross validation number of folds** specifies the number of partition folds in the cross validation process (the k defined above). Possible values range from 2 to 20. The default value is 5.

Nominal target objective function specifies the objective function to optimize for tuning parameters for a nominal target. Possible values are average squared error, area under the curve, F1 score, F0.5 score, gamma, Gini coefficient, Kolmogorov-Smirnov statistic, multi-class log loss, misclassification rate, root average squared error, and Tau. The default value is misclassification rate.

Interval target objective function specifies the objective function to optimize for tuning parameters for an interval target. Possible values are average squared error, mean absolute error, mean square logarithmic error, root average squared error, root mean absolute error, and root mean square logarithmic error. The default value is average squared error.

Model Studio: Autotuning

Maximum time (minutes) specifies the maximum time in minutes for the optimization tuner.

Maximum training time for single model (in minutes) specifies the maximum time in minutes for a single model to train. If left blank (the default), there is no maximum time.

 Demo 7.3: Improving a Decision Tree Model by Changing the Pruning Parameters

In this demonstration, you change the default settings of the Decision Tree node in the Lesson 3 pipeline. You modify the pruning parameters and compare this model performance to the model built earlier in the course.

1. To recall, the previous model, based on changings on the tree structure and the recursive partitioning parameters, achieved an average squared error of 0.0605 on the Validate partition.
2. Try to improve the model's performance by modifying some of the settings of the decision tree model. In the properties pane, expand the properties under Pruning Options.
3. Change **Subtree method** from Cost complexity to **Reduced error**.

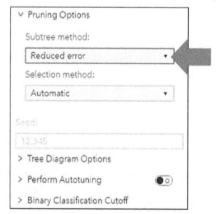

The cost complexity pruning method helps prevent overfitting by making a trade-off between the complexity (size) of a tree and the error rate. Thus, large trees with a low error rate are penalized in favor of smaller trees. On the other hand, reduced error subtree method performs pruning and subtree selection based on minimizing the error rate in the validation partition at each pruning step and then in the overall subtree sequence. The error rate is based on the misclassification rate for a categorical response variable.

4. Run the **Decision Tree** node.
5. Open the results for the node.

6. Click the **Assessment** tab.

Target ...	Data Role	Partitio...	Formatt...	Sum of ...	Averag...
churn	TRAIN	1	1	39,590	0.0610
churn	VALIDATE	0	0	16,967	0.0604

The average squared error for the tuned decision tree model is 0.0604 on the VALIDATE partition. This average squared error shows the slightest of improvements from the last model built.

7. Close the Results window.

8. Run the entire pipeline and view the results of the Model Comparison node. The Model Comparison table shows that the decision tree model is currently the champion from the Lesson 3 pipeline. This is based on the default fit statistic KS.

Champi...	Name	Algorith...	KS (You...	Misclass...
▣	Decision Tree	Decision Tree	0.5583	0.0683
	Logistic Regression	Logistic Regression	0.5488	0.0808

9. Close the results of the Model Comparison node.

End of Demonstration

Practice: Building a Decision Tree

Build a decision tree using the Autotune feature.

1. Add a Decision Tree node to the Lesson 3 pipeline, below the Variable Selection node. Use the Autotune feature. Explore the settings that are made available when **Autotune** is selected.

   Note: This practice might take several minutes to run.

2. What criteria were selected for the champion model?

   - Split criteria
   - Pruning method
   - Maximum number of branches
   - Maximum tree depth

3. How does the autotuned decision tree compare to the other models in the pipeline, particularly to the decision tree model built during the demonstration? Consider the fit statistic average squared error for this comparison.

End of Practices

Quiz

1. Which of the following statements is true regarding decision trees?

    a. The recursive partitioning used to construct decision trees leads them to being uninterpretable.

    b. The optimal split for the next input considered is the one that minimizes the logworth function for that input.

    c. The maximal decision tree is usually the one used to score new data.

    d. The logworth of a split can sometimes be negative.

2. Which of the following statements is true regarding decision trees?

    a. A well-fit tree has low bias and high variance.

    b. Accuracy is obtained by multiplying the proportion of observations falling into each leaf by the proportion of those correctly classified in the leaf and then summing across all leaves.

    c. In bottom-up pruning, the subtree with the best performance on training data is selected.

    d. Top-down pruning is usually slower but is considered more effective than bottom-up pruning.

Chapter 8: Decision Trees: Ensembles and Forests

Introduction

A *forest* is an ensemble of simple decision trees, each one able to produce its own response to a set of input variables. For classification problems, this response takes the form of a class, which classifies a set of independent variables with one of the categories in the dependent variable. Alternatively, for regression problems, the tree takes the form of an estimate of the dependent variable given the set of independent variables.

The trees that make up a forest differ from each other in two ways:

- The training data for each tree are sampled with replacement from all observations that were originally in the training data. This is known as *bagging*, and we discuss this in detail later.

- The input variables considered for splitting for any given tree are selected randomly from all available inputs.

Among these variables, only the variable most associated with the target is used when forming a split. This means that each tree is created on a sample of the inputs and from a sample of observations. Repeating this process many, many times creates a more stable model than a single tree. The reason for using a sample of the data to construct each tree is because when less than all available observations are used, the generalization error is often improved. In addition, a different sample is taken for each tree. *Boosting* is a common method used to reduce bias.

Forest Models

- The out-of-bag sample refers to the training data that are excluded during the construction of an individual tree.

- Observations in the training data that are used to construct an individual tree are the bagged sample.

- Some model assessments such as the iteration plots are computed using the out-of-bag samples as well all the training data.

In the forest algorithm, rather than taking bagging or bootstrap samples of only the rows, variables are also randomly sampled. This results in a forest, consisting of trees that use different combinations of rows and variables to determine splits. This additional perturbation (beyond bagging) leads to greater diversity in the trees, and better predictive accuracy.

A decision tree in a forest trains on new training data that are derived from the original training data presented to the model. Training different trees with different training data reduces the correlation of the predictions of the trees, which in turn should improve the predictions of the forest. The training data for an individual tree exclude some of the available data. The data that are withheld from training are called the out-of-bag sample. Observations in the training sample are called the *bagged observations*, and the training data for a specific decision tree are called the *bagged data*. For each individual tree, the out-of-bag sample is used to form predictions. These predictions are more reliable than those from training data.

Model assessment such as misclassification rates, average squared error, and iteration plots are constructed on both the entire training data set as well as the out-of-bag sample.

Building Ensemble Models: Ensembles of Trees

Even with an understanding of some of the basic guidelines for selecting an algorithm and incorporating hyperparameter tuning, determining the single most effective machine learning algorithm (and its tuning parameters) to use for a problem and data set is a daunting task. Ensemble modeling can take some of that weight off your shoulders and can give you peace of mind that the predictions are the result of a collaborative effort, or consensus, among multiple models that are trained either from different algorithms that approach the problem from different perspectives, or from the same algorithm applied to different samples or using different tuning parameter settings, or both.

As previously discussed, decision trees are unstable models. That is, small changes in the training data can cause large changes in the topology of the tree. However, the overall performance of the tree remains stable (Breiman et al. 1984). Changing the class label of one case can result in a completely different tree with nearly the same accuracy as shown in Figure 8.1.

Figure 8.1: Instability

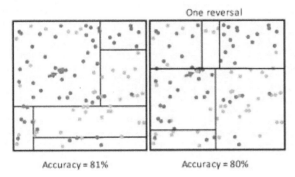

One reversal

Accuracy = 81%   Accuracy = 80%

The instability results from the large number of univariate splits considered and the fragmentation of the data. At each split, there are typically a number of splits on the same and different inputs that give similar performance (competitor splits). A small change in the data can easily result in a different split being chosen. This in turn produces different subsets in the child nodes. The changes in the data are even larger in the child nodes. The changes continue to cascade down the tree.

Figure 8.2: Competitor Splits

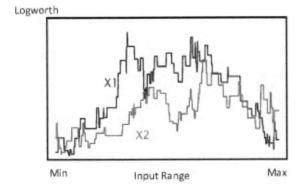

Logworth

X1

X2

Min   Input Range   Max

Methods have been devised to take advantage of the instability of trees to create models that are more powerful. *Perturb and combine (P & C)* methods generate multiple models by manipulating the distribution of the data or altering the construction method (such as changing the tree settings) and then averaging the results (Breiman 1998). The "perturb" step is illustrated in Figure 8.3, where perhaps the splitting criteria change between the trees.

Figure 8.3: Perturb Step

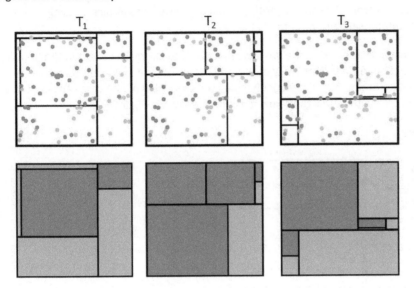

Some common perturbation methods are listed below:

- resample
- subsample
- add noise
- adaptively reweight
- randomly choose from the competitor splits

An ensemble model is the combination of the multiple models. The combinations can be formed in these ways:

- voting on the classifications
- using weighted voting, where some models have more weight
- averaging (weighted or unweighted) the predicted values

Figure 8.4 shows the "combine" step results by averaging the predicted values.

Figure 8.4: Combine Step

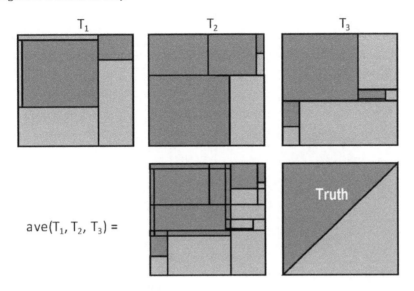

Any unstable modeling method can be used, but trees are most often chosen because of their speed and flexibility.

The attractiveness of P & C methods is their improved performance over single models. Bauer and Kohavi (1999) demonstrated the superiority of P & C methods with extensive experimentation. One reason why simple P & C methods give improved performance is variance reduction. If the base models have low bias and high variance, then averaging decreases the variance. In contrast, combining stable models can negatively affect performance. The reasons why adaptive P & C methods work go beyond simple variance reduction and are the topic of much research. (For example, see Breiman 1998.) Graphical explanations show that ensembles of trees have decision boundaries of much finer resolution than would be possible with a single tree (Rao and Potts 1997).

A new case is scored by running it down the multiple trees and averaging the results. Multiple models need to be stored and processed. The simple interpretation of a single tree is lost.

Building Forests

To recap, random forests (tree ensembles) are built using methods called *bagging* in which each decision trees are used as parallel estimators. If you use the same or very similar trees in the ensemble, then the overall result will not be much different from the result of a single tree. To avoid this, you can use bagging or *bootstrapping* and *feature randomness.* Bagging randomly selects samples from the training data with replacement. They are called bagging or bootstrapping samples.

> Bagging goes a long way towards making a silk purse out of a sow's ear, especially if the sow's ear is twitchy. …What one loses, with the trees, is a simple and interpretable structure. What one gains is increased accuracy.

> — Breiman (1996)

Figure 8.5 shows how bagging can smooth out the all-or-none bins of a single decision tree by smoothing the prediction surface.

Figure 8.5: Single Versus Bagged Trees

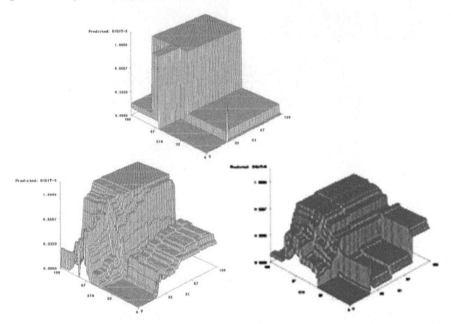

Bagging Method

The bagging method consists of the following steps:

1. **Draw K bootstrap samples.** A *bootstrap sample* is a random sample of size *n* drawn from the empirical distribution of a sample of size *n*. That is, the training data are resampled with replacement. Some of the cases are left out of the sample, and some cases are represented more than once.

2. **Build a tree on each bootstrap sample.** Pruning can be counterproductive (Bauer and Kohavi 1999). Large trees with low bias and high variance are ideal.

3. **Vote or average.** For classification problems, take the mean of the posterior probabilities or take the plurality vote of the predicted class. Bauer and Kohavi (1999) found that averaging the posterior probabilities gave slightly better performance than voting. Take a mean of the predicted values for regression.

Breiman (1996) used 50 bootstrap replicates for classification and 25 for regression and for averaging the posterior probabilities. Bauer and Kohavi (1999) used 25 replicates for both voting and averaging.

Figure 8.6: Bagging

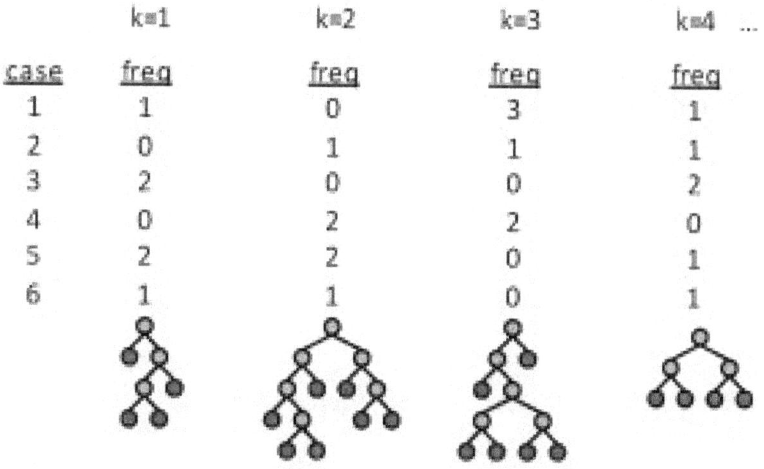

case	k=1 freq	k=2 freq	k=3 freq	k=4 freq
1	1	0	3	1
2	0	1	1	1
3	2	0	0	2
4	0	2	2	0
5	2	2	0	1
6	1	1	0	1

Boosting

Boosting is another ensemble technique to create a collection of predictors. In this method, you fit consecutive trees (random sample), and at every step, the goal is to solve for net error from the prior tree. When an input is misclassified by a hypothesis, its weight is increased so that the next hypothesis is more likely to classify it correctly. Combining the whole set at the end converts weak learners into better performing model.

Arcing (adaptive resampling and combining) methods are examples of boosting. They sequentially perturb the training data based on the results of the previous models. Cases that are incorrectly classified are given more weight in subsequent models. Arc-x4 (Breiman 1998) is a simplified version of the AdaBoost (adaptive boosting, also known as Arc-fs) algorithm of Freund and Schapire (1996). Both algorithms give similar performance (Breiman 1998, Bauer and Kohavi 1999).

In Figure 8.7, at the *k*th step, a model (decision tree) is fit using weights for each case. For the *i*th case, the arc-x4 weights (that is, the selection probabilities) are:

$$p(i) = \frac{1 + m(i)^4}{\sum\left(1 + m(i)^4\right)}$$

where $0 \le m(i) \le k$ is the number of times that the *i*th case is misclassified in the preceding steps. Unlike bagging, pruning the individual trees improves performance (Bauer and Kohavi 1999).

The weights are incorporated either by using a weighted analysis or by resampling the data such that the probability that the *i*th case is selected is $p(i)$. For convenience, the weights can be normalized to frequencies by multiplying by the sample size, *n* (as shown above). Bauer and Kohavi (1999) found that resampling performed better than reweighting for arc-x4, but it did not change the performance of AdaBoost. AdaBoost uses a different (more complicated) formula for $p(i)$. Both formulas put greater weight on cases that are frequently misclassified.

Figure 8.7: Boosting

case	k=1 freq	m	k=2 freq	m	k=3 freq	m	k=4 freq
1	1	1	1.5	1	.5	2	.97
2	1	0	.75	0	.25	0	.06
3	1	1	1.5	2	4.25	3	4.69
4	1	0	.75	1	1.5	1	.53
5	1	0	.75	0	.25	0	.06
6	1	0	.75	0	.25	1	.51

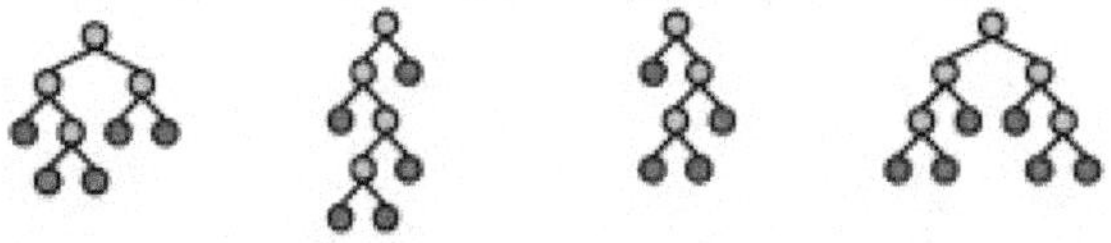

Shown is Arc-x4, one method of boosting

The process is repeated *k* times, and the *k* models are combined by voting or averaging the posterior probabilities. AdaBoost uses weighted voting where models with fewer misclassifications, particularly of the hard-to-classify cases, are given more weight. Breiman (1998) used *k*=50. Bauer and Kohavi (1999) used *k*=25.

Arcing improves performance to a greater degree than bagging, but the improvement is less consistent (Breiman 1998, Bauer and Kohavi 1999).

Gradient Boosting with Decision Trees

Gradient Boosting is similar to standard boosting except that at each iteration, the target is the residual from the previous decision tree model. At each step the accuracy is computed. Successive samples are adjusted to accommodate the previous inaccuracies.

Gradient Boosting = Gradient Descent + Boosting

It uses a gradient descent algorithm that can optimize any differentiable loss function. An ensemble of trees is built one by one, and individual trees are summed sequentially. Next, the tree tries to recover the loss (difference between actual and predicted values). In other words, gradient boosting constructs additive models by sequentially fitting a simple *parametrized function* to "pseudo" residuals by least squares at each iteration.

This additive weighted approach of trees can produce excellent fit of the predicted values to the observed values, even if the specific nature of the relationships between the inputs and the target is complex. For that reason, the method of gradient boosting by fitting a weighted additive expansion of simple trees can create general and powerful machine learning models.

Details: Gradient Boosting with an Interval Target

The gradient boosting algorithm is a weighted ($\beta_1 ... \beta_M$) linear combination of (usually) simple models ($T_1 .. T_M$). (Friedman 2001). In SAS Visual Data Mining and Machine Learning, the base model is a decision tree.

Begin with an initial guess, F_0, and proceed in a stage-wise manner fitting subsequent (m) tree models to "pseudo" residuals ($\widetilde{y}_{im}$). The residuals are computed from target values (y_i) and predictions from the function at the previous iteration ($F_{m-1}(x_i)$). The function $F_m(x)$ is updated by adding the fitted model, $v\beta_m T_m(x)$ to $F_{m-1}(x)$.

The shrinkage parameter, V (0< V <1) controls the learning rate of the algorithm. Friedman (2001) found that small values (≤ 0.1) lead to better generalization.

In regression trees with interval targets and least-square loss criterion, the "pseudo" residual, $\tilde{y}_{im}$, and the "guess," F_0, are defined as follows:

$$\tilde{y}_{im} = y_i - F_{m-1}(x_i)$$

$$F_0 = \bar{y}$$

In classification trees with a binary target ($y \in \{-1,1\}$) and binomial log-likelihood loss criterion, the "pseudo" residuals and F_0 are

$$\tilde{y}_{im} = 2y_i / (1 + \exp(2y_i F_{m-1}(x_i)))$$

$$F_0 = \frac{1}{2}\log\left(\frac{1+\bar{y}}{1-\bar{y}}\right).$$

The binary target predictions from the final approximation $F_M(x)$ can be transformed to yield probability estimates.

$$\hat{p}_{+1} = 1/(1+e^{-2F_M(x)}), \ \hat{p}_{-1} = 1/(1+e^{2F_M(x)})$$

Friedman (2002) showed that accuracy and speed can be improved by sub-sampling training data randomly (without replacement) at each iteration leading to the stochastic gradient boosting algorithm.

Gradient boosting trains a sequence of trees over multiple iterations similar to boosting. The main difference is that it minimizes a stochastic gradient descent function when oversampling to reduce the residuals of the model.

SAS Visual Data Mining and Machine Learning creates a series of trees, which form a single model. A tree in the series is fit to the residuals of the prediction from the earlier trees in the series. The residual is defined in terms of the derivative of a loss function. For squared error on an interval target, $\hat{r} = y_i - \hat{y}_i$. Each time that the data are used to grow a tree, the accuracy of the tree is computed. Successive samples are adjusted to accommodate previous inaccuracies. Each successive sample is weighted per the accuracy of the previous models. (See the SAS Visual Data Mining and Machine Learning documentation for more details.)

Model Studio: Autotuning Gradient Boosting Parameters

Autotuning searches for the best combination of the gradient boosting parameters.

Performing autotuning can substantially increase run time.

Model Studio: Autotuning Gradient Boosting Parameters

Autotuning runs based on the following options in Figure 8.8, which limit the search of all possible combinations in terms of the gradient boosting parameters.

Figure 8.8: Autotuning Options

Search for the best combination of values in different properties:

- Maximum depth
- Regularization (L1 and L2)
- Learning rate
- Number of inputs per split
- Number of iterations (trees)
- Subsample rate
- Search method – Bayesian, Genetic algorithm, Grid, Latin hypercube sample, Random
- Validation method – Partition, Cross validation
- Objective function (class and interval targets)

Note: *Quantile binning usually does better than bucket binning, which is the default.*

L1 Regularization penalizes the absolute value for the weights. Different values for L1 are tried between the range defined by From and To. The default initial value for L1 is 0. The default for the range is from 0 to 10.

L2 Regularization penalizes the square value for the weights. Different values for L2 are tried between the range established by From and To. The default initial value for L2 is 0. The default for the range is from 0 to 10.

Learning Rate controls the size of the weight changes. It ranges from 0 (exclusive) to 1. The default initial value is 0.1. The default initial value for the learning rate is 0.1. The default for the range is from 0.01 to 1.

Number of Inputs per Split specifies the number of inputs evaluated per split. The default value is 100. The default range is from 1 to 100.

Model Studio: Autotuning Gradient Boosting Parameters

Number of Iterations specifies the number of iterations of a boosting series. The default initial value is 100. The range is from 20 to 150.

Subsample Rate specifies the subsample rate. The default initial value is 0.5. The default range is from 0.1 to 1.

Search Options specifies the options for autotuning searching. The following options are available:

- **Bayesian** uses priors to seed the iterative optimization.
- **Genetic algorithm** uses an initial Latin hypercube sample that seeds a genetic algorithm. The genetic algorithm generates a new population of alternative configurations at each iteration.
- **Grid** uses the lower bound, upper bound, and midrange values for each autotuned parameter, and the initial value (or values) is used as the baseline model.
- **Latin hypercube sample** performs an optimized grid search that is uniform in each tuning parameter, but random in combinations.
- **Random** generates a single sample of purely random configurations.

Number of evaluations per iteration specifies the number of tuning evaluations in one iteration. This option is available only if the Search method is Genetic algorithm or Bayesian. The default value is 10. It ranges from 2 to 2,147,483,647.

Maximum number of evaluations specifies the maximum number of tuning evaluations. This option is available only if the Search method is Genetic algorithm or Bayesian. The default value is 50. It ranges from 3 to 2,147,483,647.

Maximum number of iterations specifies the maximum number of tuning iterations. This option is available only if the Search method is Genetic algorithm or Bayesian. The default value is 5. It ranges from 1 to 2,147,483,647.

Sample size specifies the sample size. This option is available only if the Search method is Random or Latin hypercube sample. The default value is 50. It ranges from 2 to 2,147,483,647.

There are some general options associated with the autotuning search.

Validation method specifies the validation method for finding the objective value. If your data are partitioned, then that partition is used. Validation method, Validation data proportion, and Cross validation number of folds are all ignored.

Model Studio: Autotuning Gradient Boosting Parameters

- **Partition** specifies using the partition validation method. With partition, you specify proportions to use for randomly assigning observations to each role.

  ○ **Validation data proportion** specifies the proportion of data to be used for the Partition validation method. The default value is 0.3.

- **K-fold cross validation** specifies using the cross validation method. In cross validation, each model evaluation requires k training executions (on k-1 data folds) and k scoring executions (on one holdout fold). This increases the evaluation time by approximately a factor of k.

  ○ **Cross validation number of folds** specifies the number of partition folds in the cross validation process (the k defined above). Possible values range from 2 to 20. The default value is 5.

Nominal target objective function specifies the objective function to optimize for tuning parameters for a nominal target. Possible values are average squared error, area under the curve, F1 score, F0.5 score, gamma, Gini coefficient, Kolmogorov-Smirnov statistic, multi-class log loss, misclassification rate, root average squared error, and Tau. The default value is misclassification rate.

Interval target objective function specifies the objective function to optimize for tuning parameters for an interval target. Possible values are average squared error, mean absolute error, mean square logarithmic error, root average squared error, root mean absolute error, and root mean square logarithmic error. The default value is average squared error.

Maximum time (minutes) specifies the maximum time in minutes for the optimization tuner.

Maximum training time for single model (in minutes) specifies the maximum time in minutes for a single model to train. If left blank (the default), there is no maximum time.

Demo 8.1: Building a Gradient Boosting Model

The algorithm for gradient boosting evolved from the application of boosting methods to regression trees. The main idea is to compute a sequence of simple trees, where each successive tree is built for the prediction residuals of the preceding tree. This method builds trees by partitioning the data into samples at each split node. Then, at each step of the boosting trees algorithm, a best partitioning of the data is determined, and the deviations of the observed values from the respective residuals for each partition are computed. The next trees are fitted to those residuals, to find another partition that further reduces the residual variance for the data, given the preceding sequence of trees.

This additive weighted approach of trees can produce excellent fit of the predicted values to the observed values, even if the specific nature of the relationships between the inputs and the target is complex. For that reason, the method of gradient boosting by fitting a weighted additive expansion of simple trees can create general and powerful machine learning models.

In this demonstration, you add a Gradient Boosting node to the Lesson 3 pipeline. You build a default gradient boosting model, change some of the settings, and compare the model to the other models in the pipeline.

1. In the Demo 7.3 pipeline, right-click the **Variable Selection node** and select **Add child node ▶ Supervised Learning ▶ Gradient Boosting**.

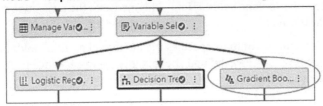

2. Keep all properties for the Gradient Boosting node at their defaults. Run the **Gradient Boosting** node.
3. Open the results for the Gradient Boosting node.
4. Click the **Assessment** tab.

Target ...	Data Role	Partitio...	Formatt...	Sum of ...	Averag...
churn	TRAIN	1	1	39,590	0.0560
churn	VALIDATE	0	0	16,967	0.0560

The Fit Statistics table, shown above, shows an average squared error of 0.0560 on the VALIDATE partition.

This performance is pretty good, even better than the decision tree tuned in the previous demonstrations. Regardless, try to improve the gradient boosting performance by changing some of the default settings.

5. Close the Results window.
6. Reduce **Number of trees** from 100 to **50**.

Generally, adding more trees to the model can be very slow to overfit. The advice is to keep adding trees until no further improvement is observed.

7. Under the Tree-splitting Options properties, increase **Maximum depth** from 4 to **8**.

Deeper trees are more complex trees and therefore you might prefer shorter trees. Generally, better results are seen with 4 to 8 levels. However, here you try more complex trees to compensate reduced number of trees in the previous setting. It's all trial-and-error!

8. Increase **Minimum leaf size** from 5 to **15**.

If you choose too small a leaf size, you can see that it might result in more splits. Too deep a tree means overfitting! On the flip side, if you choose a large leaf size (say in the above example), the tree might stop growing after few splits. ***Note that this might result in poor predictive performance.*** Let's see.

9. Increase **Number of interval bins** from 50 to **100**.

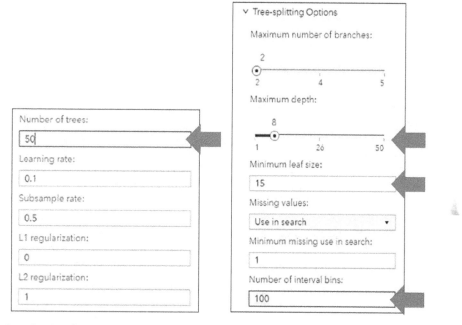

10. Run the **Gradient Boosting** node.

11. Open the results for the node.

Target ...	Data Role	Partitio...	Formatt...	Sum of ...	Averag...
churn	TRAIN	1	1	39,590	0.0490
churn	VALIDATE	0	0	16,967	0.0546

12. The average squared error for the tuned gradient boosting model is 0.0546 on the VALIDATE partition. This fit statistic is slightly better than the first model by using the default settings.

13. Close the Results window.

End of Demonstration

Practice: Building a Gradient Boosting Model

1. Build a gradient boosting model using the Autotune feature. Add a Gradient Boosting node to the Lesson 3 pipeline, below the Variable Selection node. Use the Autotune feature. Explore the settings that are made available when Autotune is selected.

   Note: This practice might take several minutes to run.

2. What criteria were selected for the champion model?

   ○ Number of trees

   ○ Number of variables per split

   ○ Number of bins

   ○ Maximum number of branches

   ○ Maximum depth

3. How does the autotuned gradient boosting compare to the other models in the pipeline, particularly to the gradient boosting model built during the demonstration? Consider the fit statistic average squared error for this comparison.

End of Practices

Model Studio: Autotuning Forest Model Options

Autotuning searches for the best combination of the forest parameters. *Performing autotuning can substantially increase run time*.

Autotuning runs based on some options, which limit the search of all possible combinations in terms of the forest parameters.

Maximum Depth specifies how deep each tree can grow. It ranges from 1 to 50. The default initial value for the maximum depth is 20. The default for the range is from 1 to 29.

Number of Trees specifies the number of trees in the forest. It ranges from 1 to 1000. The default initial value for the number of trees is 100. The default for the range is from 20 to 150.

In-bag Sample Proportion specifies the in-bag sample proportion. It ranges from 0 (exclusive) to 1. The default initial value for the proportion is 0.6. The default for the range is from 0.1 to 0.9.

Number of Inputs per Split specifies the number of inputs evaluated per split. The default value is 100. The default range is from 1 to100.

Model Studio: Autotuning Forest Model Options

Search Options specifies the options for autotuning searching. The following options are available:

- **Bayesian** uses priors to seed the iterative optimization.

- **Genetic algorithm** uses an initial Latin hypercube sample that seeds a genetic algorithm. The genetic algorithm generates a new population of alternative configurations at each iteration.

- **Grid** uses the lower bound, upper bound, and midrange values for each autotuned parameter, with the initial value (or values) used as the baseline model.

- **Latin hypercube sample** performs an optimized grid search that is uniform in each tuning parameter, but random in combinations.

- **Random** generates a single sample of purely random configurations.

Number of evaluations per iteration specifies the number of tuning evaluations in one iteration. This option is available only if the search method is Genetic algorithm or Bayesian. The default value is 10. It ranges from 2 to 2,147,483,647.

Maximum number of evaluations specifies the maximum number of tuning evaluations. This option is available only if the search method is Genetic algorithm or Bayesian. The default value is 50. It ranges from 3 to 2,147,483,647.

Maximum number of iterations specifies the maximum number of tuning iterations. This option is available only if the search method is Genetic algorithm or Bayesian. The default value is 5. It ranges from 1 to 2,147,483,647.

Sample size specifies the sample size. This option is available only if the search method is Random or Latin hypercube sample. The default value is 50. It ranges from 2 to 2,147,483,647.

There are some general options associated with the autotuning search.

Model Studio: Autotuning Forest Model Options

Validation method specifies the validation method for finding the objective value. If your data are partitioned, then that partition is used. Validation method, Validation data proportion, and Cross validation number of folds are all ignored.

- **Partition** specifies using the partition validation method. With partition, you specify proportions to use for randomly assigning observations to each role.

  - **Validation data proportion** specifies the proportion of data to be used for the Partition validation method. The default value is 0.3.

- **K-fold cross validation** specifies using the cross validation method. In cross validation, each model evaluation requires k training executions (on k-1 data folds) and k scoring executions (on one holdout fold). This increases the evaluation time by approximately a factor of k.

  - **Cross validation number of folds** specifies the number of partition folds in the cross validation process (the k defined above). Possible values range from 2 to 20. The default value is 5.

Nominal target objective function specifies the objective function to optimize for tuning parameters for a nominal target. Possible values are average squared error, area under the curve, F1 score, F0.5 score, gamma, Gini coefficient, Kolmogorov-Smirnov statistic, multi-class log loss, misclassification rate, root average squared error, and Tau. The default value is misclassification rate.

Interval target objective function specifies the objective function to optimize for tuning parameters for an interval target. Possible values are average squared error, mean absolute error, mean square logarithmic error, root average squared error, root mean absolute error, and root mean square logarithmic error. The default value is average squared error.

Maximum time (minutes) specifies the maximum time in minutes for the optimization tuner.

Maximum training time for single model (in minutes) specifies the maximum time in minutes for a single model to train. If left blank (the default), there is no maximum time.

Demo 8.2: Modeling a Binary Target with a Forest

In this demonstration, you add a Forest node to the Lesson 3 pipeline. You build a default forest model, change some of the settings, and compare the model to the other models in the pipeline.

1. In the pipeline, right-click the **Variable Selection** node and select **Add child node ▶ Supervised Learning ▶ Forest**.

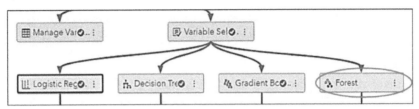

2. Keep all properties for the forest at their defaults. Run the **Forest** node.
3. Open the results for the node.
4. Click the **Assessment** tab.

Target ...	Data Role	Partitio...	Formatt...	Sum of ...	Averag...
churn	TRAIN	1	1	39,590	0.0515
churn	VALIDATE	0	0	16,967	0.0571

The Fit Statistics table shows an average squared error of 0.0571 on the VALIDATE partition.

This performance is again pretty good, better than the decision tree tuned in the earlier demonstration (but not quite as good as for the gradient boosting models). But again, try to improve the forest performance by changing some of the default settings.

5. Close the Results window.
6. The random forest is an ensemble of many decision trees, so it stands to reason that the number of trees will have a significant effect on the resulting model accuracy. Reduce **Number of trees** from 100 to **50**.

In general, the more trees you use tends to improve the performance of the forest. However, the improvement decreases as the number of trees increases. In other words, at a certain point, the benefit in prediction performance from learning more trees will be lower than the cost in computation time for learning these additional trees.

7. If you do not have any concern regarding the computation times, the more trees you have, the better (reliable) estimates you get from out-of-bag predictions. You can use OOB error rate to determine the number of trees.

Under the Tree-splitting Options properties, change **Class Target Criterion** from Information gain ratio to **Entropy**.

Information gain ratio is a measure of purity. Entropy, on the other hand, is a measure of impurity (the opposite). Entropy controls how a decision tree decides to split the data. It affects how a decision tree draws its boundaries.

8. Decrease **Maximum depth** from 20 to **12**.

9. Increase **Minimum leaf count** from 5 to **15**.

   The decision trees in a random forest are overtrained by letting them grow to a large depth (default maximum depth of 20) and small leaf size (default smallest number of observations per node of 5). The idea behind this approach is that averaging the predicted probabilities of a large number of overtrained trees is more robust than using a single fine-tuned decision tree.

10. Increase **Number of interval bins** from 20 to **100**.

11. Clear the box for the option **Use default number of inputs to consider per split**, which by default is the square root of the number of available inputs. Set this parameter to **7** (half of inputs).

    This is another key aspect of random forests: how many variables to consider for splitting each node (that is, a random subset of all variables, as opposed to considering all variables). This might reduce the bias toward the most influential variables and allows for a more generalizable model. You can manually change this option over numerous training runs.

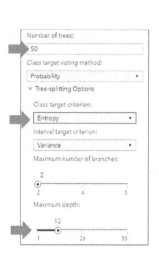

12. Run the **Forest** node.

13. Open the results for the node.

14. Click the **Assessment** tab.

Target ...	Data Role	Partitio...	Formatt...	Sum of ...	Averag...
churn	TRAIN	1	1	39,590	0.0536
churn	VALIDATE	0	0	16,967	0.0565

The average squared error for the tuned forest model is 0.0565 on the VALIDATE partition. This fit statistic is a little bit better than the first model by using the default settings.

15. Close the Results window.

16. Run the entire pipeline and view the results of model comparison.

Target ...	Data Role	Partitio...	Formatt...	Sum of ...	Averag...
churn	TRAIN	1	1	39,590	0.0536
churn	VALIDATE	0	0	16,967	0.0565

The gradient boosting model is now the champion model of the pipeline, based on default KS. The forest is a close second-place model.

17. Close the Results window.

End of Demonstration

 Practice: Building a Forest Model

1. Build a forest using the Autotune feature. Add a Forest node to your pipeline, below the Variable Selection node. Use the Autotune feature. Explore the settings that are available when **Autotune** is selected.

   Note: This practice might take several minutes to run.

2. What criteria were selected for the champion model?

   ○ Number of trees

   ○ Number of variables per split

   ○ Number of bins

   ○ Maximum number of branches

   ○ Maximum depth

3. How does the autotuned forest compare to the other models in the pipeline, particularly to the forest model built during the demonstration? Consider the fit statistic average squared error for this comparison.

   End of Practices

Pros and Cons of Tree Ensembles

To summarize, forest models are an ensemble of classification or regression trees. Forest models were developed to overcome the instability caused by minor changes in the training data.

Pros

- A powerful, highly accurate model.

- Like decision trees, tree ensembles do not require scaling of normalization.

- Like decision trees, tree ensembles can handle a mixture of different feature types.
- Runs the trees in parallel, so the performance is not affected.

Cons

- Ensemble trees are generally not a good choice for high-dimensional data; for example, test classification.

Quiz

1. Which of the following statements is true regarding tree-based models?
    a. Small changes in the training data can cause large changes in the topology of a tree.
    b. Ensemble models are used only with decision trees.
    c. In the boosting algorithm, cases that are correctly classified are given more weight in subsequent models.
    d. In the bagging algorithm, the training data is resampled without replacement.

Chapter 9: Neural Networks: Introduction and Model Architecture

Introduction

In the previous chapters, we created and refined decision tree and tree-based models. Another family of algorithms known as *neural networks* has recently seen a revival. This family includes *deep learning* and *multilayer perceptrons (MLPs)*. To introduce the algorithm, we start with the relatively simple method known as *multilayer perceptrons* for classification and regression, which form the basis of more complex deep learning models. MLPs are also known as feed-forward neural networks, or just neural networks.

In this chapter, we will describe neural networks basics, discuss options in Model Manager, train a neural network model, and begin to consider how to improve performance.

The Neural Network Model

Multilayer perceptrons can be thought of as generalizations of linear models that perform multiple stages of processing to reach a decision.

The prediction formula used to predict new cases is similar to a regression's formula, but with the addition of a *hidden unit activation function*. This addition enables a properly trained neural network to model virtually any association between input and target variables, including nonlinear relationships. However, flexibility comes at a price because the problem of input selection is not easily addressed by a neural network. The inability to select inputs is offset (*somewhat*) by a complexity optimization method named *stopped training* or *early stopping*. Stopped training can reduce the chances of overfitting, even in the presence of redundant and irrelevant inputs and will be discussed later in the next chapter.

Figure 9.1: Neural Network Prediction Formula

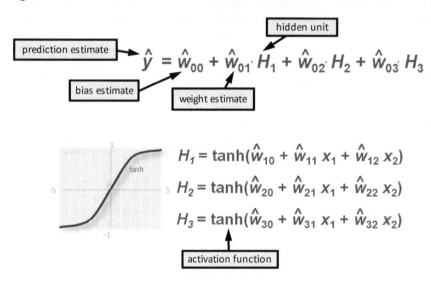

Like regressions, neural networks predict cases using a mathematical equation involving the values of the input variables.

$$\hat{y} = \hat{w}_{00} + \hat{w}_{01} \cdot H_1 + \hat{w}_{02} \cdot H_2 + \hat{w}_{03} \cdot H_3$$

The predicted estimate, $\hat{y}$, is a weighted sum of the input features x_0 to x_p, weighted by the learned coefficients, or weights, w_0 to w_p.

Details: Multilayer Perceptrons

MLP models were originally inspired by neurophysiology and the interconnections of neurons in the brain. Thus, they are often represented by a network diagram instead of an equation. The basic model arranges neurons in layers. The input layer of nodes connects to a layer of nodes called the *hidden layer*, which in turn connects to a final layer called the *target* or *output layer*. In the first layer, each node represents an input feature, the connecting lines represent the learned coefficients or weights, and the nodes on the right represent the output. The hidden layer is comprised of hidden nodes or units. In each hidden unit, after the weighted inputs and the bias are combined, the hidden unit's net input is passed through an *activation function*. The output is the weighted sum of the inputs, after passing through the hidden layers.

Figure 9.2: Network Architecture

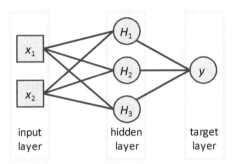

The hidden units can be thought of as neurons in the brain that fire in response to the weighted inputs. In the example shown in Figure 9.2, the tanh functions fire either 1, 0, or -1.

The neural network prediction formula can be thought of as a regression of response variable on a set of derived inputs, the hidden units. In turn, these hidden units can be thought of as regressions on the original inputs. The hidden unit "regressions" include a default link function or *activation function*, such as the *hyperbolic tangent*.

When the target variable is binary, the main neural network regression equation receives the *logit link function*.

Figure 9.3: Neural Network Binary Prediction Formula

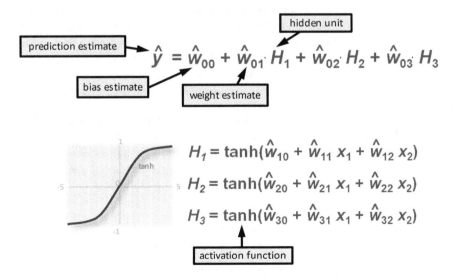

Neural Network Learning Process

The first step is to **randomly initialize** the weights of the model. The rationale for this is that wherever we start, if we are perseverant enough and through an iterative learning process, we can reach the pseudo-ideal model.

The next step is to run the model and then check its performance. You run the inputs through the network layer and calculate the actual output of the model. This step is called **forward-propagation**, because the calculation flow is going in the natural *forward* direction from the input ▶ through the neural network ▶ to the output.

In order to be able to generalize to any problem, we define what we call **loss function**. Basically, it is a performance metric on how well the model manages to reach its goal of generating outputs as close as possible to the desired target values.

The most intuitive loss function is simply *loss = (desired output – actual output)*. However, this loss function returns positive values when the network undershoots (prediction < desired output), and negative values when the network overshoots (prediction > desired output). If we want the loss function to reflect an *absolute error* on the performance regardless if it is overshooting or undershooting, we can define it as:

loss = Absolute value of (desired — actual)

Simply speaking, the machine learning goal becomes then to minimize the loss function (to reach as close as possible to 0). To do this, we use the loss function to readjust the weights in order to further reduce the loss function, and repeat until we approach zero or the results converge. This is known as **back-propagation**, where we feed the results back through the network.

Details: Forward-Propagation and Activation Functions

Forward propagation is the process of multiplying the input values of a particular neuron by their associated weights, summing the results, and scaling or "squashing" the values back between a given range before passing these signals on to the next layer of neurons. This, in turn, affects the weighted input value sums of the following layer, and so on, which then affects the computation of new weights and their distribution backward through the network. Ultimately, of course, this all affects the final output value(s) of the neural network. The activation function keeps values forward to subsequent layers within an acceptable and useful range, and forwards the output.

Activation functions perform a transformation on the input received, in order to keep values within a manageable range. Since values in the input layers are generally centered around zero and have already been appropriately scaled, they do not require transformation. However, these values, once multiplied by weights and summed, quickly get beyond the range of their original scale, which is where the activation functions come into play, forcing values back within this acceptable range and making them useful.

In order to be useful, activation functions must also be **nonlinear** and **continuously differentiable**. Nonlinearity allows the neural network to be a universal approximation; a continuously differentiable function is necessary for gradient-based optimization methods, which is what allows the efficient back propagation of errors throughout the network.

Inside the neuron, the following occurs:

- an activation function is assigned to the neuron or entire layer of neurons
- weighted sum of input values is calculated
- the activation function is applied to weighted sum of input values and transformation takes place
- the output to the next layer consists of this transformed value

Complex neural networks made up of many hidden layers are called deep learning networks. We discuss deep learning in more detail later in this chapter.

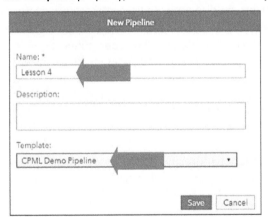

Demo 9.1: Building a Neural Network Model with Default Settings

In this demonstration, you create a new pipeline using the CPML Demo Pipeline and add a Neural Network node to it. You build the neural network model using the default settings of the node.

1. Click the plus sign (**+**) next to the pipeline tab to add a new pipeline.
2. In the New Pipeline window, enter **Lesson 4** in the **Name** field, access the menu under the **Template** property, and select **CPML Demo Pipeline**.

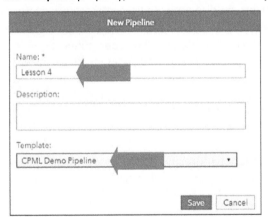

3. Click **Save**.
4. In the new pipeline, right-click the **Variable Selection** node and select **Add child node ▶ Supervised Learning ▶ Neural Network**.

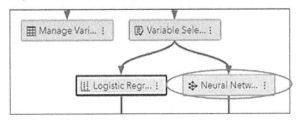

5. Keep all properties for the neural network at their defaults.
6. Run the **Neural Network** node.
7. Open the results for the node.

   There are several charts and plots to help you evaluate the model's performance. The first plot is **Network Diagram: Top 200 Weights**, which presents the final neural network structure for this model, including the hidden layer and the hidden units.

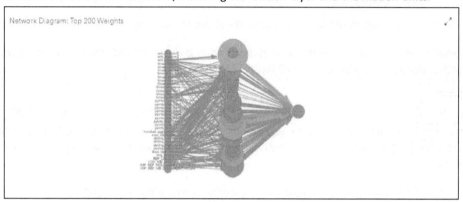

The Network Diagram: Top 200 Weights plot displays a diagram of the neural network when there are fewer than six hidden layers in the network. Only the links that correspond to the top 200 weights are displayed. You can interactively control the range of these weights to display.

The Network diagram displays the input nodes, hidden nodes, connections, and output nodes of a neural network. Nodes are represented as circles, and links between the nodes are lines connecting two circles. The size of the circle represents the magnitude of the absolute value of that node, relative to the model, and the color indicates whether that value is positive or negative. Similarly, the size of the line between two nodes indicates the strength of the link, and the color indicates whether that value is positive or negative.

The **Iteration plot** shows the model's performance based on the valid error throughout the training process when new iterations are added to achieve the final model.

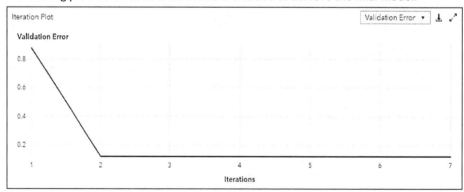

The Iteration plot displays a line graph of the validation error, if reported, as a function of the epoch. To examine the loss or objective as a function of the epoch, use the drop-down menu in the upper right corner.

The **Node Score Code window** shows the final score code that can be deployed in production.

```
Node Score Code
1      length _strfmt_ $12; drop _strfmt_;
2      _strfmt_ = ' ';
3
4      array _tlevname_55736428_{2} $2 _temporary_ ( ' 1'
5      ' 0');
6
7      length I_churn $2;
8      array _node_val_55736428_{99} _temporary_;
9
10     _badval_ = 0;
11     _dropinput_ =                    1;
12     _drop_ =                  1;
13
14     _numval_ = avg_days_susp;
15
```

Similarly, the **Training Code window** shows the train code that can be used to train the model based on different data sets or in different platforms.

```
Node Score Code
1      length _strfmt_ $12; drop _strfmt_;
2      _strfmt_ = ' ';
3
4      array _tlevname_55736428_{2} $2 _temporary_ ( ' 1'
5      ' 0');
6
7      length I_churn $2;
8      array _node_val_55736428_{99} _temporary_;
9
10     _badval_ = 0;
11     _dropinput_ =                    1;
12     _drop_ =                  1;
13
14     _numval_ = avg_days_susp;
15
```

Finally, the **Output window** shows the final neural network model parameters, the iteration history, and the optimization process. (Only a portion of the information in the Output window is shown below.)

The SAS System

The NNET Procedure

Model Information	
Model	Neural Net
Number of Observations Used	39590
Number of Observations Read	39590
Target/Response Variable	churn
Number of Nodes	99
Number of Input Nodes	47
Number of Output Nodes	2
Number of Hidden Nodes	50
Number of Hidden Layers	1
Number of Weight Parameters	2400
Number of Bias Parameters	52
Architecture	MLP
Seed for Initial Weight	12345
Optimization Technique	LBFGS
Number of Neural Nets	1
Objective Value	1.7912765327
Misclassification Rate for Validation	0.1214

8. Click the **Assessment** tab.

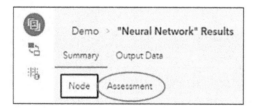

The first chart is the **Lift Report.** By default, it displays the **Cumulative Lift** plot showing the model's performance ordered by the percentage of the population. This chart is very useful for selecting the model based on a particular target of the customer base. It shows how much better the model is than the random events. Other plots, such as Lift, Gain, and Response Percentage (to name only a few), are available from a menu.

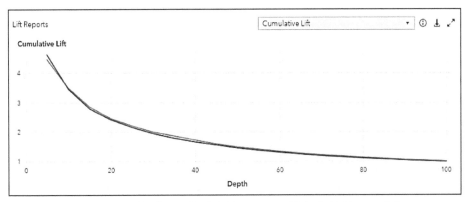

For a binary target, you also have the **ROC Reports**, which show the model's performance considering the true positive rate and the false positive rate. It is good to foresee the performance on a specific business events, when all positive cases are selected. It shows that the model's performance based on the positive cases were predicted right and the positive cases were predicted wrong. Other plots, such as those for accuracy, are available from a menu.

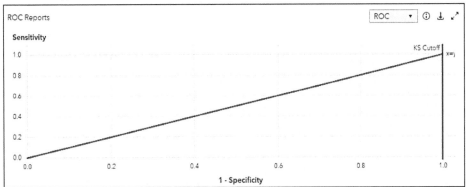

Finally, you have the **Fit Statistics** table, which shows the model's performance based on some assessment measures such as average squared error. (Only a portion of the table is shown below. You might need to maximize the table to see these values.)

Target ...	Data Role	Partitio...	Formatt...	Sum of ...	Averag...
churn	TRAIN	1	1	39,590	0.1273
churn	VALIDATE	0	0	16,967	0.1273

The fit statistics shows an average squared error of 0.1273 on the VALIDATE partition.

9. Close the Results window.

End of Demonstration

Improving the Model

After building the neural network using the default settings, we move on to the next discovery task: improving the model. There are a number of ways we can improve the performance of the model by changing the learning and optimization parameters. In the remainder of this chapter, we focus on modifying the network architecture.

Modifying Network Architecture

One way to improve neural network models is changing their architecture. By modifying the architecture, you might be able to increase model flexibility and improve model performance. Network architecture consists of the following aspects:

- Different connection types

- Number of layers

- Activation functions

- Number of neurons in each layer

Network Architecture

There are three layers in the basic multilayer perceptron (MLP) neural network as shown in Figure 9.4.

Figure 9.4: Multilayer Perceptron

$$g^{-1}(\hat{y}) = w_0 + \sum_{i=1}^{h} w_i g_i \underbrace{\left(w_{0i} + \sum_{j=1}^{d} w_{ij} x_j \right)}_{\text{hidden layer}}$$

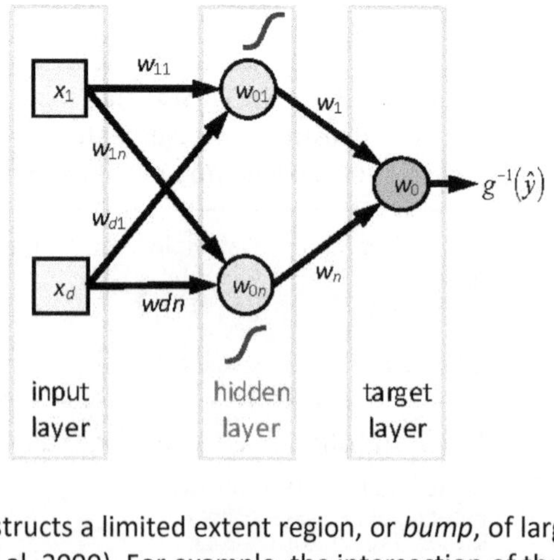

A single hidden-layer multilayer perceptron constructs a limited extent region, or *bump*, of large values surrounded by smaller values (Principe et al. 2000). For example, the intersection of the hyperplanes created by a hidden layer consisting of three hidden units forms a triangle-shaped bump.

Different Connection Types

The hidden and output layers *must* be connected by a nonlinear function in order to act as separate layers. Otherwise, the multilayer perceptron collapses into a linear perceptron. More formally, if matrix **A** is the set of weights that transforms input matrix **X** into the hidden layer output values, and matrix **B** is the set of weights that transforms the hidden unit output into the final estimates **Y**, then the linearly connected multilayer network can be represented as **Y=B[A(X)]**. However, if a single-layer weight matrix **C=BA** is created, exactly the same output can be obtained from the single-layer network: **Y=C(X)**.

The number of parameters in an MLP with *k* interval inputs grows quickly with the number of hidden units, *h*, considered. The number of parameters is given by the equation.

The "number of parameters" equations in this chapter assume that the inputs are interval or ratio level. Each nominal or ordinal input increases *k* by the number of classes in the variable, minus 1.

Skip-Layer Perceptron

By adding direct connections from the input to output layers, bypassing the hidden layer, it is possible to combine the linear and nonlinear neural network paradigms. The result is known as a *skip-layer network*.

Figure 9.5: Skip-Layer Perceptron

$$g^{-1}(\hat{y}) = w_0 + \sum_{i=1}^{h} w_i g_i \left(w_{0i} + \sum_{j=1}^{d} w_{ij} x_j \right) + \sum_{k=1}^{d} w_{1 1k} x_k$$

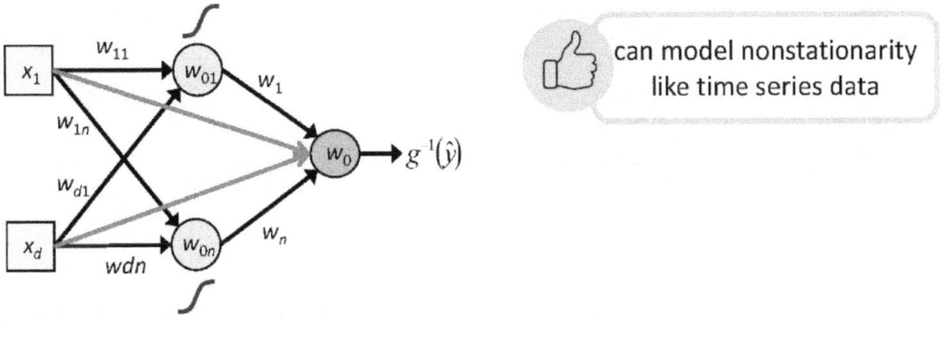

Because a multilayer perceptron is already a universal approximator, in general there is little to be gained by adding direct connections. Adding direct connections does *not* make it any more universal. However, a multilayer perceptron is inherently stationary (Leisch et al. 1999). This means that it tends to perform poorly when applied to nonstationary data. In this case, adding direct connections can help.

The number of parameters in a skip-layer network with *k* inputs and *h* hidden units is:

$$h(k + 2) + k + 1$$

In Model Studio, skip-layer perceptrons are constructed when the property **Allow direct connections between input and target neurons**, located on the Options tab, is selected.

Number of Layers

A neural network is a *universal approximator*, which means that it can model any continuous input-to-output relationships no matter how complex. Adding a second layer can model both continuous and discontinuous input-to-output relationships no matter how complex. You need at most two hidden layers to approximate any function!

As Sarle (1997) writes in his Neural Network FAQ, "If you have only one input, there seems to be no advantage to using more than one hidden layer. But things get much more complicated when there are two or more inputs."

Figure 9.6: MLP with Two Hidden Layers

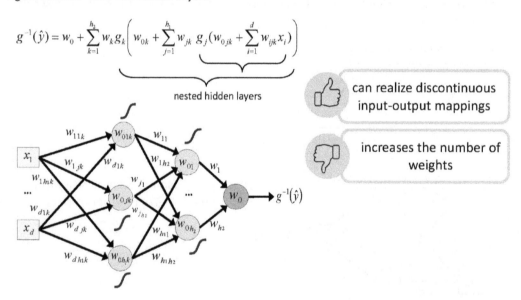

When a second layer of hidden units is added, the single layer network's bumps form disjoint regions (Principe et al. 2000). The number of neurons in the second hidden layer determines the number of bumps formed in the input space (Principe et al. 2000). Now approximations in different areas of the input space can be adjusted independently of each other. This gives an MLP with two hidden layers the ability to realize discontinuous input-output mappings.

Unfortunately, the number of parameters in a two-layer network grows very quickly. If there are h_1 and h_2 units in the first and second hidden layers respectively, and k (interval) inputs, the number of parameters is given by the following equation:

$$h_1(k + 1) + h_2(h_1 + 1) + h_2 + 1$$

Details: More Than Two Hidden Layers and Deep Learning

You need at most two hidden layers to approximate any function (Cybenko 1988). In fact, with gradient-based learning methods, it has been found that when more than two hidden layers are used, learning often slows to a crawl. This is known as the *vanishing gradient problem*. This problem arises because the chain rule, used to update the hidden unit weights, has the effect of multiplying *n* small numbers to compute the gradients of the front layers in an *n*-layer network. The gradient therefore decreases exponentially with *n*.

The term *deep learning* refers to the numerous hidden layers used in a neural network. However, **the true essence of deep learning is the methods that enable the increased extraction of information** derived from a neural network with more than one hidden layer. Adding more hidden layers to a neural network would provide little benefit without deep learning methods that underpin the efficient extraction of information. SAS Viya provides the key elements that enable learning to persist in the presence of many hidden layers. These elements are listed below:

- activation functions that are more resistant to saturation than conventional activation functions

- weight initializations that consider the amount of incoming information

- new regularization techniques such as dropout and batch normalization

- fast moving gradient-based optimizations such as Stochastic Gradient Descent

> **Neuron saturation** is when the output of an activation function results in a near-zero gradient (in other words, when the derivative is zero).

Needless to say, deep learning has shown impressive promise in solving problems that were previously considered infeasible to solve. The process of deep learning is to formulate an outcome from engineering new glimpses of the input space and then reengineering these engineered projections with the next hidden layer. This process is repeated for each hidden layer until the output layers are reached. The output layers reconcile the final layer of incoming hidden unit information to produce a set of outputs. The classic example of this process is facial recognition. The first hidden layer captures shades of the image. The next hidden layer combines the shades to formulate edges. The next hidden layer combines these edges to create projections of ears, mouths, noses, and other distinct aspects that define a human face. The next layer combines these distinct formulations to create a projection of a more complete human face. And so on.

> The possible number of hidden layers in SAS Visual Data Mining and Machine Learning ranges from 0 to 10. The default is 1.

Modifying Activation Functions

Another parameter that you can modify is the activation function.

Figure 9.7: Activation Function

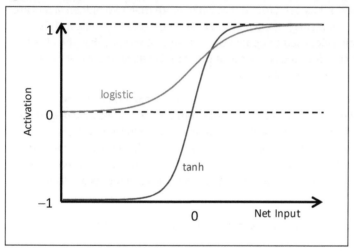

After the weighted inputs and the bias have been combined, the neuron's net input is passed through an activation function. Many of the defining hidden unit activation functions are members of the sigmoid family. The most famous member of the sigmoid family is the logistic function:

$$\text{logistic}(net) = \frac{1}{1 + e^{-net}} = \hat{p},$$

where

$$net = w_0 + \sum_{i=1}^{d} w_i x_i$$

The logistic activation function constrains its output to the range 0:1, making it an ideal for generating probability ($\hat{p}$) estimates. In statistics, the logistic function is better known as the *logit-link* function:

$$\text{logit}(\hat{p}) = \ln(\frac{\hat{p}}{1-\hat{p}}) = \ln(odds)$$

Although the logistic activation function was used in early neural network research, many other sigmoidal activation functions exist. One that plays a key role in the Neural Network node is the *hyperbolic tangent* (tanh). In fact, *it is the default hidden unit activation function.*

$$\tanh(net) = \frac{e^{net} - e^{-net}}{e^{net} + e^{-net}}$$

The hyperbolic tangent ranges from -1 to 1. This means that the inflection point is at 0 rather than at 0.5, as it is in the logistic sigmoid. This offers a small advantage during network initialization.

The strength of neural networks is their ability to model nonlinear relationships. The hidden unit activation function is the key contributor to the model's ability to model nonlinearities. In each hidden unit, after the weighted inputs and the bias are combined, the hidden unit's net input is passed through an activation function.

Figure 9.9: Hidden Layer Activation Functions

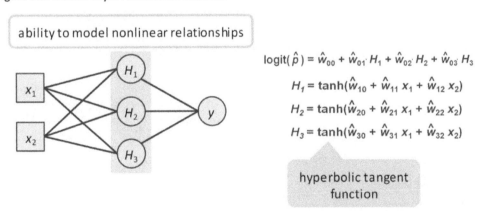

Activation functions can also be used in the target layer to model outcome distributions for different types of targets. In this example, the target is binary. The *target layer link function* (also known as the *target layer activation function*) is the logistic function, which is typically used with a binary target. The logistic function is the inverse of the logistic activation function. The logistic activation function constrains its output to the range of 0 to 1, so it is an ideal candidate for generating probability estimates when used in the target layer.

Figure 9.9: Target Layer Activation

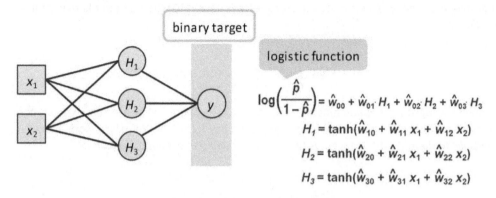

Interestingly, with respect to the hidden layer neurons, it does not seem to matter which of the sigmoid activation functions is used. The logistic and the hyperbolic tangent activation functions perform more or less equivalently.

Table 9.1: Activation Functions

Function	Plot	Equation	Range
Exponential		$f(x) = e^x$	$[0, \infty)$
Identity		$f(x) = x$	$(-\infty, \infty)$
Logistic		$f(x) = \dfrac{1}{1 + e^{-x}}$	$(0,1)$
Rectified Linear Unit (ReLU)		$f(x) = \begin{cases} 0 \ for \ x < 0 \\ x \ for \ x \geq 0 \end{cases}$	$[0, \infty)$
Sine		$f(x) = \sin(x)$	$[-1,1]$

Function	Plot	Equation	Range
Softplus		$f(x) = \ln(1 + e^x)$	$[0, \infty)$
Hyperbolic Tangent (Tanh)		$f(x) = \dfrac{(e^x - e^{-x})}{(e^x + e^{-x})}$	$(-1, 1)$

Several useful non-sigmoidal activation functions are also available. For example, the *exponential* activation function generates values that range from 0 to ¥. This is particularly useful when fitting distributions that are undefined for negative input values (for example, Poisson or gamma distributions).

$$exponential(net) = e^{net}$$

Sigmoid and hyperbolic tangent functions have lower and upper limits. The softplus activation function returns nonnegative values. Softplus values range from zero to infinity.

$$softplus(net) = \ln(1 + e^{net})$$

The identity activation function does not transform its argument at all. (See below.) This is useful when the desired response range is -¥ to ¥, such as when a normal target distribution is assumed.

$$identity(net) = net$$

Identity is the default output activation function.

Another activation function is the rectifier. The *rectifier* has now become the *de facto* standard in neural networks. Although many variants exist, the rectifier activation function is usually defined by the following equation:

$$rectifier(net) = max(0, net)$$

The rectifier activation function has been argued to be more biologically plausible than the widely used *logistic sigmoid* and its more practical counterpart, the *hyperbolic tangent*. A neuron using the rectifier activation function is called a *rectified linear unit* or, simply, a *rectilinear unit* (ReLU).

And finally, the sine activation function is also available. This is a well-known mathematical function. There are many ways to define the sine function. For example, the sine function can be defined using a right-angled triangle or a unit circle (LeCun et al. 1998).

Change the Number of Neurons in Each Layer

The question of the number of hidden units or neurons required is more difficult to answer than the required number of layers. If the network has too many hidden units, it models random variation (noise) as well as the desired pattern (signal). This means that the model will fail to generalize. Conversely, having too few hidden units will fail to adequately capture the underlying signal. This means that the error value will tend to stabilize at a high value. Again, the model will fail to generalize.

Figure 9.10: Number of Hidden Units to Use

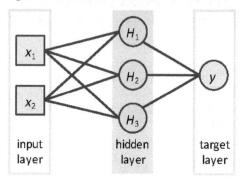

Hidden Units	Result
Too many	• Models noise • Fails to generalize
Too few	• Fails to capture the signal • Fails to generalize

The appropriate number of hidden units is, perhaps, best determined empirically. You start with a linear network and measure its performance on some appropriate metric, like the Schwarz-Bayesian criterion. Then increase the number of hidden units by one and observe the impact on the network's fit. Continue adding hidden units until the network's performance drops. The final network is given by the number of hidden units in the network prior to the hidden unit addition that degraded the model's performance.

Figure 9.11: Guidelines for Number of Neurons

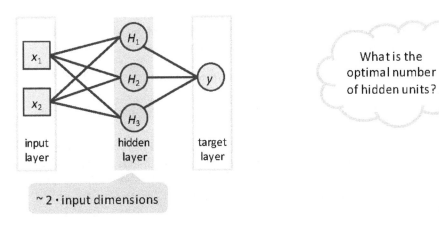

Unfortunately, *the optimal number of hidden units is problem-specific*. However, there are guidelines. For example, Principe et al. (2000) suggest that the number of units in the first hidden layer should be about twice the number of input dimensions. This will reflect the number of discriminant functions in the input space.

Figure 9.12: Guidelines for Number of Neurons

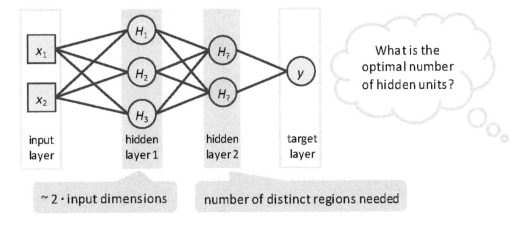

If a second hidden layer is required, then the number of hidden units in the second layer should reflect the number of distinct regions needed (Principe et al. 2000).

Demo 9.2: Improving a Neural Network Model by Changing the Network Architecture Parameters

In this demonstration, you change the default settings of the Neural Network node in the pipeline. You modify the network architecture parameters.

1. Recall that the average squared error of the previous model, based on the default settings, was 0.1273 on the VALIDATE partition.

   Try to improve the neural network performance by changing some of the default settings assigned to the network architecture.

2. Change **Input standardization** from Midrange to **Z score**. In this way, you rescale your data to have a mean of 0 and a standard deviation of 1. Midrange standardization results in the range values with a minimum of -1 and maximum of +1. Midrange standardization is usually applied to the tanh, arctangent, Elliott, sine, and cosine activation functions.

3. Clear the box for **Use the same number of neurons in hidden layers**. This enables you to use a different number of neurons in each hidden layer. However, this setting is redundant here because we are using only one hidden layer.

4. Under **Custom Hidden Layer Options**, enter **26** for **Hidden layer 1: number of neurons** (twice as many as the number of inputs). This specifies the number of hidden neurons in the first hidden layer for a network with one or more hidden layers. Because you have only one hidden layer, this can also be accomplished by directly using the **Number of neurons per hidden layer** property (which is inactive in the image below).

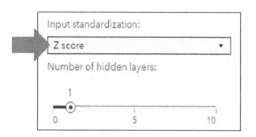
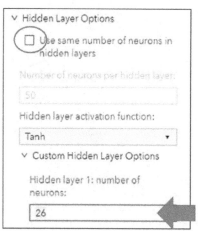

5. Run the **Neural Network** node.
6. Open the results for the node.

7. Click the **Assessment** tab.

Target ...	Data Role	Partitio...	Formatt...	Sum of ...	Averag...
churn	TRAIN	1	1	39,590	0.0705
churn	VALIDATE	0	0	16,967	0.0691

The average squared error for the tuned neural network model is 0.0691 on the VALIDATE partition. This fit statistic is much better than the first model, which was fit by using the default settings. (But keep in mind, results like this are data dependent! We cannot expect such large improvements every time that we try change settings for a model.)

8. Close the Results window.

End of Demonstration

Strengths, Weaknesses, and Parameters of Neural Networks

One of the main advantages of neural networks is that they are able to build very complex models that capture information or patterns contained in large amounts of data. Given enough time, computational power, data, and careful tuning pf parameters, they often out-perform other machine learning algorithms.

To understand the flexibility of neural networks, let's first look at the advantages and disadvantages of more traditional regression models, including nonlinear models. When an input variable x has a linear relationship with a target y, x appears in the model with no transformation. If the relationship is nonlinear, but you can specify a hypothetical relationship between x and y, you can build a parametric nonlinear regression model.

Figure 9.13: Traditional Regression Model

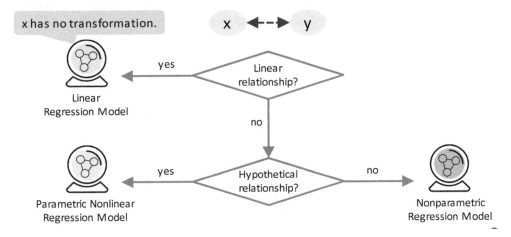

When it is not practical to specify the hypothetical relationship, you can build a nonparametric regression model.

Assuming that the functional form (that is, the equation) defining the nonlinear relationship between *y* and *x* is known *a priori*, and that only the parameters are unknown, then the parameters can be estimated using a technique known as *nonlinear regression* (Seber and Wild 1989).

> If the nonlinear equation is **not** known, one option is to assume that the input-output relationship takes on some hypothesized functional form. A popular choice is a polynomial. A single input, *x*, polynomial of degree *d* is given by the equation:
>
> $$\hat{y} = w_0 + w_1 x + w_2 x^2 + \cdots + w_d x^d = w_0 + \sum_{k=1}^{d} w_k x^k$$
>
> One reason for the polynomial's popularity is the *Weierstrass approximation theorem*. The theorem asserts that any continuous-valued function on a real interval [a:b], can be approximated arbitrarily closely by a polynomial function. This means that a linear regression model using polynomials of sufficient complexity is actually a universal approximator.

Nonlinear regression models are more difficult to estimate than linear models. Not only must you specify the full nonlinear regression expression to be modeled, an optimization method must be used to efficiently guide the parameter search process. You must also provide initial parameter estimates. The value of these initial parameter estimates is critical. Starting at a bad location in the parameter space results in an inferior solution or, perhaps, even failure to achieve convergence at all.

A nonparametric regression model has no functional form and, therefore, no parameters.

Traditional nonlinear regression models, which are parametric, and nonparametric regression models have several limitations. Nonlinear regression models are more difficult to estimate than linear models. In addition to specifying the functional form, it is necessary to use an optimization method to efficiently guide the parameter search process. It is essential for the optimization process to start with good parameter estimates. Starting at bad locations in the parameter space results in an inferior model.

Traditional nonlinear modeling techniques become vastly more difficult as the number of inputs increase. Remember that this is called *the curse of dimensionality*. It is uncommon to see parametric nonlinear regression models with more than a few inputs because deriving a suitable functional form becomes increasingly difficult as the number of inputs increases. Higher-dimension input spaces are also a challenge for nonparametric regression models.

Neural networks were developed to overcome these challenges. Although neural networks are parametric nonlinear models, they are similar to nonparametric models in one way: neural networks do not require the functional form to be specified. This enables you to construct models when the relationship between the inputs and outputs is unknown.

However, like other parametric nonlinear models, neural networks do require the use of an optimization process with initial parameter estimates. Also, unlike nonlinear parametric regression models and nonparametric regression models, neural networks generally perform well in sparse, high-dimensional spaces.

Advantages of Neural Networks

A major benefit of neural networks is their unlimited flexibility. A neural network is a universal approximator, which means that it can model any input-output relationship, no matter how complex. Neural networks overcome the main limitations of traditional regression methods, but they have a few limitations of their own: lack of interpretability and the need for a strong signal in the data.

Figure 9.14: Advantages and Disadvantages of Neural Networks

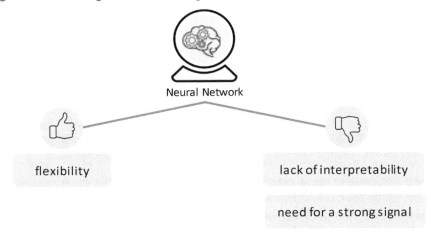

Although neural networks are parametric nonlinear regression models, they behave like nonparametric regression (smoothing splines) in that it is not necessary to specify the functional form of the model. This enables construction of models when the relationship between the inputs and outputs is unknown.

Disadvantages of Neural Networks

Large, powerful neural networks often take a long time to train. They require careful preprocessing of data, as discussed above. Similar to SVM, they work best with *homogeneous* data where all features have similar meanings. For data with very different features, trees might work better. Networks require careful tuning, and there are many ways to tune.

It is also very hard to interpret or analyze neural networks. This is known as the black box objection, meaning that it is impossible to see or understand what is going on inside the model, inputs are fed into a *black box,* and outputs are spat out. However, in many tasks, pure prediction is the goal. Understanding how the inputs affect the prediction is of secondary importance. In other applications, the opposite is true: Predictive power is a consideration only to the extent that it validates the interpretive power of the model. Neural networks are most appropriate for pure prediction tasks.

Recently, the black box has been "opened," at least partially. Two approaches are direct weight examination through Hinton diagrams and input sensitivity assessment. A particularly interesting method of opening the black box is *decomposition* (Tsukimoto 2000), which contends that the weights in a neural network can be approximated by a set of IF-THEN rules. A related approach is to use a decision tree to interpret the neural network's predictions.

SAS Visual Data Mining and Machine Learning provides model interpretability capabilities. Three methods that are model neutral and visual and can be used to compare models are Variable Importance Rankings, Local Interpretable Model Agnostic Explanations (LIME), and Individual Conditional Expectation (ICE) plots. Partial Dependency plots can also help with the interpretation of complex models. These are discussed in Chapter 11.

Impact of Noisy Data

Sometimes neural networks do not outperform simpler and easier-to-implement models like regression. This has led to disenchantment with the more complex neural networks. A possible explanation for this failure was suggested by David Shepard Associates (1999) in *The New Direct Marketing*:

"...if marketers think they can blindly use [neural networks] without the aid of an experienced statistician or an AI expert, they are making, in our opinion, a very serious mistake ..."

Not only is there a wide array of neural network architectures available today, the staggering number of options within any given architecture makes successful model construction less likely if the modeler is unfamiliar with the theoretical and practical implications of each option. Also, the poor relative performance of neural networks in some situations can be due to the signal-to-noise ratio.

To illustrate, in the left panel of Figure 9.15, the nonlinear model that is produced by the nonlinear neural network would clearly produce a superior fit to the data, as compared to the fit produced by the linear regression model. There is a strong pattern (signal) relative to the amount of variation (noise) around the pattern. The signal-to-noise ratio is high.

Figure 9.15: Impact of Noisy Data

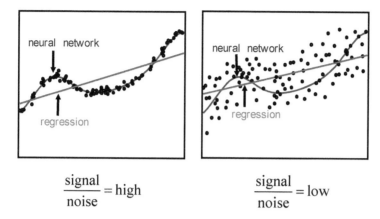

$$\frac{\text{signal}}{\text{noise}} = \text{high} \qquad \frac{\text{signal}}{\text{noise}} = \text{low}$$

The situation in the right panel of Figure 9.15 is different. The signal-to-noise ratio is low. The regression and neural network models will likely offer a comparable fit to the data. Therefore, Ockham's razor would imply that, in this case, there would be no advantage to using the more complex neural network.

Ockham's razor states that "entities must not be multiplied beyond necessity." Thus, if competing hypotheses are equal in other respects, Ockham's razor recommends choosing the hypothesis with the fewest postulates. In short, the simplest hypothesis is usually the correct one.

An important property of neural networks is that their weights are set randomly before learning is started, and this random initialization affects the model. This means that even when using exactly the same model parameters, you can obtain very different models when using different random seeds. This should not be a problem for very large networks but could affect accuracy for smaller networks.

Quiz

1. Which of the following statements is true regarding neural networks?
   a. Neural networks are one of the slowest scoring models.
   b. Neural networks cannot handle large volumes of data.
   c. Neural networks are most appropriate for pure prediction tasks.
   d. Neural networks perform well when the signal-to-noise ratio is low.

Chapter 10: Neural Networks: Optimizing the Model and Learning

Optimizing the Model

Now that we have changed the model architecture (in an attempt to improve the model), we are ready to optimize the complexity of the model. The way in which neural network models optimize complexity is very different from other algorithms. For example, there is not a clear "sequence of models that increase in complexity" in the same way that there is for decision trees and regression models using a stepwise method. For neural networks, optimizing complexity does not involve adding more terms or more rules to the model. Instead, optimizing the complexity of a neural network involves controlling the magnitude of the weights. If the weights grow too large, the model will be overfit and will not generalize well. The two main methods of avoiding overfitting are *weight decay* and *early stopping*. These methods are often used together.

Remember, a neural network uses a numerical optimization method that you specify to estimate the weights that minimize the error function. This process is called *learning*. Two steps are very important in the learning process for a neural network. The first one is to find a good set of parameters that minimizes the error (avoid bad local minima). The second one is to ensure that this set of parameters performs well (minimize the error) in different (new) data sets. (In other words, avoid overfitting of the training data.) It is also important to discuss the *parameter estimation process* and available *numerical optimization methods* in SAS Visual Data Mining and Machine Learning.

Figure 10.1: Network Learning

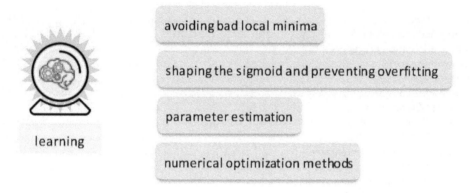

Avoiding Bad Local Minima

A *global minimum* is a set of weights that generates the smallest amount of error. A simple strategy to ensure that a global minimum has been attained is a brute-force search of the parameter space. Unfortunately, the curse of dimensionality quickly makes this method infeasible.

Figure 10.2: Global and Local Minima

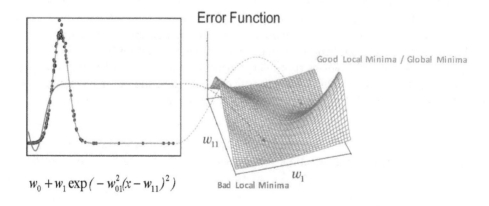

$$w_0 + w_1 \exp\left(-w_{01}^2 (x - w_{11})^2\right)$$

Many optimization algorithms are not guaranteed to converge to a global error minimum. Rather, many search optimization algorithms are heuristic methods that key on local features of the error surface when making their decisions. This makes them vulnerable to *local* minima (that is, areas of the error surface generating non-optimal error values). See Figure 10.3.

Figure 10.3: Local Minimum

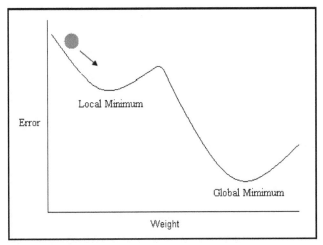

From the optimization algorithm's perspective, when a local minimum is reached, any movement away from the bottom leads to an increase in error. Because this is unacceptable, the search stops.

Unlike the parabolic error surface of a generalized linear model fit using least squares (which has no local minima), the error surface of a nonlinear model is plagued with local minima. Fortunately, many of these local minima have nearly the global error value. It is only the worst of them that must be avoided.

> In Model Studio, the **Number of tries** property specifies the number of times the network is to be trained using a different starting point. Specifying this option helps ensure that the optimizer finds the table of weights that truly minimizes the objective function and does not return a local minimum. By default, **Number of tries** is 1.

Details: Initialization Procedure

One way to avoid the worst local minima is to start with good weight values. In the Neural Network node, this is accomplished by means of the following five-step initialization process:

1. Standardize the inputs to have a midrange of 0, a minimum value of -1, and a maximum value of 1 (midrange).
2. Set the input-to-hidden weights to a small random number.
3. Use the hyperbolic tangent activation function so that the inflection point is at zero. The Elliott or arctangent functions are acceptable alternatives because they also have a zero inflection point.
4. Set the hidden-to-output connection weights to zero.

5. Because the hidden-to-output weights are set to zero in step 4, the output activation is given solely by the output bias on the first iteration. Therefore, the output bias is initialized to the mean of the target.

Figure 10.4: Initialization Procedure

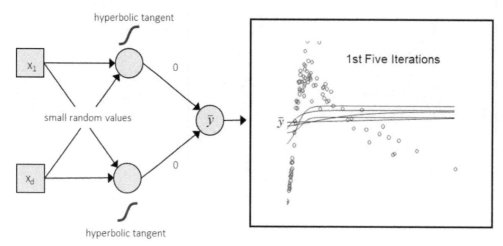

These initializations help prevent the optimization algorithms from stepping into treacherous regions of the parameter space (that is, regions of the parameter space with many bad local minima).

Shaping the Sigmoid

The weights and biases give the sigmoidal surfaces their range. For example, because the maximum value returned by the hyperbolic tangent activation function is 1, the upper bound of the hyperbolic tangent's activation range is given by the output unit's bias plus its weight:

$$w_0 + w_1 \tanh(w_{01} + w_{11}x) = w_0 + w_1(1) = w_0 + w_1$$

Figure 10.5: Shaping the Sigmoid

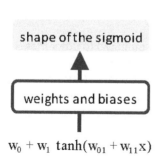

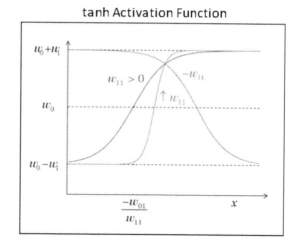

Conversely, the minimum activation value of the hyperbolic tangent function is −1, which means that the lower bound of the hyperbolic tangent's activation range is as follows:

$$w_0 + w_1 \tanh(w_{01} + w_{11}x) = w_0 + w_1(-1) = w_0 - w_1$$

The weights and biases also give the sigmoid surfaces their flexibility. The sign of the weight associated with input x controls the direction of the sigmoid. Positive weight values produce the familiar s-shaped curve, and a negative weight value flips the sigmoid horizontally. The larger the absolute value of the weight, the steeper the curve. *Steep sigmoids are often held to be responsible for overfitting.*

Figure 10.6: Shaping the Sigmoid—Flexibility

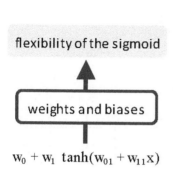

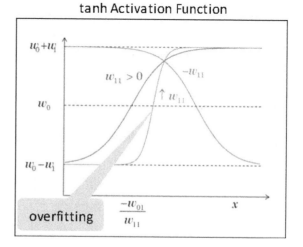

Note: Early stopping is one way to help keep the sigmoids from becoming too steep. Overfitting is controlled by the regularization terms L1 and L2 and the annealing rate, which you will learn about later.

Parameter Estimation

Recall that for neural networks, optimizing complexity is different compared to other models that we have seen thus far. Optimizing the complexity of a neural network model does not involve adding more terms (as for a regression model) or more rules (as for a decision tree). Here, it is the size of the weight estimates that are important in optimizing complexity.

Figure 10.7: Preventing Overfitting

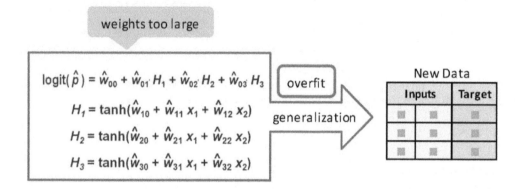

If the weights grow too large, the model will be overfit to the training data and not generalize well to new data. Weight decay and early stopping are the two primary methods to help avoid overfitting. These two methods are often used in tandem and are discussed next.

Figure 10.8: Preventing Overfitting—Weight Decay

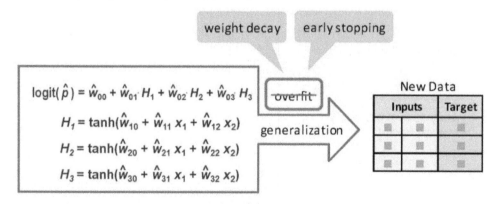

Bartlett (1997) demonstrated that generalization depends more on the magnitude of the weights than on the number of weights. Very large magnitude weights tend to generate an irregular fit to the data as the model adapts to noise (random variation). In other words, large weights are responsible for overfitting.

Figure 10.9: Weight Decay

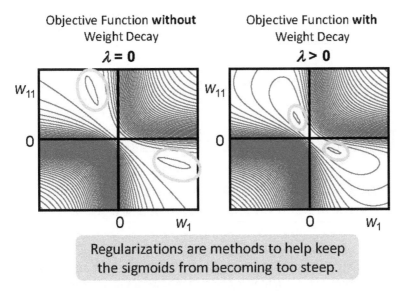

The graph on the left side of Figure 10.9 shows the objective function without weight decay. The graph on the right shows the objective function with weight decay. In both graphs, the horizontal axis shows the magnitude of the weight w1, and the vertical axis shows the magnitude of the weight w11.

In the graph on the left, with no weight decay, the minima are farther from the origin, so the weights used to find the minima are large. In the graph on the right, the minima are constrained closer to the origin, so the weights used to find the minima are smaller (and thus, less likely to overfit).

Regularization

Weight decay is one way to keep the weights from growing too large. L1 regularization is similar to L2 regularization in that both methods penalize the objective function for large network weights. The two regularizations differ in that L2 regularization penalizes the objective function by an amount proportional to the weight size, whereas L1's penalty is constant relative to changes in the weights. This means that L2 is likely to penalize larger weights to a greater degree than L1, but to a lesser degree than L1 when the weights are small. L1 regularization encourages sparsity because it is found to "concentrate the weight of the network in a relatively small number of high-importance connections, while the other weights are driven toward zero" (Nielsen 2015). L2 regularization is viewed as shrinking weights toward zero and can be considered not as robust as L1 regularization due to the large penalty that can arise from outliers.

Figure 10.10: Regularizations

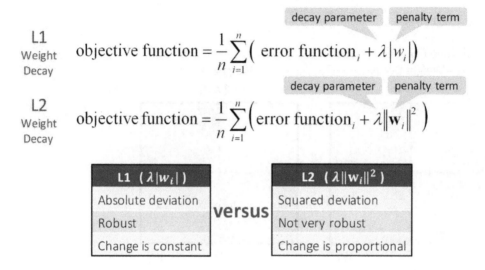

The decay parameter *lambda,* which can range from 0 to 1, controls the relative importance of the penalty term. Specifying too large of a penalty term risks the model underfitting the data. However, as Ripley (1996) points out, the advantages of weight decay far outweigh its risks [emphasis added]:

> Weight decay helps the optimization in several ways. When weight decay terms are included, it is normal to find fewer local minima, and as the objective function is more nearly quadratic, the quasi-Newton and conjugate gradient methods exhibit super-linear convergence in many fewer iterations. *There seems no reason to ever exclude a regularizer such as weight decay.* (pp. 159–160)

In any event, the influence of the penalty term is usually kept extremely small. In many published studies, the magnitude of the decay parameter (lambda) is on the order of 0.000001.

Early Stopping

Early stopping is another way to keep the weights from growing too large. It is closely related to ridge regression (Sarle 1995). Complexity optimization is an integral part of neural network modeling. Other modeling methods select an optimal model from a sequence of possible models. In the Neural Network node, only one model is estimated, so what is compared?

SAS Visual Data Mining and Machine Learning treats each iteration in the optimization
process as a separate model. The iteration with the smallest value of the selected fit
statistic is chosen as the final model. This method of model optimization is also called
stopped training.

To begin model optimization, model weights are given initial values. The weights multiplying the
hidden units in the logit equation are set to zero, and the bias in the logit equation is set equal to
the logit(π1), where π1 equals the primary outcome proportion. The remaining weights
(corresponding to the hidden units) are given random initial values (near zero).

Figure 10.10: Initial values

Initial hidden unit weights

$$\text{logit}(\hat{p}) = 0 + 0 \cdot H_1 + 0 \cdot H_2 + 0 \cdot H_3$$

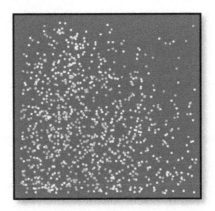

This "model" assigns each case a prediction estimate: $\hat{p}_i = \pi_1$. An initial fit statistic is calculated
on training and validation data. For a binary target, this is proportional to the log likelihood
function:

$$\sum_{\substack{primary \\ outcomes}} \log(\hat{p}_i(\hat{\mathbf{w}})) + \sum_{\substack{\sec ondary \\ outcomes}} \log(1 - \hat{p}_i(\hat{\mathbf{w}}))$$

where

$\hat{p}_i$ is the predicted target value.

$\hat{\mathbf{w}}$ is the current estimate of the model parameters.

Figure 10.11: Random Initial Input Weights and Biases

Initial hidden unit weights

$$\text{logit}(\hat{p}) = 0 + 0 \cdot H_1 + 0 \cdot H_2 + 0 \cdot H_3$$

$$H_1 = \tanh(-1.5 - .03x_1 - .07x_2)$$

$$H_2 = \tanh(.79 - .17x_1 - .16x_2)$$

$$H_3 = \tanh(.57 + .05x_1 + .35x_2)$$

Random initial
input weights and biases

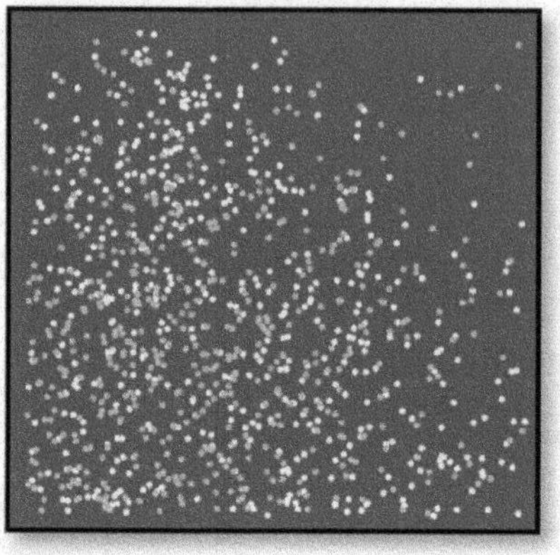

Training proceeds by updating the parameter estimates in a manner that decreases the value of the objective function. This process is repeated until one of the two following conditions is met:

- The objective function that is computed using the training partition stops improving.
- The objective function that is computed using the validation partition stops improving.

The process has been repeated the number of times specified in the **Maximum iterations** and **Maximum time** properties, which are found in the Common Optimization Options group of properties in the Neural Network node.

Figure 10.12: Early Stopping – Initial Step Set up to Predict the Overall Average Response

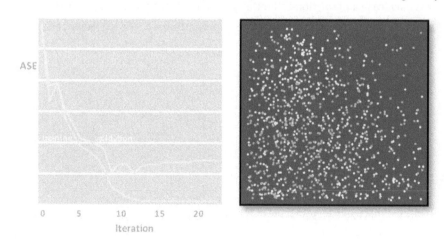

As stated previously, in the initial step of the training procedure, the neural network model is set up to predict the overall average response rate for all cases.

Follow the iterations in Figure 10.13. One step substantially decreases the value average squared error (ASE). Amazingly, the model that corresponds to this one-iteration neural network closely resembles the standard regression model, as seen from the fitted isoclines. The second iteration step goes slightly astray. The model actually becomes slightly worse on the training and validation data. Things are back on track in the third iteration step. The fitted model is already exhibiting nonlinear and nonadditive predictions. Half of the improvement in ASE is realized by the third step.

Most of the improvement in validation ASE occurred by the ninth step. (Training ASE continues to improve until convergence in step 23.) The predictions are close to their final form. Step 12 brings the minimum value for validation ASE. Although this model is ultimately chosen as the final model, the algorithm for the model continues to train until the likelihood objective function changes by a negligible amount on the training data. In step 23, as seen below, training is declared complete due to lack of change in the objective function from step 22. Notice that between step 13 and step 23, ASE actually increased for the validation data. This is an indication of overfitting.

Figure 10.13: Early Stopping – ASE Error for Each Iteration

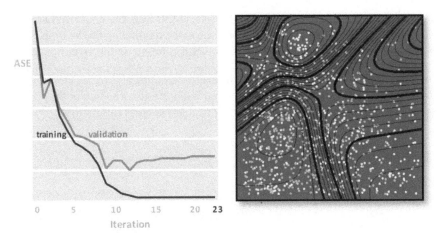

The Neural Network node selects the modeling weights from iteration 13 for the final model. In this iteration, the validation ASE is minimized. You can also configure the Neural Network node to select the iteration with minimum misclassification for final weight estimates.

Note: The name *stopped training* comes from the fact that the final model is selected as if training were stopped on the optimal iteration. Detecting when this optimal iteration occurs (while actually training) is somewhat problematic. To avoid stopping too early, the Neural Network node continues to train until convergence on the training data or until reaching the maximum iteration count, whichever comes first.

Model Studio: Early Stopping

In Model Studio, the **Perform Early Stopping** property specifies whether to stop training when the model begins to overfit. The training stops after N consecutive iterations (stagnation) without improvement in the validation partition. Early stopping cannot be used if there is no validation partition. By default, this option is selected. The following options are available:

- **Stagnation**—Specifies the number of consecutive iterations (N) for early stopping. The default value is 5.

- **Validation error goal**—Specifies a goal for early stopping based on the validation error rate. When the error gets below this value, the optimization stops. This option is in effect only for networks with fewer than 6 hidden layers. The value of 0 indicates that no validation error goal is set. The default value is 0.

Parameter Estimation: Iterative Updating

The *error function* defines the surface of the parameter space. In this way, the neural network learns or searches for the best set of weights to minimize the error, depending on the type of the surface. Then the numerical method to estimate the weights is based on the error function.

A *global minimum* is a set of weights that generates the smallest amount of error. A simple strategy to ensure that a global minimum has been attained is a brute-force search of the parameter space. Unfortunately, the curse of dimensionality quickly makes this method infeasible.

Figure 10.14: Parameter Estimate—Iterative Updating

The objective function
is minimized.

$$Q(\mathbf{w}) = (y - \mu(\mathbf{w}))^2$$

Weight estimates are
adjusted using numerical
optimization techniques.

$$\mathbf{w}^{(t+1)} = \mathbf{w}^{(t)} + \delta^{(t)}$$

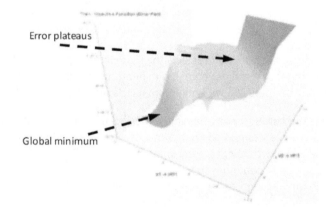

Error plateaus

Global minimum

Search optimization algorithms are *heuristic* methods that key on *local* features of the error surface when making their decisions. This makes them vulnerable to *error plateaus* (that is, areas of the error surface generating non-optimal error values). An error plateau is an area of the error space in which very little improvement is attained, given the current dot product of the inputs and weights. Previously, error plateaus were viewed as *local minima.* It is possible for a model to get stuck at a local minima, but this occurs only if the process has arrived at a saddle point for each model degree of freedom. Therefore, local minima are highly unlikely in higher-dimensional spaces.

From the optimization algorithm's perspective, when an error plateaus is reached, any further movements yield very little improvement in the error. And at this point, the search stops.

Unlike the parabolic error surface of a generalized linear model fit using least squares (which has no local minima), the error surface of a nonlinear model is plagued with error plateaus. Fortunately, many of these error plateaus have nearly the global error value. It is only the worst of them that must be avoided.

To efficiently search this landscape for an error minimum, optimization must be used. The optimization methods use local features of the error surface to guide their descent. Specifically, the weights associated with a given error minimum are located using the following procedure:

1. Initialize the weight vector to small random values, $\mathbf{w}^{(0)}$.
2. Use an optimization method to determine the update vector, $\delta^{(t)}$.
3. Add the update vector to the weight values from the previous iteration to generate new estimates:

   $$\mathbf{w}^{(t+1)} = \mathbf{w}^{(t)} + \delta^{(t)}$$

4. If none of the specified convergence criteria have been achieved, then go to step 2.

In the example in Figure 10.15, shown earlier, weight estimates for a binary target are produced by minimizing the error, which is -2 * log-likelihood. This particular error function is known as the Bernoulli function. In Model Studio, the error function is always a deviance function. Deviance is a generalization of the idea of using the sum of squares of residuals in ordinary least squares on cases where model-fitting is achieved by maximum likelihood. The deviance function returns the deviance from a binomial distribution, with a probability of primary outcome $\hat{p}$, and a number of independent Bernoulli trials *n*.

Figure 10.15: Parameter Estimation Example

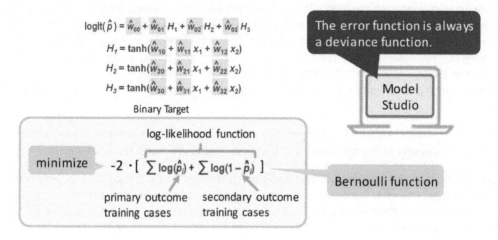

Deviance

Deviance defines the error function (that is, the deviance measure) to be minimized. The table in Figure 10.16 summarizes the error functions used in Model Studio. A single neuron implements a generalized linear model. This means that a single neuron can model many common target distributions including Poisson, gamma, binary, multinomial, and ordinal targets. Moreover, there is no need to perform target transformations. You simply fit the desired target distribution by selecting the appropriate error (deviance) function.

Figure 10.16: Deviance

$$Q(\mathbf{w}) = 2\phi\left[\ln\left(l_{staturated}\right) - \ln(l(\mathbf{w}))\right]$$

Distribution	Deviance Measure
Normal	$Q(\mathbf{w}) = \sum (y - \mu(\mathbf{w}))^2$
Poisson	$Q(\mathbf{w}) = 2\sum \left[y\ln(y/\mu(\mathbf{w})) - (y - \mu(\mathbf{w}))\right]$
Gamma	$Q(\mathbf{w}) = 2\sum \left[-\ln(y/\mu(\mathbf{w})) + (y - \mu(\mathbf{w}))/\mu(\mathbf{w})\right]$
Entropy	$Q(\mathbf{w}) = 2\left[y\ln\left(\dfrac{y}{\mu(\mathbf{w})}\right) + (1 - y)/\ln\left(\dfrac{1 - y}{1 - \mu(\mathbf{w})}\right)\right]$

If the probability distribution is a member of the exponential family, minimizing deviance is equivalent to maximizing likelihood. But deviance offers the advantage that it does not require a probability density function, which makes the calculation of deviance more efficient. Deviance also offers other numerical advantages. For example, the deviance measures are automatically scaled.

The default method for fitting an interval target is a *normal* distribution. The deviance measure used to fit a normal distribution is the familiar ordinary least squares equation below.

$$Q(\textbf{w}) = \sum (y - \mu(\textbf{w}))^2$$

A *Poisson* distribution is usually thought of as the appropriate distribution for count data. Because the variance is proportional to the mean, the deviance function for a Poisson distribution is the following:

$$Q(\textbf{w}) = 2 \sum [y \, ln(\, y/\mu(\textbf{w})) - (y - \mu(\textbf{w}))]$$

In a *gamma* distribution, the variance is proportional to the square of the mean. It is often used when the target represents an amount. The gamma deviance function is given by the following:

$$Q(\textbf{w}) = 2 \sum [- \, ln(\, y/\mu(\textbf{w})) + (y - \mu(\textbf{w}))/\mu(\textbf{w})]$$

Entropy

Cross or relative entropy is for independent interval targets with values between zero and 1 (inclusive). *Identical to the Bernoulli distribution if the target is binary*, it offers some advantages over the Bernoulli distribution when the data are proportions. The entropy deviance estimate is given by the following:

$$Q(\textbf{w}) = 2 \left[y \, ln \left(\frac{y}{\mu(\textbf{w})}\right) + (1 - y)/ \, ln \left(\frac{1 - y}{1 - \mu(\textbf{w})}\right)\right]$$

Table 10.1 summarizes the appropriate activation and error function combinations.

Table 10.1: Target Activation Function and Error Function Combinations

Target	Activation Function	Error Function
	Identity	Normal
	Sine	Normal
Interval	Hyperbolic tangent	Normal
	Exponential	Poisson
	Exponential	Gamma

Target	Activation Function	Error Function
Nominal	Softmax	Entropy

If the target is interval, there are four possible activation functions to be used: Identity, Sine, Hyperbolic Tangent, and Exponential. If the target distribution is normal, the error function should be Normal. If the target distribution is exponential, the error function can be Poisson or Gamma. If the target is nominal, the activation function should be Softmax, and the error function should be Entropy.

Numerical Optimization

There are two optimization methods available in the Neural Network node of Model Studio: limited memory Broyden-Fletcher-Goldfarb_Shanno optimization algorithm (LBFGS) and stochastic gradient descent.

LBFGS

Limited-Memory Broyden-Fletcher-Goldfarb-Shanno optimization algorithm:

- LBFGS is the default optimization method for the Neural Network node when two or fewer hidden layers are used.

- An estimation of the inverse Hessian matrix is used to steer the search.

- Rather than a full *nxn* (*n* = number of variables) approximation to the inverse Hessian, only a few vectors are stored to represent the approximation.

This method is well suited for optimization problems with a large number of variables.

The LBFGS is an optimization algorithm in the family of quasi-newton methods that approximates the BFGS algorithm using only some specific gradients to represent the approximation implicitly. It uses less computer memory due to its linear memory requirement. The algorithm starts with initial estimates of the optimal value of weights and progresses continuously to improve the estimates of the weights. The derivatives of the function of the estimates are used to drive the algorithm to find the direction of the steepest descent. The derivatives are also used to find the estimate of the Hessian matrix (second derivative).

Batch Gradient Descent

Re-invented several times, the back propagation (backprop) algorithm initially used only *gradient descent* to determine an appropriate set of weights. The gradient, $\nabla \mathbf{g}^{(t)}$, is the vector of partial derivatives of the error function with respect to the weights. It points in the steepest direction uphill. By negating the step size (that is, *learning rate*) parameter, *h*, a step is made in the direction that is locally steepest downhill:

$$\delta^{(t)} = -\eta \nabla g^{(t)}$$

Unfortunately, as gradient descent approaches the desired weights, it exhibits numerous back-and-forth movements known as *hemstitching*. To control the training iterations wasted in this hemstitching, later versions of back propagation included a momentum term, yielding the modern update rule:

$$\delta^{(t)} = -\eta g^{(t)} + \alpha \delta^{(t-1)}$$

The *momentum* term retains the last update vector, $\delta^{(t-1)}$, using this information to "dampen" potentially oscillating search paths. The cost is an extra learning rate parameter ($0 \leq \alpha \leq 1$) that must be set.

Figure 10.17: Batch Gradient Descent

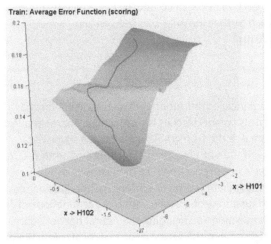

Train: Average Error Function (scoring)

$$\delta^{(t)} = -\eta \nabla g^{(t)} + \alpha \delta^{(t-1)}$$

- Uses a partial (fraction) of the training observations to calculate the gradient on each descent step

- Results in a smooth progression to the error minima

Note: The default value of α is 0. This means that, by default, backprop performs gradient descent.

In the (default) batch variant of the gradient descent algorithm, generation of the weight update vector is determined by using all of the examples in the training set. That is, the exact gradient is calculated, ensuring a relatively smooth progression to the error minima.

> For a linear neuron, with squared error, the error surface is a quadratic bowl. The vertical cross-sections are parabolas, and the horizontal cross-sections are ellipses. For multilayer networks, the error surface is much more complicated. But provided that the weights are not too big, locally the error surface can be well approximated by a piece of a quadratic bowl (Hinton 2013).

However, when the training data set is large, computing the exact gradient is computationally expensive. The entire training data set must be assessed on each step down the gradient. Moreover, if the data are redundant, the error gradient on the second half of the data will be almost identical to the gradient on the first half. In this event, it would be a waste of time to compute the gradient on the whole data set. You would be better off computing the gradient on a subset of the weights, updating the weights, and then repeating on a new subset. In this case, each weight update is based on an approximation to the true gradient. But as long as it points in approximately the same direction as the exact gradient, the approximate gradient is a useful alternative to computing the exact gradient (Hinton et al. 2006).

A compromise between batch gradient descent and single-case stochastic gradient descent is to divide the training data into small batches, compute the gradient using a single batch, make an update, and then move to the next batch of observations. This is known as *mini-batch gradient descent*. Like single-case stochastic gradient descent, mini-batch gradient descent is typically faster than batch gradient descent. And because the weights are updated less often than when single-observation stochastic gradient descent is used, mini-batch gradient descent typically uses less computation updating the weights, that is, each mini-batch computes the gradients for a number of cases in parallel. However, it is important that the mini-batches contain approximately balanced classes (Hinton et al. 2013).

Stochastic Gradient Descent (SGD)

Stochastic gradient descent (SGD) is another numerical optimization method available for the Neural Network node in Model Studio. Stochastic gradient descent is a stochastic approximation of the gradient descent optimization. It approximates the true gradient by using a single data point in the training data set. The gradient descent is an optimization algorithm to find the minimum value for a function iteratively. It takes steps proportional to the negative of the gradient of the function at the current point. The gradient is a multi-variable generalization of the derivative. The derivative can be defined on functions of a single variable. For functions of several variables, which is the case of the predictive models, including the neural networks, the gradient is defined. As the gradient represent the slope of the tangent for a particular function, it points in the direction of the greatest rate of increase of the function, which in the neural network case would be the point that minimize the loss function.

Figure 10.18: Stochastic Gradient Descent (SGD)

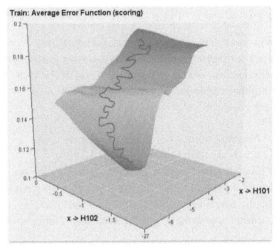

$$\delta^{(i)} = -\eta \nabla g^{(i)} + \alpha \delta^{(i-1)}$$

- Uses a single training observation to calculate an approximate gradient for each descent step
- Results in a chaotic progression to the error minima

If a multi-variable function *F(x)* is differentiable in a neighborhood of a point *a*, *F(x)* decreases fastest if it goes from a point *a* in the direction of the negative gradient of *F(x)* at *a*.

> In Model Studio, the Minibatch size property specifies the size of the minibatches used for SGD optimization. The default value is 50.

Model Studio: Numerical Optimization Methods

There are two optimization methods available in the Neural Network node of Model Studio: limited memory BFGS and stochastic gradient descent.

Figure 10.19: Numerical Methods in Model Studio

- Limited-Memory Broyden-Fletcher-Goldfarb-Shanno (**LBFGS**)

- Stochastic Gradient Descent (**SGD**)

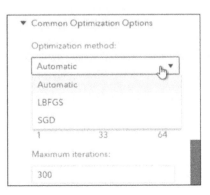

Model Studio: Numerical Optimization Methods

In the Neural Network properties panel, you can select a numerical optimization method under **Common Optimization Options**. The menu for **Optimization method** is shown in Figure 10.19. The default setting of Optimization method is **Automatic**, which selects one of the two available optimization methods based on the number of hidden layers. LBFGS is used when there are 2 or less hidden layers. SGD is used otherwise.

The default optimization method in the Neural Network node when there are two or fewer hidden layers is a variant of the BFGS method known as limited memory BFGS. Like the original BFGS, the limited memory BFGS (L-BFGS) uses an estimation of the inverse Hessian to steer the search. But, whereas BFGS stores an n by n approximation to the Hessian (where n is the number of variables), the L-BFGS variant stores only a few vectors that represent the approximation implicitly. Thus, L-BFGS is well suited for optimization problems with a large number of variables (Byrd et al. 1995).

Note: The default optimization method for the Neural Network node is **Automatic**. Automatic uses LBFGS if the network has two or fewer hidden layers. Otherwise, **Stochastic Gradient Decent**, discussed next, is used. LBFGS cannot be used in networks with more than two hidden layers.

Which Optimization Method Should You Use?

The LBFGS algorithm uses a limited amount of computer memory. It can often get the better solution than the SGD with fewer iterations. A strength of SGDs is that they are simple to implement and faster for problems that have many training examples and many predictor variables.

However, SGD methods have many disadvantages. One key disadvantage of SGDs is that they require much manual tuning of optimization parameters such as learning rates and convergence criteria. If you do not know the task at hand well, it is very difficult to find a good learning rate or a good convergence criterion. A standard strategy in this case is to run the learning algorithm with many optimization parameters and choose the model that gives the best performance on a validation set. Because you need to search over the large space of possible optimization parameters, this makes SGDs difficult to train in settings where running the optimization procedure many times is computationally expensive. We will discuss optimization parameters for SGD and in general, in the following chapter.

For more details, see "Alternatives to SGD: L-BFGS" at
https://raberrytv.wordpress.com/2015/06/20/alternatives-to-sgd-l-bfgs/

Regularize and Tune Model Hyperparameters

One of the hardest components in neural network modeling is finding the model parameters that minimize the loss function. In the preceding chapter, we briefly discussed these parameters that are associated with the number of hidden layers, the number of hidden units, the activation function, the target function, and so on. As the complexity of your model increases, its predictive abilities often decrease after a certain point due to overfitting and multicollinearity issues. Therefore, the resulting models often do not generalize well to new data, and they yield unstable parameter estimates. Some of the machine learning procedures in SAS Viya offer the **Autotune** option, which searches the optimal combination of hyperparameters to fit the best model under certain conditions.

The Learning Rate

The **learning rate** is a training parameter that controls the size of weight and bias changes in learning of the training algorithm. Neural networks are often trained by weight decay methods. This means that at each iteration, we calculate the derivative of the loss function with respect to each weight and subtract it from that weight. However, by doing that, the weights can change too much in each iteration, making the weights too big and tending to overfit the model. One way to avoid that is to multiply each derivative by a small value, the learning rate described above, before subtracting it from its corresponding weight.

Figure 10.20: Network Learning Hyperparameters for SGD

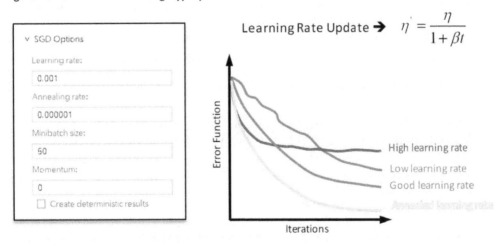

Learning Rate Update ➜ $\eta' = \dfrac{\eta}{1 + \beta t}$

You can think of a loss function as a surface where each direction that you can move in represents the value of a weight. Gradient descent is like taking leaps in the current direction of the slope, and the learning rate is like the length of the leap that you take. Setting the learning rate too high yields great progress in decreasing the error function in the first few iterations, but at a risk of diverging later in the training process. On the other hand, setting the learning rate too small can result in very long training times. A "good" learning rate is a balance between the two and is considered to be problem-specific.

A learning rate schedule is one approach used to optimize the learning process. The idea behind a learning rate schedule is to train the model for a few iterations using a large learning rate. Afterward, adjust the learning rate to a lower value and train the model for a few more iterations. This process is repeated until convergence. An alternative to a learning rate schedule uses an *annealing rate*. Annealing is a way to automatically reduce the learning rate as SGD progresses, causing smaller steps as SGD approaches a solution. Effectively, it replaces the learning rate parameter, h, with $\eta' = \eta / (1 + \beta t)$, where t is the number of iterations that SGD has performed and is the annealing parameter.

Setting the annealing rate too small results in very long training times, and setting it too large can result in movement away from the desired solution (that is, divergence).

> If you see a very large objective value with SGD, especially with small data set, it is likely that the learning rate is set too large.

Summary of Hyperparameters

Below is a summary of the hyperparameters found in Model Studio:

- **Learning rate** controls the the size of the changes in weights and biases during the learning process for the SGD optimizer.

- **Annealing Rate** automatically reduces the learning rate as SGD progresses, causing smaller steps as SGD approaches a solution. Effectively, it replaces the learning rate parameter as a function of the number of iterations that SGD has performed.

- **Regularization 1 (L1)** shrinks the weights by a constant amount toward 0.

- **Regularization 2 (L2)** shrinks the weight by an amount proportional to the weight size. It is the weight decay.

- **Momentum** is the current weight update is a function of the previous one. The momentum parameter is used to prevent the system from converging to a local minima.

Model Studio: Autotuning

When the Autotune feature is used, SAS Visual Data Mining and Machine Learning returns the optimal number of units for each hidden layer. Autotuning is invoked by selecting the **Performing Autotuning** property on the Options tab in the Neural Network node. Autotuning is available only when the number of hidden layers is less than six.

Model Studio: Autotuning

The Autotuning statement activates the tuning optimization algorithm, which searches for the best hidden layers and regularization parameters based on the problem and specified options. If the algorithm used to train the neural network is based on the Stochastic Gradient Descent, the Autotune feature also searches for the best values of the learning rate and annealing rate. In addition, the Autotune feature searches for the best hyperparameter values for the following:

- Number of hidden layers
- Number of neurons
- L1 and L2 regularizations
- Learning rate
- Annealing rate
- Search method—Bayesian, Genetic algorithm, Grid, Latin hypercube sample, Random
- Validation method—Partition, Cross validation
- Objective function (class and interval targets)

You can also define the search method for the hyperparameters, as **Bayesian, Genetic algorithm**, **Latin hypercube sample**, or **Random sample**. The genetic algorithm method uses an initial Latin hypercube sample that seeds a genetic algorithm to generate a new population of alternative configurations at each iteration. The Latin Hypercube method performs an optimized grid search that is uniform in each tuning parameter, but random in combinations. The Random method generates a single sample of purely random configurations. The Bayesian method uses priors to seed the iterative optimization.

You can specify the number of tuning evaluations in one iteration. This option is available only if the Search method is Genetic algorithm or Bayesian. Similarly, you can specify the maximum number of tuning evaluations and the maximum number of tuning iterations. For the search method, Random or Latin hypercube is also possible to specify a sample size.

Finally, you can specify the validation method for finding the objective value, including partition and cross validation—including the proportion of the validation data set and the number of folds for cross validation —and the objective function, depending on the level of the target variable. Autotuning searches for the best combination of the neural network parameters. *Performing autotuning can substantially increase run time.* It runs based on some options, which limit the search of all possible combinations in terms of the neural network parameters.

Number of Hidden Layers specifies whether to autotune the number of hidden layers. It ranges from 1 to 5. The default initial value is 1. The default range is from 0 to 2.

Model Studio: Autotuning

Number of Neurons specifies whether to autotune the number of neurons. It ranges from 1 to 1000. The default initial value is 1. The default range is from 1 to 100.

L1 Weight Decay specifies whether to autotune the L1 weight decay parameter. It penalizes the absolute value for the weights. Different values of L1 are tried between the range defined by From and To. The default initial value for the L1 is 0. The default range is from 0 to 10.

L2 Weight Decay specifies whether to autotune the L2 weight decay parameter. It penalizes the square value for the weights. Different values of L2 are tried between the range established by From and To. The default initial value for the L2 is 0. The default range is from 0 to 10.

Learning Rate specifies whether to autotune the learning rate for the hidden layers. It controls the size of the weight changes. It ranges from 0 (exclusive) to 1. The default initial value is 0.1. The default initial value for the learning rate is 0.1. The default for the range is from 0.01 to 1. It works just for the SGD algorithm.

Annealing Rate specifies whether to autotune the annealing rate for the hidden layers. It automatically reduces the learning rate as SGD progresses. The default initial value is 0.001. The default range is from 0.000001 to 0.1. It works just for the SGD algorithm.

Search Options specifies the options for autotuning searching. The following options are available:

- **Bayesian** uses priors to seed the iterative optimization.
- **Genetic algorithm** uses an initial Latin hypercube sample that seeds a genetic algorithm. The genetic algorithm generates a new population of alternative configurations at each iteration.
- **Grid** uses the lower bound, upper bound, and midrange values for each autotuned parameter, with the initial value (or values) used as the baseline model.
- **Latin hypercube sample** performs an optimized grid search that is uniform in each tuning parameter, but random in combinations.
- **Random** generates a single sample of purely random configurations.

Number of evaluations per iteration specifies the number of tuning evaluations in one iteration. This option is available only if the Search method is Genetic algorithm or Bayesian. The default value is 10. It ranges from 2 to 2,147,483,647.

Maximum number of evaluations specifies the maximum number of tuning evaluations. This option is available only if the Search method is Genetic algorithm or Bayesian. The default value is 50. It ranges from 3 to 2,147,483,647.

Model Studio: Autotuning

Maximum number of iterations specifies the maximum number of tuning iterations. This option is available only if the Search method is Genetic algorithm or Bayesian. The default value is 5. It ranges from 1 to 2,147,483,647.

Sample size specifies the sample size. This option is available only if the Search method is Random or Latin Hypercube sample. The default value is 50. It ranges from 2 to 2,147,483,647.

There are some general options associated with the autotuning search.

Validation method specifies the validation method for finding the objective value. If your data is partitioned, then that partition is used. Validation method, Validation data proportion, and Cross validation number of folds are all ignored.

- **Partition** specifies using the partition validation method. With partition, you specify proportions to use for randomly assigning observations to each role.

  - **Validation data proportion** specifies the proportion of data to be used for the Partition validation method. The default value is 0.3.

- **K-fold cross validation** specifies using the cross validation method. In cross validation, each model evaluation requires k training executions (on k-1 data folds) and k scoring executions (on one holdout fold). This increases the evaluation time by approximately a factor of k.

  - **Cross validation number of folds** specifies the number of partition folds in the cross validation process (the k defined above). Possible values range from 2 to 20. The default value is 5.

Nominal target objective function specifies the objective function to optimize for tuning parameters for a nominal target. Possible values are average squared error, area under the curve, F1 score, F0.5 score, gamma, Gini coefficient, Kolmogorov-Smirnov statistic, multi-class log loss, misclassification rate, root average squared error, and Tau. The default value is misclassification rate.

Interval target objective function specifies the objective function to optimize for tuning parameters for an interval target. Possible values are average squared error, mean absolute error, mean squared logarithmic error, root average squared error, root mean absolute error, and root mean squared logarithmic error. The default value is average squared error.

Maximum time (minutes) specifies the maximum time in minutes for the optimization tuner.

Maximum training time for single model (in minutes) specifies the maximum time in minutes for a single model to train. If left blank (the default), there is no maximum time.

Demo 10.1: Improving a Neural Network Model by Changing the Network Learning and Optimization Parameters

In this demonstration, you change the previous settings of the Neural Network node in the pipeline. You modify the learning and optimization parameters and compare this model performance to the other model in the pipeline.

1. Recall that the previous model, based on changes in the network architecture, achieved an average squared error of 0.0691 on the VALIDATE partition. This fit statistic showed quite an improvement over the first model built by using the default settings.

   Try to improve the neural network performance by changing now some of the default settings assigned to the learning and optimization parameters.

2. Under the Common Optimization Options properties, increase **L1 weight decay** from 0 to **0.01**.

3. Decrease **L2 weight decay** from 0.1 to **0.0001**.

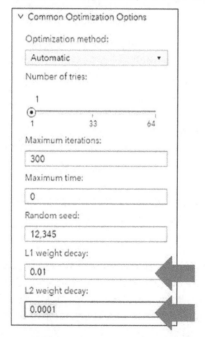

In L1, we penalize the absolute value of the weights. Unlike L2, the weights can be reduced to zero here. Hence, it is very useful when we are trying to compress our model. Otherwise, we usually prefer L2 over it.

Mathematically speaking, weight decay adds a regularization term in order to prevent the coefficients to fit so perfectly as to overfit. The difference between the L1 and L2 is just that L2 is the sum of the square of the weights, while L1 is just the sum of the weights.

4. Run the **Neural Network** node.
5. Open the results for the node.

6. Click the **Assessment** tab.

Target ...	Data Role	Partitio...	Formatt...	Sum of ...	Averag...
churn	TRAIN	1	1	39,590	0.0702
churn	VALIDATE	0	0	16,967	0.0685

The average squared error for the tuned neural network model is 0.0685 on the VALIDATE partition. This fit statistic is slightly better than the previous model trained in the last demonstration.

7. Close the Results window.
8. Run the entire pipeline and view the results of model comparison.

Champi...	Name	Algorith...	KS (You...	Misclas...
▣	Neural Network	Neural Network	0.5536	0.0799
	Logistic Regressio n	Logistic Regressio n	0.5488	0.0808

The neural network model is the champion of the pipeline based on default KS.

9. Close the Results window.

End of Demonstration

Quiz

1. Which of the following statements is true regarding neural networks?

   a. Neural networks in SAS Visual Data Mining and Machine Learning have a built-in method for selecting useful inputs.

   b. The algorithms in neural networks are guaranteed to converge to a global error minimum.

   c. The initial weight values in a neural network have no impact on whether the optimization algorithm is vulnerable to local minima.

   d. There are two optimization methods available for neural networks in Visual Data Mining and Machine Learning: limited memory Broyden-Fletcher-Goldfarb-Shanno (LBFGS) and stochastic gradient descent (SGD).

Chapter 11: Support Vector Machines

Introduction

Support vector machines (SVMs) are the newest of the machine learning models that are presented in this book. Like neural networks, these models tend to be black boxes (that is, harder to interpret), but they are very flexible. Support vector machines automatically discover any relationship between the inputs and the target, which means that you do not need to specify the relationship before modeling. However, SVM is most commonly used as a *supervised machine learning algorithm* that can be used for both classification or regression challenges. Unlike trees and neurons, a support vector is not something that most people can easily visualize. In this chapter, we learn what a support vector is and how to build support vector machine models.

Support Vector Machine Algorithm

Support vector machines (SVMs) were originally developed for pure classification tasks to solve pattern recognition problems. In other words, the model makes decision predictions instead of ranks or estimates. Support vector machines have been broadly used in fields such as image classification, handwriting recognition, financial decision, and text mining. They have since expanded and now can be used for regression tasks as well (Vapnik, Golowich, and Smola 1997). However, in Model Studio, currently only classification tasks are possible for binary targets and can provide decisions, ranks, and probability estimates. In the simple example shown in Figure 11.1, a support vector machine separates the outcomes of a binary target into two classes, red (black) and green (gray).

Figure 11.1: Support Vector Machines

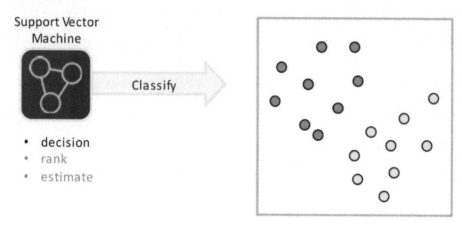

In this simple illustration, the goal is to classify red (the dots in the upper left on the slide above) versus green (in the lower right). There are many classification rules (lines) that could be used to perfectly separate the red and green cases. In fact, when data are perfectly linearly separable, as is the case above, there are infinitely many solutions. So how will a unique solution be discovered?

Figure 11.2: Classifying Red (Black) Versus Green (Gray)

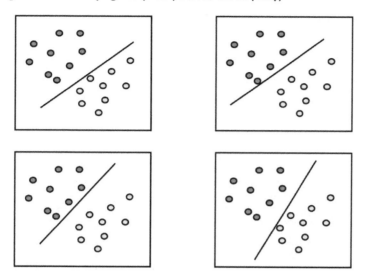

Given two input variables (as shown in Figures 11.1 and 11.2), the support vector machine is a line. Given three input variables, the support vector is a plane. And with more than three input variables, the support vector is a hyperplane.

For mathematical convenience, the binary target is defined by values +1 and -1, rather than the usual 1 and 0. The renumbering is done automatically by Model Studio. Because the linear separator equals 0, classification is determined by a point falling on the positive or negative side of the line.

This is a simple linear problem to start with. Finding the best solution to a linear classification problem is a mathematical problem, so let's look at the mathematical definition of a support vector machine model. Later, you see a more complex nonlinear problem. In the illustration below, think of the vector w as the mechanism that affects the slope of H. The bias parameter, b, is the measure of offset of the separating line (or plane, in higher dimensions) from the origin.

Figure 11.3: Linear Separation of the Training Data

- A separating hyperplane H is given by the following:
  - the normal vector *w*
  - an additional parameter, *b*, called *bias*

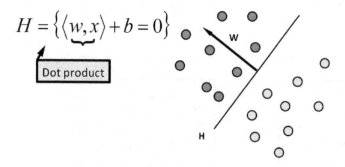

$$H = \left\{ \langle \underbrace{w, x} \rangle + b = 0 \right\}$$

Dot product

A dot product is a way to multiply vectors that result in a scalar, or a single number, as the answer. It is an element-by-element multiplication and then a sum across the products. Consider the following example:

If $\underline{a} = \begin{bmatrix} a_1 \\ a_2 \\ a_3 \end{bmatrix}$ and $\underline{b} = \begin{bmatrix} b_1 \\ b_2 \\ b_3 \end{bmatrix}$ then $\langle \underline{a}, \underline{b} \rangle = a_1 b_1 + a_2 b_2 + a_3 b_3$.

In Figure 11.4, data points located in the direction of the normal vector are diagnosed as positive. Data points on the other side of the hyperplane are diagnosed as negative.

Figure 11.4: Training Versus Prediction

- Training:

  Select *w* and *b* in such a way that the hyperplane separates the training data – that is, construction of a hyperplane.

- Prediction of the class for a new observation:

  On which side of the hyperplane (+/-) is the new data point located?

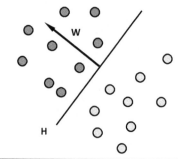

Choosing the Best Hyperplane

As discussed above, if the data points are *linearly separable,* then an infinite number of separating hyperplanes (that is, classification rules) exist. to choose the best and achieve a unique solution is to think of a "fat" hyperplane. This leads to a separator that has the largest margin of error, essentially wiggle room, on either side.

Figure 11.5: A "Fat" Hyperplane

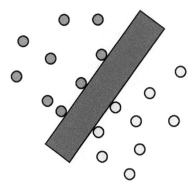

Among all these hyperplanes, only one of them has the *maximum margin.* It is essentially the median of the fat hyperplane.

Figure 11.6: A Maximum-Margin Hyperplane

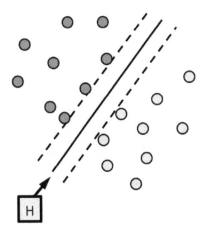

What Are the Support Vectors?

The normal vector for the maximum-margin separating hyperplane is:

$$w = \sum_{i=1}^{\#sv} \alpha_i y_i x_i^{sv}$$

(The mathematical details of this solution are provided in the next section.)

The support vectors describe the properties of the maximum-margin hyperplane. The construction of the maximum-margin hyperplane is not explicitly dependent on the dimension of the input space. Because of this, the curse of dimensionality is avoided. The curse of dimensionality states that the more input variables a model uses, the more data points are needed to fit the model. In Figure 11.7, only the five points that are the carrying vectors are used to determine *w*.

Figure 11.7: What Are the Support Vectors?

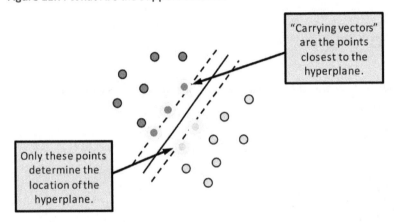

Demo 11.1: Building a Support Vector Machine Based on Default Settings

In this demonstration, you create a new pipeline using the CPML Demo Pipeline and add a Support Vector Machine node to it. You build the support vector machine model using the default settings of the node.

1. Click the plus sign (**+**) next to the Lesson 4 pipeline tab to add a new pipeline.

2. In the New Pipeline window, enter **Lesson 5** in the **Name** field. For **Template**, select **CPML Demo Pipeline**.

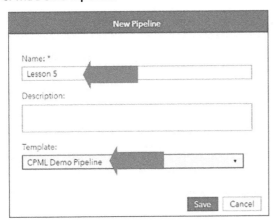

3. Click **Save**.
4. In the Lesson 5 pipeline, right-click the **Variable Selection** node and select **Add child node ▶ Supervised Learning ▶ SVM**.

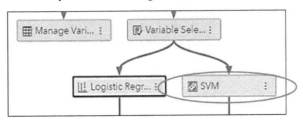

5. Keep all properties for the support vector machine at their defaults.
6. Run the **SVM** node.
7. Open the results for the support vector machine model.

    There are several charts and plots to help you evaluate the model's performance. The first table is Fit Statistics, which presents the support vector machine's performance considering several assessment measures.

Fit Statistics

Statistic	Training	Validation
Accuracy	0.9152	0.9156
Error	0.0848	0.0844
Sensitivity	0.3689	0.3706
Specificity	0.9906	0.9909

The Training Results table shows the parameters for the final support vector machine model, such as the support vectors and the margin, among others.

Training Results

Statistic	Description	Value
WW	Inner Product of Weights	43.6941
Beta	Bias	0.0672
TotalSlack	Total Slack (Constraint Violations)	8,794.5304
LongVector	Norm of Longest Vector	2.8267
nSupport	Number of Support Vectors	39,590
nSupportInM	Number of Support Vectors on Margin	0
MaximumF	Maximum F	3.2365
MinimumF	Minimum F	-3.7650

The Path EP Score Code window shows the final score code that can be deployed in production.

Path EP Score Code

```
1    data sasep.out;
2        dcl double "REP_BILL_DATA_USG_M03" having label n'Replacement: 3M Avg Billed Data Usag
3        dcl double "REP_BILL_DATA_USG_M06" having label n'Replacement: 6M Avg Billed Data Usag
4        dcl double "REP_CALLS_IN_OFFPK" having label n'Replacement: Calls Incoming Off-Peak' f
5        dcl double "REP_CALLS_IN_PK" having label n'Replacement: Calls Incoming Peak' format C
6        dcl double "REP_CALLS_OUT_OFFPK" having label n'Replacement: Calls Outgoing Off-Peak'
7        dcl double "REP_CALLS_OUT_PK" having label n'Replacement: Calls Outgoing Peak' format
8        dcl double "REP_DATA_DEVICE_AGE" having label n'Replacement: Avg Age of Devices on Pla
9        dcl double "REP_LIFETIME_VALUE" having label n'Replacement: Lifetime Value' format DOL
10       dcl double "REP_MB_DATA_NDIST_M06M" having label n'Replacement: 6M Avg Billed Data Usa
11       dcl double "REP_MB_DATA_USG_M01" having label n'Replacement: MB Data Usage 1 Mth Prior
12       dcl double "REP_MB_DATA_USG_M02" having label n'Replacement: MB Data Usage 2 Mths Prio
13       dcl double "REP_MB_DATA_USG_M03" having label n'Replacement: MB Data Usage 3 Mths Prio
14       dcl double "REP_MB_DATA_USG_ROAMM01" having label n'Replacement: MB Data Usage Roam 1
15
```

Similarly, the **Training Code window** shows the train code that can be used to train the model based on different data sets or on different platforms.

Training Code

```
1    *------------------------------------------------------*;
2    * Macro Variables for input, output data and files;
3        %let dm_datalib =;
4        %let dm_lib     = WORK;
5        %let dm_folder  = %sysfunc(pathname(work));
6    *------------------------------------------------------*;
7    *------------------------------------------------------*;
8      * Training for svm;
9    *------------------------------------------------------*;
10   *------------------------------------------------------*;
11     * Initializing Variable Macros;
12   *------------------------------------------------------*;
13   %macro dm_unary_input;
14       %mend dm_unary_input;
15       %global dm_num_unary_input;
```

Finally, the **Output window** shows the final support vector machine model parameters, the training results, the iteration history, the misclassification matrix, the fit statistics, and the predicted probability variables.

The SAS System

The SVMACHINE Procedure

Model Information	
Task Type	C_CLAS
Optimization Technique	Interior Point
Scale	YES
Kernel Function	Linear
Penalty Method	C
Penalty Parameter	1
Maximum Iterations	25
Tolerance	1e-06

8. Click the **Assessment** tab.

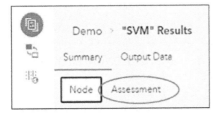

The first chart is **Lift Reports**, which by default shows **Cumulative Lift**. Cumulative Lift shows the model's performance ordered by the percentage of the population. This chart is very useful for selecting the model based on a particular target of the customer base. It shows how much better the model is than the random events.

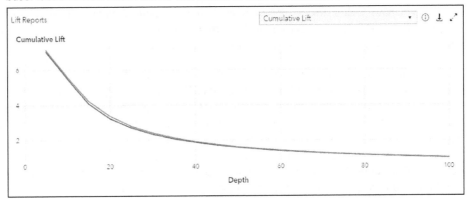

For a binary target, you also have the **ROC Reports** output, which shows the model's performance in terms of ROC curve by considering the true positive rate and the false positive rate. It is good to foresee the performance on a specific business event when all positive cases are selected. It shows that the model's performance based on the positive cases were predicted right and the positive cases were predicted wrong.

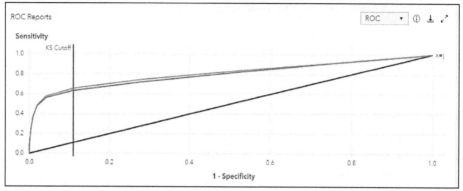

Finally, you have the Fit Statistics output, which shows the model's performance based on some assessment measures, such as average squared error.

Target ...	Data Role	Partitio...	Formatt...	Sum of ...	Averag...
churn	TRAIN	1	1	39,590	0.1079
churn	VALIDATE	0	0	16,967	0.1076

The Fit Statistics table shows an average squared error of 0.1076 on the VALIDATE partition.

9. Close the Results window.

End of Demonstration

Improve the Model and Optimizing Complexity

Now that you have built a support vector machine model using the default settings, you are ready to refine it. For support vector machines, there is no clear distinction between the next two Discovery tasks: improving the model and optimizing complexity.

Training a support vector machine does not involve a sequence of models, as with decision trees, or a sequence of iterations, as with neural networks. This means that, for support vector machines, there is no way to optimize complexity by assessing performance on validation data across multiple models or iterations. Instead, you can adjust a few key hyperparameters and then look at the performance of the support vector machine model on validation data. In this chapter, you learn to increase the flexibility of a support vector machine model by modifying the settings of three critical options in Model Studio: **penalty, kernel,** and **tolerance**. The penalty is a term that accounts for misclassification errors in model optimization. The kernel is a mathematical function that operates as a dot product on transformed data in a higher dimension. The tolerance value balances the number of support vectors and model accuracy.

Figure 11.8: Improving the Support Vector Machine Model

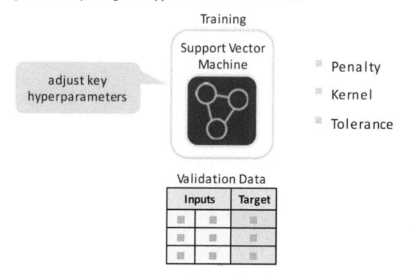

The Optimization Problem

In Figure 11.9, if the target variable equals 1, then *H* must be greater than or equal to 1. If the target is -1, then *H* must be less than or equal to -1. The optimal hyperplane satisfies these conditions and also has minimal norm.

Figure 11.9: Optimization Problem

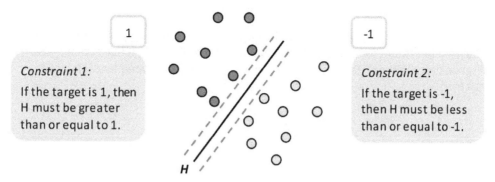

The binary target is written as +/- 1 for mathematical convenience.

The denoting of the binary target as +1 or -1 is simply for ease in mathematical details. This trick enables the combination of the two constraints into a single constraint. Optimization problems with a single constraint are mathematically easier to solve than optimization problems under two constraints.

Details: The Optimization Problem

Mathematically, these constraints are written as follows:

$$\langle w, x_i \rangle + b \geq 1$$

if $y_i = 1$ and

$$\langle w, x_i \rangle + b \leq -1$$

if $y_i = -1$.

However, these two constraints can be combined into a single constraint where

$$y_i \cdot \left(\langle w, x_i \rangle + b \right) \geq 1$$

for $i = 1, 2, ...n$.

The width of this *maximum margin hyperplane* is determined by the usual calculation of a point to a line. In general, the distance from a point (x_0, y_0) to a line $Ax + By + C = 0$ is given by

$$|Ax_0 + By_0 + C| / sqrt(A^2 + B^2)$$

Using this calculation, the maximum margin hyperplane is found by maximizing $2/||w||$, where $||w||$ is the *norm* of the vector w, which is defined as $||w|| = sqrt(w'w)$. The norm of a vector is a measure of length.

Maximizing $2/||w||$ is equivalent to minimizing $||w||$. Because $||w||$ is defined by using a square root, it becomes mathematically simpler to minimize the square of $||w||$. The solution is the same.

If the data points are not linearly separable, we have a so-called *soft margin* hyperplane. In this case, we need to account for errors that the separating hyperplane might make. During the optimization process, the distance between a point in error and the hyperplane is typically denoted by ξ.

Figure 11.10: Training Data Not Linearly Separable

Errors are accounted for during the optimization process:

- Penalty: C*(distance to hyperplane)

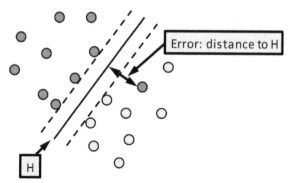

- C is an error weight (regularization parameter).

For large values of C, the optimization will choose a smaller-margin hyperplane if that hyperplane does a better job of getting all the training points classified correctly. Conversely, a very small value of C causes the optimizer to look for a larger-margin separating hyperplane, even if that hyperplane misclassifies more points. For very tiny values of C, you should get misclassified examples, often even if your training data is linearly separable.

Details: The Solution

Given the need to account for errors, the optimization problem is solved by minimizing

$$\| w \|^2 + C \cdot \sum_i \xi_i$$

under the single constraint

$$y_i \cdot \left(\langle w, x_i \rangle + b \right) \geq 1 - \xi_i, \quad \xi_i \geq 0$$

.

The method used to solve the optimization problem is the Lagrange approach. Here, Lagrange multipliers $\alpha_i \geq 0$ are introduced. They summarize the problem in a Lagrange function. Constraints: $\xi_i \geq 0$ and $\alpha_i \geq 0$, so you must find the saddle point of the Lagrange function.

For the optimization problem above, the Lagrange function becomes

$$L(w,b,\alpha,\xi) = \frac{1}{2} \| w \|^2 + C \cdot \sum_{i=1}^{n} \xi_i - \sum_{i=1}^{n} \alpha_i \left(\xi_i + y_i \left(\langle w, x_i \rangle + b \right) - 1 \right)$$

.

In order to find the saddle point, $L(w,b,\alpha,\xi)$ is minimized with respect to *w*, *b*, and *ξ* but maximized with respect to α_i .

The Lagrange Approach

Take the following derivatives of the Lagrange function:

$$\frac{\partial}{\partial b} L(w,b,\alpha,\xi) = 0 \quad \frac{\partial}{\partial w} L(w,b,\alpha,\xi) = 0$$

and obtain

$$\sum_{i=1}^{n} \alpha_i y_i = 0 \quad w = \sum_{i=1}^{n} \alpha_i y_i x_i$$

This leads to the so-called *dual problem*. Maximize

$$W(\alpha) = \sum_{i=1}^{n} \alpha_i - \frac{1}{2} \sum_{i,j=1}^{n} \alpha_i \alpha_j y_i y_j \langle x_i, x_j \rangle$$

under the constraints

$$0 \le \alpha_i \le C \quad \text{and} \quad \sum_{i=1}^{n} \alpha_i y_i = 0$$

After plugging back into the Lagrange function and reformulating, you have the classification function:

$$f(x_{new}) = sign\left(\langle w, x_{new} \rangle + b\right)$$
$$= sign\left(\sum_{i=1}^{n} \alpha_i y_i \langle x_i, x_{new} \rangle + b\right)$$

Demo 11.2: Changing the Methods of Solution for a Support Vector Machine

In this demonstration, you change the default settings of the Support Vector Machine node in the Lesson 5 pipeline. You modify the methods of solution parameters for the Support Vector Machine node.

1. Recall that the average squared error of the previous model, based on the default settings, was 0.1076 on the VALIDATE partition.

    Try to improve the support vector machine performance by changing some of the default settings assigned to the methods of solution.

2. Change the **Penalty** property from 1 to **0.1**.

    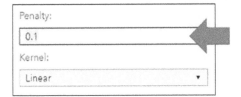

    The Penalty (C parameter) tells the SVM optimization how much you want to avoid misclassifying each training example. A smaller value of C causes the optimizer to look for a larger-margin separating hyperplane, even if that hyperplane misclassifies more points. A larger penalty value usually provides a more robust model. However, it might overfit.

3. Run the **Support Vector Machine** node.

4. Open the results for the node.

5. Click the **Assessment** tab. Examine the Fit Statistics window.

Target ...	Data Role	Partitio...	Formatt...	Sum of ...	Averag...
churn	TRAIN	1	1	39,590	0.0937
churn	VALIDATE	0	0	16,967	0.0932

6. The average squared error for the tuned support vector machine model is 0.0932 on the VALIDATE partition. This fit statistic is better (smaller) than the first model, which used the default settings.

7. Close the Results window.

    End of Demonstration

The Kernel Trick

In the previous section, we attempted to refine the model by changing the penalty term. Remember that the penalty term accounts for misclassification errors that inevitably occur when the data are not linearly separable. Suppose we decide that our model's performance is not yet satisfactory. We want to go beyond a soft-margin classifier. Next, we apply a kernel function to improve classification. One method to optimize the complexity in support vector machine models is changing the margins.

In most realistic scenarios, not only is data not linearly separable, but a soft margin classifier would make too many mistakes to be a viable solution.

Figure 11.11: Data Points Unable to Be Separated Linearly

Input space 2-D

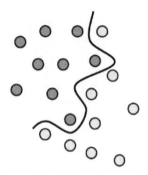

One solution requires transforming the data to a higher dimension and then finding the maximum margin hyperplane in this higher dimension.

Below is an example that is not linearly separable in two dimensions, but it is easy to separate in three dimensions. This can be generalized to higher dimensions.

Figure 11.12: Using the Feature Space Transformation

Input space 2-D   Feature space 3-D

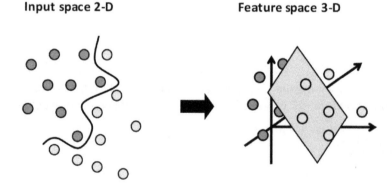

Details: Dot Products in Feature Spaces Are Mathematically Difficult to Calculate

The original data points occur only in dot products. So, whether solving for the parameters of *H* or when scoring a new observation, the calculations depend on dot products.

Here is the equation used to solve the dual optimization problem:

$$W(\alpha) = \sum_{i=1}^{n} \alpha_i - \frac{1}{2} \sum_{i,j=1}^{n} \alpha_i \alpha_j y_i y_j \langle x_i, x_j \rangle$$

Here is the equation used to classify a new case:

$$f(x_{new}) = sign \left(\sum_{i=1}^{n} \alpha_i y_i \langle x_i, x_{new} \rangle + b \right)$$

Both equations rely on dot products of the data.

For data that are not linearly separable, the data points are transformed to a *feature space* with a function Φ. Then we separate the data points Φ(x) in the feature space. Usually, the dimension of the feature space is *much* higher than the dimension of the input space. If the classification really is easier in the high-dimensional feature space, you want to construct the separating hyperplane there. This requires dot product calculations in the feature space. This creates a problem because dot products in feature spaces are mathematically difficult to calculate.

Details: The Solution

You can overcome the curse of dimensionality because you need to calculate only inner products between vectors in the feature space. Φ(x) is the transformation from the input space to the feature space. You do not need to perform the mapping explicitly. If K satisfies Mercer's theorem, it describes an inner product.

These are the two kernel functions available in Model Studio. Why do we call it a *trick*? You do not have to know exactly what the feature space looks like. It is enough to specify the kernel function as a measure of similarity. You do not perform the exact kernel calculations but consider the result. Still, you have the geometric interpretation in the form of a separating hyperplane (that is, more transparency as for a neural network).

In Figure 11.13, the points are not linearly separable in two dimensions but are in three dimensions. Using a kernel function in the input space when there is nonlinear separation is equivalent to performing dot products in a higher-dimensional feature space that does have linear separation.

Figure 11.13: The Kernel Trick

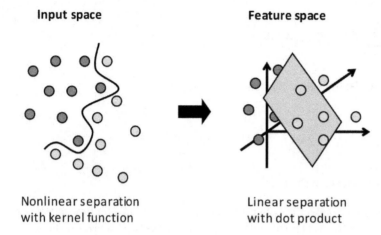

Nonlinear separation
with kernel function

Linear separation
with dot product

Model Studio: Kernel Parameters

In Model Studio, for polynomial kernels, only degrees of 2 and 3 are available. The kernel function is used for spatial classification.

- Linear $K(u, v) = u^T v$.

- Quadratic $K(u, v) = (u^T v + 1)^2$. The 1 is added to avoid zero-value entries in the Hessian matrix.

- Cubic $K(u, v) = (u^T v + 1)^3$. The 1 is added to avoid zero-value entries in the Hessian matrix.

The penalty value balances model complexity and training error. A larger penalty value creates a more robust model at the risk of overfitting the training data.

The tolerance value balances the number of support vectors and model accuracy. Tolerance is a user-defined value that controls the absolute error of the objective function. A tolerance value that is too large creates too few support vectors, and a value that is too small overfits the training data. The iteration stops if the absolute error is less than or equal to the tolerance value.

Model Interpretability

In theory, support vector machines have a geometric interpretation because they are hyperplanes. However, in practice, many analysts consider support vector machine models to be black boxes, much like neural networks. Thus, there is often a trade-off between model accuracy and model interpretability. Machine learning algorithms are good at generating accurate and generalizable predictive models, but it is often nearly impossible to understand how the algorithms arrived at those predictions or even what the behavior or trend of the model is. We cannot gain much insight into support vector machines, as well as some other machine learning models, by analyzing the model parameters. However, we can learn a great deal by analyzing the predictions from these models. In the next demonstration, you learn how to use Model Studio's model interpretability feature to interpret your results.

There is almost always a trade-off in terms of accuracy versus interpretability.

Machine learning algorithms are good at generating very accurate (and generalizable) predictive models using quite complex combinations of mathematical and logical elements. They provide very good predictions, but it can be nearly impossible to understand how they arrived at those predictions or in general what the behavior or trend of the model is. This is a big problem in regulated industries and other applications where it is important to be able to explain **why** a model gave a certain answer. So model interpretability (understanding the predictions) is the usual criticism of machine learning models. As machine learning models become more sophisticated, the ability to quickly and accurately interpret these models can diminish.

This criticism stems from the complex parameterizations found in the model. Although it is true that little insight can be gained by analyzing the actual parameters of the model, much can be gained by analyzing the resulting prediction decisions.

Model Studio: Model Interpretability

SAS Visual Data Mining and Machine Learning provides three plots that help users interpret model results:

- **Partial Dependence**—A PD plot depicts the functional relationship between the model inputs and the model's predictions. A PD plot shows how the model's predictions partially depend on the values of the input variables of interest. To create a one-way PD plot, identify the plot variable and the complementary variables. Next, create a replicate of the training data for each unique value of the plot variable. In each replicate, the plot variable is replaced by the current unique value. Finally, score each replicate with your model and compute the average predicted value within each replicate. The final result is a view of how the prediction changes with respect to the plot variable.

  PD plots from various machine learning models can also be used for model comparison.

Model Studio: Model Interpretability

- **Individual Conditional Expectation**—An ICE plot presents a disaggregation of the PD plot to reveal interactions and differences at the observation level. The ICE plot is generated by choosing a plot variable and replicating each observation for every unique value of the plot variable. Then each replicate is scored. SAS Visual Data Mining and Machine Learning creates a segmented ICE plot. A segmented ICE plot is created from a cluster of observations instead of on individual observations.

- **Local Interpretable Model-Agnostic Explanations (LIME)**—A LIME plot creates a localized linear regression model around a particular observation (or a cluster centroid) based on a perturbed sample set of data. That is, near the observation of interest, a sample set of data is created. This data set is based on the distribution of the original input data. The sample set is scored by the original model, and sample observations are weighted based on proximity to the observation of interest. Next, variable selection is performed using the LASSO technique. Finally, a linear regression is created to explain the relationship between the perturbed input data and the perturbed target variable. The final result is an easily interpreted linear regression model that is valid near the observation of interest.

Figure 11.14: Model Interpretability in Model Studio

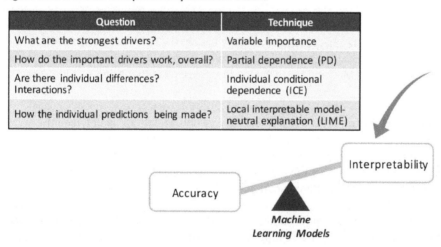

Question	Technique
What are the strongest drivers?	Variable importance
How do the important drivers work, overall?	Partial dependence (PD)
Are there individual differences? Interactions?	Individual conditional dependence (ICE)
How the individual predictions being made?	Local interpretable model-neutral explanation (LIME)

Each of these plots work for all models and are used to compare results across many different models.

Model Studio: Model Interpretability

For more details, refer to the following resources:

- Blog series "Interpretability" at https://blogs.sas.com/content/tag/interpretability/

- SAS paper "Interpreting Black-Box Machine Learning Models Using Partial Dependence and Individual Conditional Expectation Plots" by Ray Wright at https://www.sas.com/content/dam/SAS/support/en/sas-global-forum-proceedings/2018/1950-2018.pdf

- SAS Communities Library "LIME and ICE in SAS Viya 3.4: Interpreting Machine Learning Models" at https://communities.sas.com/t5/SAS-Communities-Library/LIME-and-ICE-in-SAS-Viya-3-4-Interpreting-Machine-Learning/ta-p/510915

Demo 11.3: Changing the Kernel Function for a Support Vector Machine and Adding Model Interpretability

In this demonstration, you change the previous settings of the Support Vector Machine node in the Lesson 5 pipeline. You modify the kernel function and other parameters and compare this model performance to the other model in the pipeline. Later, you use the Model Interpretability capability to add some explanation to the support vector machine model.

1. Recall that the previous model, based on changing the penalty term, achieved an average squared error of 0.0932 on the VALIDATE partition. Changing only the penalty term led to a model that was an improvement (at least based on ASE) compared to the SVM model built under the defaults.

   Try to improve the support vector machine performance by changing some of the default settings assigned to the kernel function parameters.

2. For **Kernel**, change the function from Linear to **Polynomial**. Leave **Polynomial degree** as **2**.

   We are just trying to make the hyperplane decision boundary between the classes different by changing the kernel. Linear kernels usually work fine for data that are linearly separable. However, if the data are not linearly separable, a linear kernel does not classify well.

3. For **Tolerance**, change 0.000001 to **0.5**. Tolerance specifies the minimum number at which the iteration stops.

4. For **Maximum iterations**, change 25 to **10**. This property specifies the maximum number of iterations allowed with each try. In some cases, you can obtain a good model in fewer than five iterations.

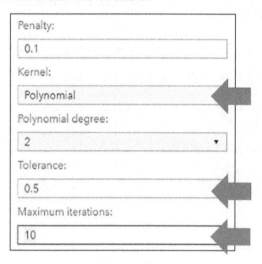

5. Run the **Support Vector Machine** node.
6. Open the results for the node.
7. Click the **Assessment** tab. Examine the Fit Statistics window.

Target ...	Data Role	Partitio...	Formatt...	Sum of ...	Averag...
churn	TRAIN	1	1	39,590	0.0917
churn	VALIDATE	0	0	16,967	0.0912

The average squared error for the tuned support vector machine model is 0.0912 on the VALIDATE partition. This fit statistic is slightly better than the previous model.

8. Close the Results window.

Some improvement in the model performance has been observed. However, model interpretation is still a challenging task in machine learning models, which include support vector machines.

9. Under **Post-training Properties**, expand **Model Interpretability**. Expand **Global Interpretability** and select the check box for **PD Plots**. Expand **Local Interpretability** and select the check box for **ICE plots**. Finally, turn on the property for **LIME** plots.

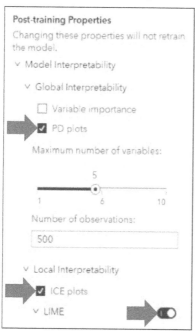

10. Scroll to the bottom of the Post-training Properties and expand **General ICE/LIME Options**. Notice that, by default, the ICE and LIME plots are used to interpret cluster centroids, rather than individual observations. Also, by default, two clusters are generated from the observations for these plots.

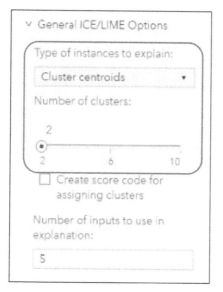

11. Run the Support Vector Machine node.

12. Open the results for the node.

13. Now you see an additional tab along with the Node and Assessment tabs. Click the **Model Interpretability** tab.

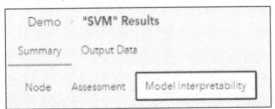

14. Expand the Partial Dependence plot.

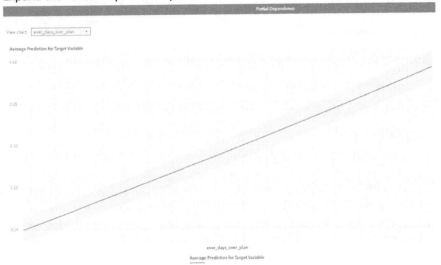

The Partial Dependence plot shows the marginal effect of a feature on the predicted outcome of a previously fit model. The prediction function is fixed at a few values of the chosen features and averaged over the other features. A Partial Dependence plot can show whether the relationship between the target and a feature is linear, monotonic, or more complex.

The plot above shows the relationship between **Total Days Over Plan** and the model's prediction. There is a positive linear relationship. On average, the more time (days) that customers use their devices over their specified plan, there is an increase in the probability of churn. This is an important insight for the business.

15. To see the relationship between the model's predictions and other variables, click the drop-down arrow next to **View chart**.

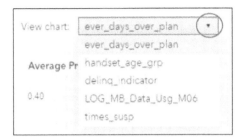

These are the five most important inputs in the model, based on a one-level decision tree for all inputs used to predict the predicted values from the model.

16. Select the **Handset Age Group** variable.

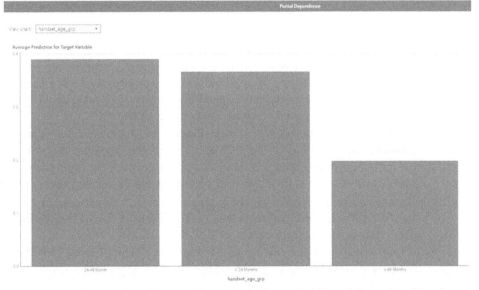

This PD plot indicates that there is a decrease in the probability of churn the older the handset is. Does this make business sense?

17. Exit the maximized view of the Partial Dependence plot.

18. Expand the Individual Conditional Expectation plot.

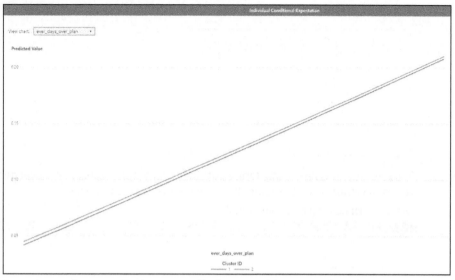

For a chosen feature, ICE plots generally draw one line per instance, representing how the instance's prediction changes when the feature changes. SAS Visual Data Mining and Machine Learning creates an ICE plot for the most representative clusters of observations instead of on individual observations, by default.

Above is the segmented ICE plot of churn probability by total days over plan. Each line represents the conditional expectation for one customer segment. The plot indicates that for both customer segments, there is a consistent increase in the probability of churn, for an increase in total days over plan, given that other features are constant.

ICE plots help resolve interesting subgroups and interactions between model variables. The most useful feature to observe when evaluating an ICE plot of an interval input is intersecting slopes. Intersecting slopes indicate that there is an interaction between the plot variable and one or more complementary variables. **Total Days Over Plan** does not show any interactions.

19. Click the drop-down arrow next to **View chart** to see ICE plots of other variables. Select the **Handset Age Group** variable.

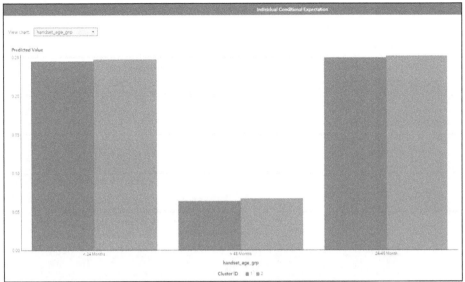

A segmented ICE plot is created from a cluster of observations instead of on individual observations. The most useful feature to observe when evaluating an ICE plot of a categorical input is significant differences between clusters in each group. Significant differences between each cluster's plot between groups indicate group effects.

There are two clusters represented in this plot, with the average predicted probability of churn calculated separately for each cluster, across all levels of **Handset Age Group**. For this variable, the trend of observing the lowest probability of churn for the oldest handset age group holds true for both clusters, and the average predicted probability of churn for the oldest handset group is slightly smaller in cluster 1 compared to cluster 2. In fact, for all levels of Handset Age Group, the probability of churn in cluster 1 is slightly smaller than that for cluster 2.

20. Exit the maximized view of the Individual Conditional Expectation plot. Although PD and ICE plots provide only indirect approximations of a model's workings, they are popular and highly visual tools for obtaining a working understanding of increasingly complicated machine learning models.

21. Expand the **Local Model** table.

A local logistic regression model was fit around Cluster Centroid: 1 for a perturbed sample of the data. The Cluster centroid is treated as the observation of interest for calculating distance for the perturbed samples. The column of estimates is the estimated parameter coefficients for the local logistic regression model for Cluster Centroid: 1.

The **View chart** menu is used to see the local logistic regression model fit around Cluster Centroid: 2 as well.

22. Restore the **Local Model** table.

23. Expand the **Local Explanation for Nominal Variables** plot.

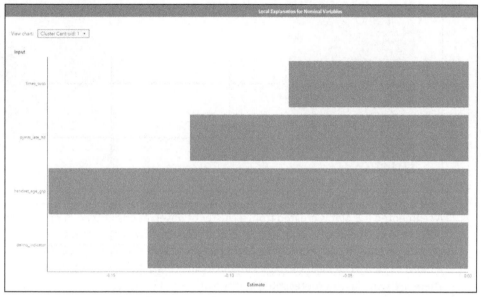

This plot shows the estimated regression coefficients for each nominal input for Cluster Centroid: 1. You see that the nominal input with the largest effect on the probability of churn for this cluster is **Handset Age Group**. Hovering over the bar for **Handset Age Group** reveals a tooltip that shows that the coefficient shown is for the oldest handset age group (>48 months). The negative coefficient indicates that the largest decrease in the probability of churn is for the oldest handset group for this cluster. This agrees with what is shown in the ICE plot.

Use the **View Charts** menu to see the results for Cluster Centroid: 2.

24. Restore the **Local Explanation for Nominal Variables** plot.

25. Maximize the **Local Explanation for Interval Variables** plot.

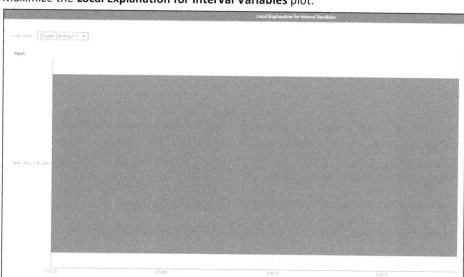

This plot shows the estimated regression coefficient for total days over plan for Cluster Centroid: 1. For this cluster, the estimated regression coefficient is positive, which indicates that there is an increase in the predicted probability of churn as total days over plan increases for this cluster. This also agrees with what is shown in the ICE plot.

Use the **View Charts** menu to see the results for Cluster Centroid: 2.

26. Restore the **Local Explanation for Interval Variables** plot.
27. Close the Results window.
28. Run the entire pipeline and view the results of model comparison.

Champi...	Name	Algorith...	KS (You...	Misclas...
⊙	SVM	SVM	0.5662	0.0729
	Logistic Regressio n	Logistic Regressio n	0.5488	0.0808

The support vector machine model is the champion of this pipeline based on default KS.

29. Close the Results window.

End of Demonstration

Regularize and Tune Hyperparameters of the Model

One of the hardest processes in support vector machine models is to find the model parameters that minimize the loss function.

Model Studio: Autotuning

When the autotuning feature is used, SAS Visual Data Mining and Machine Learning returns the penalty, the kernel function, and the degree of the kernel function if it is a polynomial function. Autotuning is invoked by selecting the Performing Autotuning option property on the Options tab in the Support Vector Machine node.

Note: Performing autotuning can substantially increase run time.

Autotuning searches for the best combination of the following support vector machine parameters.

Penalty specifies whether to autotune the penalty value. The initial value is 1. The search process can be ranged from 0.000001 to 100, defined by the From and To options.

Polynomial degree specifies whether to autotune the polynomial degree for the SVM model. The initial value is 1. The search process can be ranged from 1 to 3, defined by From and To options.

Search Options specifies the options for autotuning searching. The following options are available:

- **Bayesian** uses priors to seed the iterative optimization.

- **Genetic algorithm** uses an initial Latin hypercube sample that seeds a genetic algorithm. The genetic algorithm generates a new population of alternative configurations at each iteration.

- **Grid** uses the lower bound, upper bound, and midrange values for each autotuned parameter, with the initial value (or values) used as the baseline model.

- **Latin hypercube sample** performs an optimized grid search that is uniform in each tuning parameter, but random in combinations.

- **Random** generates a single sample of purely random configurations.

Number of evaluations per iteration specifies the number of tuning evaluations in one iteration. This option is available only if the Search method is Genetic algorithm or Bayesian. The default value is 10. It ranges from 2 to 2,147,483,647.

Model Studio: Autotuning

Maximum number of evaluations specifies the maximum number of tuning evaluations. This option is available only if the Search method is Genetic algorithm or Bayesian. The default value is 50. It ranges from 3 to 2,147,483,647.

Maximum number of iterations specifies the maximum number of tuning iterations. This option is available only if the Search method is Genetic algorithm or Bayesian. The default value is 5. It ranges from 1 to 2,147,483,647.

Sample size specifies the sample size. This option is available only if the Search method is Random or Latin hypercube sample. The default value is 50. It ranges from 2 to 2,147,483,647.

There are some general options associated with the autotuning search.

Validation method specifies the validation method for finding the objective value. If your data is partitioned, then that partition is used. Validation method, Validation data proportion, and Cross validation number of folds are all ignored.

- **Partition** specifies using the partition validation method. With partition, you specify proportions to use for randomly assigning observations to each role.

    - **Validation data proportion** specifies the proportion of data to be used for the Partition validation method. The default value is 0.3.

- **K-fold cross validation** specifies using the cross validation method. In cross validation, each model evaluation requires k training executions (on k-1 data folds) and k scoring executions (on one holdout fold). This increases the evaluation time by approximately a factor of k.

    - **Cross validation number of folds** specifies the number of partition folds in the cross validation process (the k defined above). Possible values range from 2 to 20. The default value is 5.

Nominal target objective function specifies the objective function to optimize for tuning parameters for a nominal target. Possible values are average squared error, area under the curve, F1 score, F0.5 score, gamma, Gini coefficient, Kolmogorov-Smirnov statistic, multi-class log loss, misclassification rate, root average squared error, and Tau. The default value is misclassification rate.

Interval target objective function specifies the objective function to optimize for tuning parameters for an interval target. Possible values are average squared error, mean absolute error, mean square logarithmic error, root average squared error, root mean absolute error, and root mean squared logarithmic error. The default value is average squared error.

Maximum time (minutes) specifies the maximum time in minutes for the optimization tuner.

Model Studio: Autotuning

Maximum training time for single model (in minutes) specifies the maximum time in minutes for a single model to train. If left blank (the default), there is no maximum time.

 Practice: Building a Support Vector Machine Mode.

1. Build a support vector machine model using the Autotune feature. Add a Support Vector Machine node to the Lesson 5 pipeline, connected to the Variable Selection node. Use the Autotune feature. Explore the settings that are made available on when **Autotune** is selected, but keep all properties at their defaults, *except the polynomial degree*. Under the autotune properties, set the maximum value for the polynomial degree to be 2.

   Note: This practice might take several minutes to run.

2. What kernel was selected during the autotune process? What is the value of the penalty parameter, and is it much different from the default value (1) used for the other SVMs?

3. How does the autotuned SVM compare to the other models in the pipeline? Consider the fit statistic average squared error for this comparison.

End of Practices

Quiz

1. Because only the observations closest to the separating hyperplane are used to construct the support vector machine, the curse of dimensionality is reduced.

- True
- False

Chapter 12: Model Assessment and Deployment

Introduction

The concept of model deployment in machine learning refers to the application of a model for prediction using a new data.

Building a model is generally not the end of the project. Making predictions on an individual's local machine is a good idea only for a limited time in most cases. If a model is useful, it needs to be used by an organization in an operational manner to make decisions quickly, if not automatically. The models are built in order to solve a business problem, so they need to eventually be deployed into a business environment. Even if the purpose of the model is to increase knowledge of the data, the knowledge gained will need to be organized and presented in a way that the customer can use it. Depending on the requirements, the deployment phase can be as simple as generating a report or as complex as implementing a repeatable prediction process. In many cases, it is the customer, not the data analyst, who will carry out the deployment steps. For example, a credit card company might want to deploy a trained model or set of models (neural networks, meta-learner, and so on) to quickly identify transactions that have a high probability of being fraudulent.

However, even if the analyst will not carry out the deployment effort, it is important for the customer to understand up front what actions will need to be carried out in order to actually use the created models. Keep in mind that some level of data preparation has likely been applied to the data set in its original, raw form, and this must be accounted for when making predictions on new observations. Moving the logic that defines all the necessary data preparation and mathematical expressions of a sophisticated predictive model from a development environment such as a personal computer into an operational database is one of the most difficult and tedious aspects of machine learning. Mature, successful organizations are masters of this process, which is called model deployment, deployment, or model production.

The deployment phase can be broken into several tasks:

- Model Assessment
- Model Comparison
- Monitoring Model Performance over time
- Updating the Model as necessary

We typically build several models, often using different algorithms as ensembles. We first assess individual models and then compare them to determine the best model, typically called a *champion* model. The champion model is then deployed into production, a process called *scoring.* After a model has been deployed, it is important to monitor performance and then update per requirements. In this chapter, we discuss the different tasks in detail.

Model Assessment

During model assessment, you evaluate the efficacy of the models built.

Figure 12.1: Evaluation of Model Performance

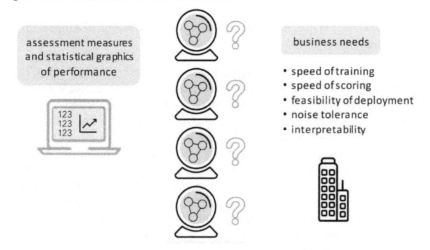

No model is uniformly the best, particularly when considering the deployment over time, when data changes. You select a model primarily based on assessment measures and statistical graphics of performance. All models are based somehow on the data provided. The data describe the problem or the business scenario analyzed. When the scenario changes, the data change, and the model can degrade in terms of predictions.

It is also important to evaluate the model according to the business needs. What is more important to a problem? The ability to explain the prediction, the model's accuracy, the speed to score, or the speed to train? In well-regulated industries, you need to explain the prediction, so some techniques are more suitable. In some business scenarios, the target might change dynamically, so the models need to be trained very fast. In some cases, the model needs to be scored in real time, so the scoring process is the most important variable in this equation. There is no universal best model. It depends on what is required in terms of problem solving and business needs.

The purpose of predictive modeling is generalization, which is the performance of the model on new data. As was stated before, evaluating the model on the same data on which the model was fit usually leads to an optimistically biased assessment. The simplest strategy for correcting the optimism bias is data splitting, where a portion of the data is used to fit the model and the rest is held out for empirical validation.

It is important that the validation data set is used to optimize the model hyperparameters. The training data set will be used to fit the model. The test data set is used to evaluate how the model would perform based on new data. It is useful to assess how the model can generalize to new data, which most likely will differ from the data used to train and validate the model.

The cases in these data sets (training, validation, and test) should be distinct. No case should be assigned to more than one data set. This technique is known as *Honest Assessment*.

Figure 12.2: Honest Assessment

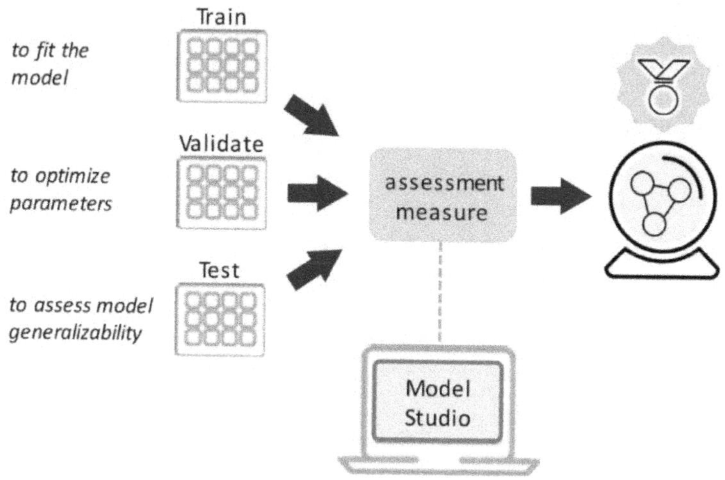

Model Studio: Assessment

To compare across several modes, Model Studio uses a default assessment measure, which varies by the type of target. If you want, you can specify a different assessment measure. Model Studio computes all assessment measures for each available data partition (train, validate, and test).

By default, Model Studio selects a champion model based on the validation data set unless a test data set is available. If you want, you can specify a different data set.

Cross Validation

Another aspect of parameter tuning involves cross validation. For small data sets, a single validation partition might leave insufficient data for validation in addition to training. Keeping the training and validation data representative can be a challenge. For this reason, cross validation is typically recommended for model validation given small data sets.

Data splitting is a simple but costly technique. When the data set is too small to split into training and validation, we can use cross validation. Cross validation avoids overlapping test sets.

- First step: Data are split into k subsets of equal size.
- Second step: Each subset in turn is used for validation and the remainder for training.

This is called k-fold cross validation.

In a k-fold cross validation, the data set is divided into k subsets. For example, in a five-fold cross validation, the initial data set is divided into A, B, C, D, and E subsets. On the first run, the subsets B, C, D, and E are used to train the model, and the subset A is used to validate the model. Then the subsets A, C, D, and E are used to train the model, and the subset B is used to validate. The process goes on until all subsets are used for training and validation.

Figure 12.3: Cross Validation

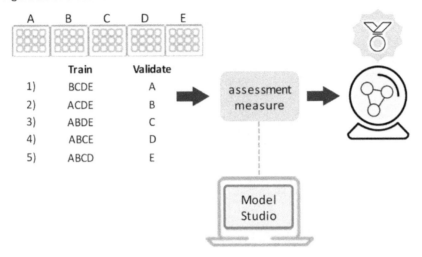

Often the subsets are stratified before the cross validation is performed. The error estimates are averaged to yield an overall error estimate. This process can produce a better representation of error across the entire data set, because all observations are used for training and validation. With this cross-validation process, the trade-off is increased processing time.

Assessment Measures

Numeric measures used to evaluate model performance are called *assessment measures* or *fit statistics*, but which assessment measure should you use? To compare models, you select an appropriate assessment measure based on the following two factors:

- the target measurement scale
- the prediction type

An assessment measure that is appropriate for a binary target might not make sense for an interval target. Similarly, an assessment measure that is suitable for decision predictions cannot be used for estimate predictions. Figure 12.4 shows some common assessment measures for a binary target, given different prediction types. The type of prediction is one factor (along with the target type) that you must consider when you choose a model selection statistic.

Figure 12.4: Assessment Measures

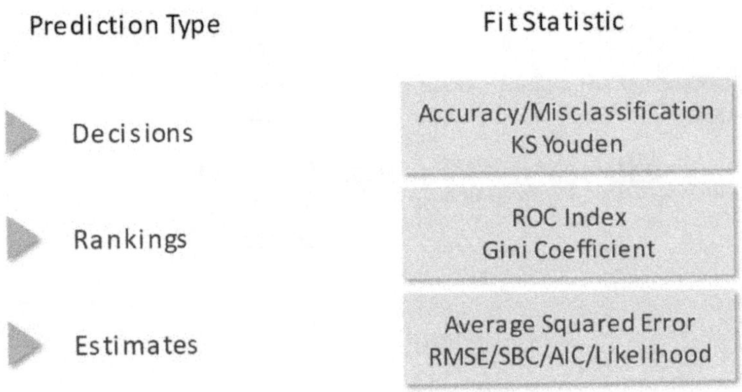

Prediction Type	Fit Statistic

- Decisions — Accuracy/Misclassification / KS Youden
- Rankings — ROC Index / Gini Coefficient
- Estimates — Average Squared Error / RMSE/SBC/AIC/Likelihood

Decision Predictions

With a binary target, you typically consider the following two decision types:

- the primary decision, corresponding to the primary outcome
- the secondary decision, corresponding to the secondary outcome

Matching the primary decision with the primary outcome yields a correct decision called a *true positive*. Likewise, matching the secondary decision to the secondary outcome yields a correct decision called a *true negative*. Decision predictions can be rated by their accuracy (that is, the proportion of agreement between prediction and outcome). Mismatching the secondary decision with the primary outcome yields an incorrect decision called a *false negative*. Likewise, mismatching the primary decision to the secondary outcome yields an incorrect decision called a *false positive*. A decision prediction can be rated by its misclassification (that is, the proportion of disagreement between the prediction and the outcome).

In summary, decisions require high accuracy or low misclassification.

Ranking Predictions

Consider ranking predictions for binary targets. With ranking predictions, a score is assigned to each case. The basic idea is to rank the cases based on their likelihood of being a primary or secondary outcome. Likely primary outcomes receive high scores, and likely secondary outcomes receive low scores.

When a pair of primary and secondary cases is correctly ordered, the pair is said to be *in concordance*. Ranking predictions can be rated by their degree of concordance (that is, the proportion of such pairs whose scores are correctly ordered). When a pair of primary and secondary cases is incorrectly ordered, the pair is said to be *in discordance*. Ranking predictions can be rated by their degree of discordance (that is, the proportion of such pairs whose scores are incorrectly ordered). When a pair of primary and secondary cases are ordered equal, the pair is said to be a *tied pair*. This implies that your model is not able to differentiate between primary and secondary outcomes. The fewer tied pairs, the better.

In summary, rankings require high concordance or low discordance.

Estimate Predictions

Finally, consider estimate predictions. For a binary target, estimate predictions are the probability of the primary outcome for each case. Primary outcome cases should have a high predicted probability. Secondary outcome cases should have a low predicted probability. The squared difference between a target and an estimate is called the *squared error*. Averaged over all cases, squared error is a fundamental assessment measure of model performance. When calculated in an unbiased fashion, the average squared error is related to the amount of bias in a predictive model. A model with a lower average squared error is less biased than a model with a higher average squared error.

In summary, estimates require low (average) squared error.

Selecting Model Fit Statistics by Prediction Type

Model fit statistics can be grouped by prediction type.

For *decision* predictions, the Model Comparison tool rates model performance based on accuracy or misclassification, profit or loss, and by the Kolmogorov-Smirnov (KS) statistic. Accuracy and misclassification tally the correct or incorrect prediction decisions. The Kolmogorov-Smirnov statistic describes the ability of the model to separate the primary and secondary outcomes.

The Kolmogorov-Smirnov (Youden) statistic is a goodness-of-fit statistic that represents the maximum distance between the model ROC curve and the baseline ROC curve.

For *ranking* predictions, two closely related measures of model fit are commonly used. The ROC index is like concordance (described above). The Gini coefficient (for binary prediction) equals 2 * (ROC Index − 0.5).

The ROC index equals the percent of concordant cases plus one-half times the percent of tied cases.

For *estimate* predictions, there are at least two commonly used performance statistics. The Schwarz's Bayesian criterion (SBC) is a penalized likelihood statistic. This likelihood statistic can be thought of as a weighted average squared error.

The *confusion matrix* is a common format for calculating and displaying assessment measures of model performance for decision predictions on a binary target. This matrix is a crosstabulation of the actual and predicted outcomes, based on a decision rule. A simple decision rule allocates cases to the target class with the greatest posterior probability. For binary targets, this corresponds to a 50% cutoff on the posterior probability. A confusion matrix displays four counts: true positives, true negatives, false positives, and false negatives. A true positive (or TP) is a case known to be a primary outcome and also predicted as a primary outcome. A true negative (or TN) is a known secondary case predicted as a secondary case. A false positive (or FP) is a case that is predicted as a primary outcome but is actually a known secondary outcome. And a false negative (or FN) case is a case that is predicted as a secondary outcome but known to be a primary outcome.

Figure 12.5: Confusion Matrix

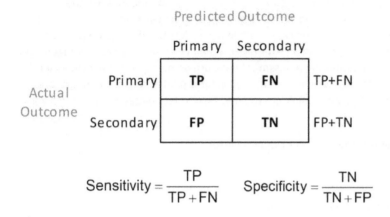

True and false positives and true and false negatives are used to calculate various assessment measures such as sensitivity and specificity. *Sensitivity*, the true positive rate, is the number of true positive decisions divided by the total number of known primary cases. *Specificity*, the true negative rate, is the number of true negative decisions divided by the total number of known secondary cases. These measures are the basis for the ROC chart, which you learn about next.

In addition to numeric measures of model performance, data scientists often use graphical tools to assess models as well. The *receiver operating characteristic chart* (ROC chart) is a commonly used graphical representation of model performance for a binary target. ROC charts are based on measures of sensitivity and specificity. The sensitivity of a model is the true positive rate. The specificity of a model is the true negative rate.

Figure 12.6: ROC Chart

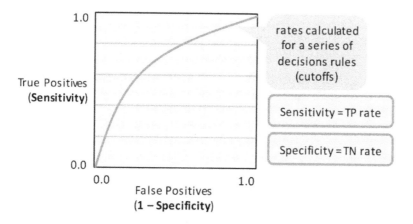

It is easier to interpret ROC charts when you understand how they are constructed. To create an ROC chart, predictions are generated for a set of validation data. These predictions must be rankings or estimates. Then the validation data are sorted by the ranks or estimates, from high to low. This creates a list of cases, sorted in order of importance. Each point on the ROC chart corresponds to a specific fraction of the sorted data. The sample point on this ROC chart corresponds to the selection of 40% of the validation data with the highest predicted probabilities. The selection value of this point cannot be seen from the chart. In the ROC chart, the Y axis represents the cumulative rate of true positives (that is, Sensitivity). The X axis represents the cumulative rate of false positives, which is 1 minus Specificity. The rate on each axis ranges from 0 to 1, so the plot is contained within a unit square. The rates are calculated for a series of decision rules (in other words, cutoffs) between 0% and 100%. However, the cutoffs are not shown in the chart.

Figure 12.7: ROC Chart

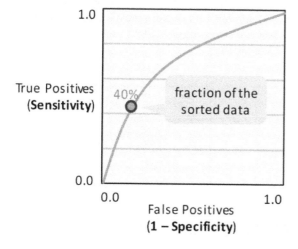

For example, in Figure 12.8, the orange point on the ROC chart corresponds to the selection of 40% of the validation data with the highest predicted probabilities.

The vertical, or *y*, coordinate of the red point indicates the fraction of primary outcome cases captured in the gray region (here, approximately 45%).

The horizontal, or *x*, coordinate of the red point indicates the fraction of secondary outcome cases captured in the gray region (here, approximately 25%).

Figure 12.8: ROC Chart

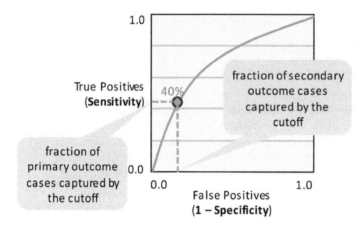

The ROC chart represents the union of similar calculations for all selection fractions.

ROC Index / C-Statistic

The ROC chart provides a nearly universal diagnostic for predictive models. Models that capture primary and secondary outcome cases in a proportion approximately equal to the selection fraction are weak models (left side of Figure 12.9). Models that capture mostly primary outcome cases without capturing secondary outcome cases are strong models (right side of Figure 12.9).

Figure 12.9: ROC Index / C-Statistic

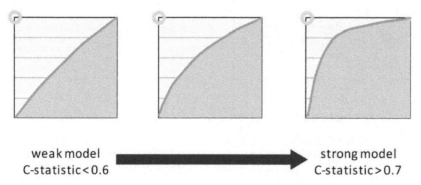

The tradeoff between primary and secondary case capture can be summarized by the area under the ROC curve. This area can be referred to as the *C-Statistic*. (In machine learning literature, it is more commonly called the *ROC Index*.) Perhaps surprisingly, the C-Statistic is closely related to concordance, the measure of correct case ordering.

Response Rates Charts

Suppose that you are running a direct marketing campaign where you are trying to target members of your customer base with an offer in the hope that they will respond and purchase a new product or subscribe to an additional service. A predictive model can predict the probability of each customer responding based on their characteristics and behaviors. To assess the model performance, you measure the benefit that the predictive model can offer in predicting which customers will be responders in a new campaign compared to targeting them at random (using no predictive model). This can be achieved by examining the *cumulative gains* and *lift* associated with the model.

Figure 12.10: Charts Based on Response Rate

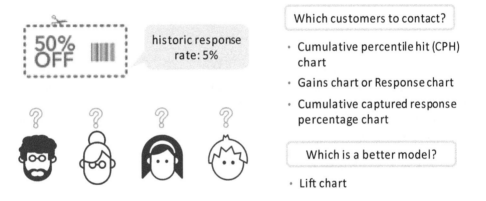

Gains Chart

The *Gains chart* illustrates the advantage of using a predictive model to make business decisions as compared to not using a model (that is, having a baseline or random model). The Gains chart is also known as a *cumulative percentile hits* (or *CPH) chart,* and in Model Studio, this chart is called the *cumulative percent captured response chart.*

Lift Chart

In addition, the *lift chart,* often called a *cumulative lift chart,* helps you decide which models are better to use. If cost/benefit values are not available or changing, you can use lift to select a better model. The model with the highest lift curve is generally better for model deployment. The lift chart illustrates graphically the advantage of using a predictive model as compared to not using a model. Cumulative lift is a ratio of response rates. The response rate in the numerator equals the cumulative percentile hits for a given percentile (P) from a given model (M). The response rate in the denominator equals the cumulative percentile hits for the same percentile given no model.

Figure 12.11: Cumulative Lift Chart

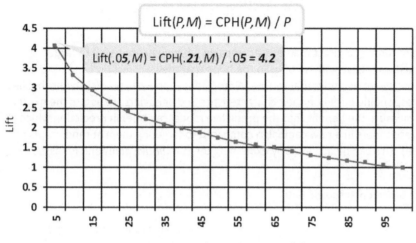

Cumulative Percentiles from List

A lift chart can contain lines for multiple models, which is helpful for selecting the best model in a specific business scenario. The model with the highest lift curve is generally better for model deployment. However, the best model can vary depending on the percentile. For the customer response example, if you expect to contact 20% of your customers, you want to choose the model that performs best on this percentile.

Figure 12.12: Cumulative Lift Chart for Multiple Models

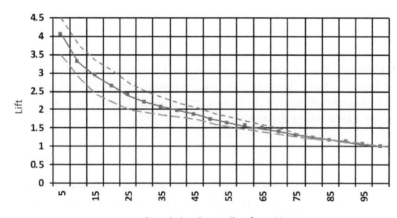

Cumulative Percentiles from List

Example

Suppose we want to choose which customers to contact for a direct marketing campaign. The historic response rate is 5%. Figure 12.13 shows the cumulative percentile hits when we do not use a model. The Y axis represents the cumulative percentile hits. The X axis represents the cumulative percentiles from the list of cases (in this example, customers). This particular chart has 20 percentiles (that is, 20 bars). The first bar shows that 5% of the event cases are captured in the top 5% of customers. The selected fraction of cases (in this example, 5%) is known as the *depth*. Because the graph is cumulative, the second bar shows that 10% of the event cases are captured in the top 10% of customers.

Figure 12.13: Cumulative Captured Response Percentage Chart

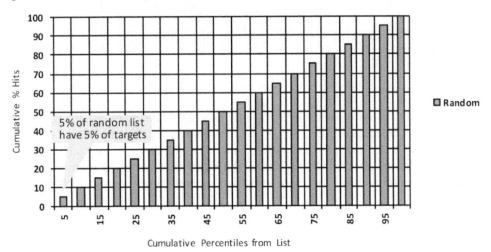

The cumulative percentile hits based on a predictive model are now added to the chart. For the top 5% of customers ranked on their posterior probabilities, the model found that 21% responded. For the top 10% of customers (again, ranked by their posterior probabilities), the model found that 32% responded, when calculated cumulatively. For all fractions of customers, the chart shows that the model captures more responders than not using a model.

Figure 12.14: Cumulative Captured Response Percentage Chart

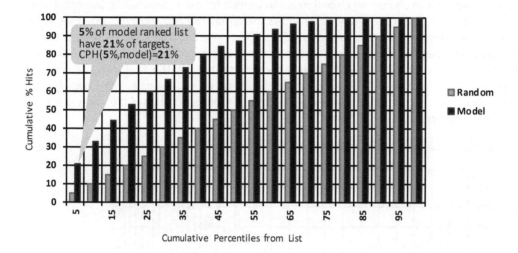

The CPH for the top 5% of customers, given the model, was 21%. Given no model, the response rate for the top 5% of customers (from a randomly ordered list) is 5%. Thus, the lift at 5% is 21% divided by 5%, which is 4.2. This indicates that, for the top 5% of customers, the model captured 4.2 times as many responders, compared to not using a model. Below is the lift chart for the customer response example. The Y axis represents the lift, and the X axis represents the cumulative percentiles from the list. Notice the lift value 4.2 for the 5% percentile.

Model Comparison

As discussed earlier in this chapter, we build several models, assess individual models, and then compare them to determine the best model, typically called a *champion* model.

Model Studio: Model Comparison in

In Model Studio, you can compare models within a pipeline as well as across several pipelines using a **Model Comparison** node and the **Pipeline Comparison** tab, respectively.

Model Studio: Model Comparison in

Figure 12.15: Comparing Models

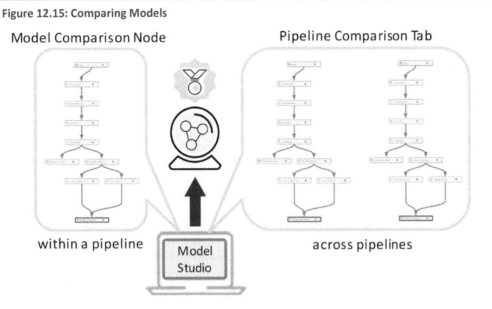

The **Model Comparison** node is automatically added to a pipeline when a **Supervised Learning** node is added. The Model Comparison node enables you to compare the performance of competing models using various benchmarking criteria. There are many assessment criteria that can be used to compare models. For class targets, these include measures of error, lift-based measures, and measures derived from the ROC curve. You can select the measure and specify the depth to use when applying a lift-based measure or the cutoff to use when applying an ROC-based measure. For interval targets, there are various measures of error available for choosing the champion model. All measures of assessment are computed for each of the data partitions that are available (train, validate, and test). You can also select which data partition to use for selecting the champion.

The **Pipeline Comparison** tab compares only the champion models for each pipeline. The selected model from the Model Comparison node of each pipeline is added to the Pipeline Comparison tab. This enables you to compare models from the different pipelines in your project and select a champion model. To add models that were not selected by the Model Comparison node to the Pipeline Comparison tab, right-click the given model, and select **Add challenger model**.

Model Studio gives you several options of model assessment and comparison. Below is a glossary of assessment measures offered.

Model Studio: Model Comparison in

Class selection statistics:

- **Accuracy** is a measure of how many observations are correctly classified for each value of the response variable. It is the number of event and non-event cases classified correctly, divided by all cases.

- **Area under the curve (C statistic)** is a measure of goodness of fit for binary outcome. It is the concordance rate, and it is calculated as the area under the curve.

- **Average squared error** is the sum of squared errors (SSE) divided by the number of observations.

- **Captured response** is the number of events in each bin divided by the total number of events.

- **Cumulative captured response** is the cumulative value of the captured response rate.

- **Cumulative lift** is cumulative lift up to and including the specified percentile bin of the data, sorted in descending order of the predicted event probabilities.

- **F1 score** is the weighted average of precision (positive predicted value) and recall (sensitivity). It is also known as the F-score or F-measure.

- **False discovery rate** is the expected proportion of type error I—incorrectly reject the null hypothesis (false positive rate).

- **False positive rate** is the number of positive cases misclassified (as negative).

- **Gain** is similar to a lift chart. It equals the expected response rate using the predictive model divided by the expected response rate from using no model at all.

- **Gini** is a measure of the quality of the model. It has values between -1 and 1. Closer to 1 is better. It is also known as Somers' D.

- **Kolmogorov-Smirnov statistic (KS)** is a goodness-of-fit statistic that represents the maximum separation between the model ROC curve and the baseline ROC curve.

- **KS (Youden)** is a goodness-of-fit index that represents the maximum separation between the model ROC curve and the baseline ROC curve.

- **Lift** is a measure of the advantage (or lift) of using a predictive model to improve on the target response versus not using a model. It is a measure of the effectiveness of a predictive model calculated as the ratio between the results obtained with and without the predictive model. The higher the lift in the lower percentiles of the chart, the better the model is.

Model Studio: Model Comparison in

- **Misclassification (Event)** is considers only the classification of the event level versus all other levels. Thus, a non-event level classified as another non-event level does not count in the misclassification. For binary targets, these two measures are the same. It is computed in the context of the ROC report. That is, at each cutoff value, this measure is calculated.

- **Misclassification (MCE)** is a measure of how many observations are incorrectly classified for each value of the response variable. This is the true misclassification rate. That is, every observation where the observed target level is predicted to be a different level counts in the misclassification rate.

- **Multiclass log loss** is the loss function applied to multinomial target. It is the negative log-likelihood of the true labels given a probabilistic classifier's prediction.

- **ROC separation** is the area under the ROC curve is the accuracy. The ROC separation enables you to change the ROC-based cutoff and evaluate the model's performance under different ranges of accuracy.

- **Root average squared error** is the square root of the average differences between the prediction and the actual observation.

Interval Selection Statistics:

- **Average squared error** is the sum of squared errors (SSE) divided by the number of observations.

- **Root average squared error** is the square root of the average squared differences between the prediction and the actual observation.

- **Root mean absolute error** is the square root of the average differences between the prediction and the actual observation, not considering the direction of the error.

- **Root mean squared logarithmic error** is the square root of the average squared differences between the prediction and the actual observation. The differences between the prediction and actual observation is measure by the log function.

Demo 12.1: Comparing Multiple Models in a Single Pipeline

In this demonstration, you run the Model Comparison node in the Lesson 3 pipeline. You compare the models' performances based on different fit statistics.

Note: Although not shown here, you could look at the results of the Model Comparison node from any of the other pipelines where models were built.

The Model Comparison node enables you to compare the performance of competing models using various assessment measures. There are many criteria that can be used to compare models. For class targets, there are 18 different measures, including measures of error, lift, and ROC. You can select the measure and specify the depth to use when applying a lift-based measure or the cutoff to use when applying an ROC-based measure. For interval targets, there are four measures of error: ASE, RASE, RMAE, and RMSLE. All measures of assessment are computed for each of the data partitions that are available (train, validate, and test). You can also select which data partition to use for selecting the champion.

Note: If multiple supervised learning nodes are connected to the Model Comparison node, then only successfully completed models are compared. Models that have failed or been stopped are not considered. The selected model from the Model Comparison node of each pipeline is added to the Pipeline Comparison tab. This enables you to compare models from the different pipelines in your project and to select a champion model.

1. You can change the default assessment measures on the **Project settings** option under the **Rules** property. (Recall that the shortcut button for **Project settings** ⚙ˇ is found in the upper right corner of the project window.)

2. Click **Cancel** if you opened the Project settings window.

3. You can also change the default settings under the properties for the Model Comparison node. Click the **Lesson 3** pipeline tab to open it. Select the **Model Comparison** node. Its properties are shown below.

Note: The complete list of assessment measures was described earlier in this chapter.

4. It is possible that tree-based models were built and assessed individually, but the Model Comparison node was not run. Right-click the **Model Comparison** node and select **Run**.

5. When the Model Comparison node is done (the green check mark is visible), right-click the **Model Comparison** node and select **Results**.

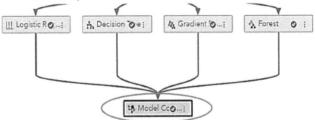

The first results table shows the champion model based on the assessment measure selected. (This comparison does not include the models developed during the practices by using the Autotune feature.)

Model Comparison

Champion	Name	Algorithm Name	KS (Youden)	Misclassification Rate
☒	Gradient Boosting	Gradient Boosting	0.5925	0.0618
	Forest	Forest	0.5903	0.0646
	Decision Tree	Decision Tree	0.5563	0.0683
	Logistic Regression	Logistic Regression	0.5488	0.0808

The criteria used to evaluate the models and select the champion are shown in the Properties table.

Property Name	Property Value
selectionCriteriaClass	Kolmogorov-Smirnov statistic (KS)
selectionCriteriaInterval	Average squared error
selectionTable	Validate
selectionDepth	10
cutoff	0.5000

Properties

6. Click the **Assessment** tab to see more results.

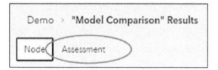

On the Assessment tab, you can find two plots and one table that present the performance and the fit statistics for all the models compared. The first plot is **Lift Reports,** which displays Response Percentage by default. From a menu, you also have the options to see the models' performance based on the Captured Response Percentage, Cumulative Captured Response Percentage, Cumulative Response Percentage, Cumulative Lift, Gain, and Lift.

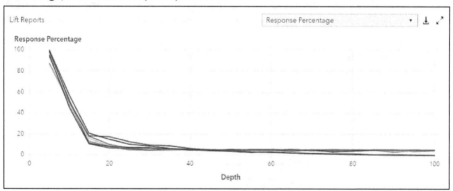

Note: The chart must be expanded to reveal the legend that indicates which colored line represents which model and on what partition.

The Lift Reports chart by default shows the performance for all models in the pipeline for all data partitions. You can also change the chart so that it displays the performance of only a single model or for the performance of all models only for a certain partition by expanding it.

7. Expand the **Lift Reports** chart.

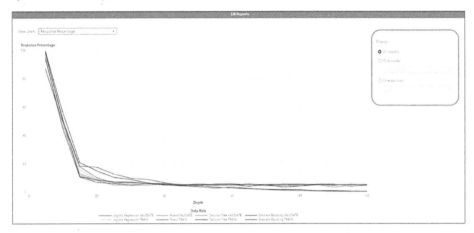

First, notice that the legend is now visible at the bottom of the plot, indicating the color of line corresponding with each model and on what partition. Also, from the column on the right, you can choose to display the results for a single model or the results for all models based on a single partition. Make different selections to see how the chart is affected.

8. Restore the Lift Reports chart.

The second plot is **ROC Reports**, which is based on **Accuracy** by default. The menu provides options to enable you to see the models' performances based on the F1 Score and ROC from the drop-down menu.

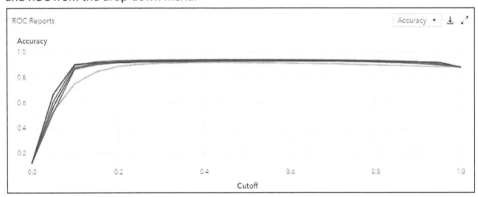

Here is the ROC Reports chart showing ROC.

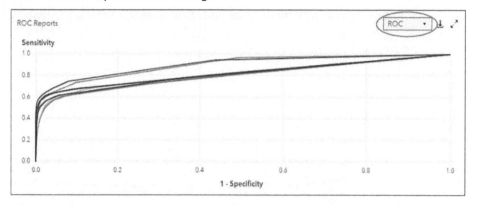

Note: Just as with the Lift Reports chart, you can expand the ROC Reports chart to review the color legend. You can also choose to view a single model or a certain partition from the expanded view.

Finally, the **Fit Statistics table** shows all models' performances based on the data partitions defined in the project (train, validate, and test) for a series of fit statistics, such as Area Under ROC, Average Squared Error, Gini Coefficient, and KS.

Fit Statistics				
Statistics Label	Train: Gradient Boo...	Validate: Gradient ...	Train: Decision Tree	Validate: Decision T...
Area Under ROC	0.9023	0.8221	0.8014	0.8098
Average Squared Error	0.0490	0.0545	0.0609	0.0603
Divisor for ASE	39,590	16,967	39,590	16,967
Formatted Partition	1	0	1	0
Gamma	0.9001	0.7616	0.7590	0.7719
Gini Coefficient	0.8046	0.6442	0.6028	0.6196
KS (Youden)	0.6658	0.5924	0.5442	0.5583

9. Close the results.

End of Demonstration

Demo 12.2: Comparing Multiple Models across Pipelines and Registering the Champion Model

The Pipeline Comparison tab enables you to compare the best models from each pipeline created. In addition, it enables you to register the champion model and use it in the Manage Models tool.

Note: The models built in practices are ignored in this demonstration.

1. Click Pipeline Comparison.

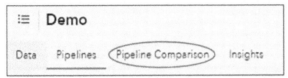

At the top of the Pipeline Comparison tab, you see the champion model from each pipeline as well as the model deemed the overall champion in the pipeline comparison—that is, the champion of champions. In addition, several charts and tables are provided that summarize the performance of the overall champion model, show the variable importance list of the model, provide training and score codes, and show other outcomes from the selected best model. The default assessment measure for Pipeline Comparison is Kolmogorov-Smirnov (KS).

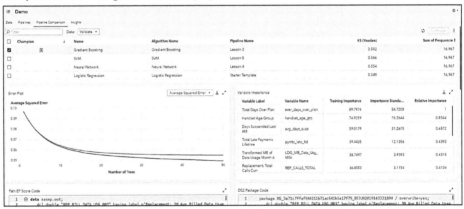

All the results shown are for the overall champion model only. There might be a need to perform a model comparison of each of the models shown.

2. Select the check boxes next to all the models shown at the top of the Results page. You can also select the check box next to **Champion** at the top of the table.

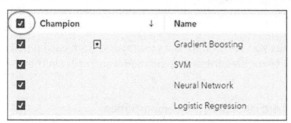

3. When multiple models are selected, the Compare button in the upper right corner is activated. Click the **Compare** button.

The Compare results are shown, where assessment statistics and graphics can be compared across all champion models from each of the pipelines.

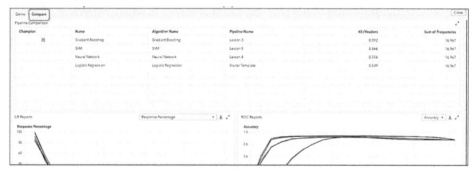

Note: Just as with the graphical displays from the Model Comparison node within a pipeline, the graphical displays here can be expanded to review the legend as well as select subsets of the information to display.

4. Close the Compare results window and deselect models in the table at the top of the window until only the overall champion model is selected. The overall project champion model is indicated with the star symbol in the Champion column.

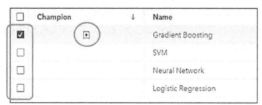

5. Before the champion model is registered in preparation for deployment, let's look at the summary information provided by the Insights tab. Click the **Insights** tab.

The Insights tab contains summary information in the form of a report for the project, the champion model, and any challenger models. For the purposes of the Insights tab, a champion model is the overall project champion model, and a challenger model is one that is a pipeline champion, but not the overall project champion.

At the top of the report is a summary of the project and a list of any project notes. Summary information about the project includes the target variable, the champion model, the event rate, and the number of pipelines in the project.

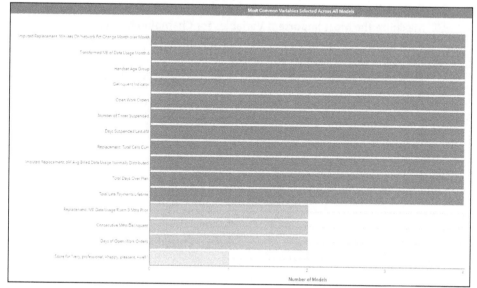

6. Maximize the plot for **Most Common Variables Selected Across All Models**. This plot summarizes common variables used in the project by displaying the number of pipeline champion models that the variables end up in. Only variables that appear in models used in the pipeline comparison are displayed.

The plot shows that many variables were used by all four models in the pipeline comparison. These variables are listed at the top of the plot. Only a single variable was used in only one model in the pipeline comparison. This variable is listed at the bottom of the plot.

7. Restore the **Most Common Variables Selected Across All Models** plot.

8. Maximize the **Assessment for All Models** plot. This plot summaries model performance for the champion model across each pipeline and the overall project champion.

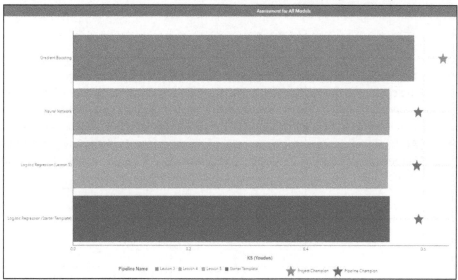

The plot shows that the overall project champion model is the gradient boosting model, which came from pipeline Lesson 3. The KS value for this model is nearly 0.6. The orange star next to the model indicates that it is the project champion.

9. Restore the Assessment for All Models plot.

10. Maximize the **Most Important Variables for Champion Model** plot. This plot shows the most important variables, as determined by the relative importance calculated using the actual overall champion model.

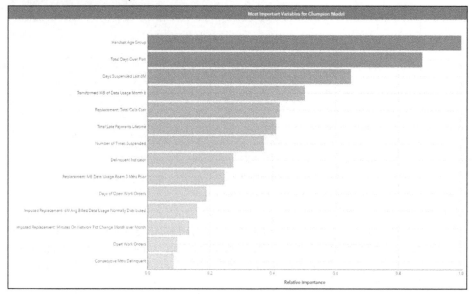

The plot shows that the most important variable for the overall champion model is **Handset Age Group**. The relative importance of the variable **Total Days Over Plan** is about 87% of the importance for **Handset Age Group**. This means that **Total Days Over Plan** is 0.87 times as important as **Handset Age Group** for this model.

11. Restore the Most Important Variables for Champion Model plot.

12. Finally, at the bottom of the report is the **Cumulative Lift for Champion Model** plot. This plot displays the cumulative lift for the overall project champion model for both the training and validation partitions.

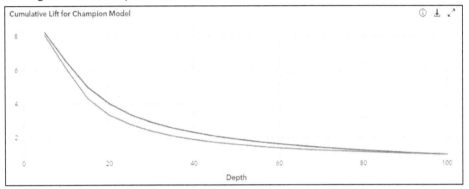

13. Now that we have gained additional insights into the project and the models that it contains, we prepare for model deployment. Return to the pipeline comparison results by clicking the **Pipeline Comparison** tab.

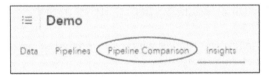

14. Make sure that only the champion model is selected. Click the three vertical dots in the right top corner to access the Project pipeline menu. Note that Manage Models is not available.

15. Select **Register models**.

The **Register Models** window appears.

The spinning circle next to **Registering** in the Status column indicates that the selected model (in this case, **Gradient Boosting**) is actively being registered so that the model is available to other SAS applications.

After registration is complete, the Register Models window is updated to indicate that the registration process has successfully completed.

When the champion model is registered, it can be viewed and used in SAS Model Manager where you can export the score code in different formats, deploy the model, and manage its performance over time.

16. Close the Register Models window after the model is registered successfully.

End of Demonstration

Model Deployment

After selecting a champion model, it is time to put the model to use by scoring new data. The scoring process is sometimes referred to as *model deployment*, *model production*, or *model implementation*.

Scoring the Champion Model

All tasks performed earlier in the analytics life cycle lead to this task: generating predictions through scoring. An organization gets value from the model when it is in production. To maximize that value, it is necessary to monitor model performance over time and update the model as needed.

Model Studio: Scoring

For scoring, the model is first translated into another format (typically, score code). In the SAS Viya environment, score code is a SAS program that you can easily run on a scoring data set. Then the model is applied to the scoring data set to obtain predicted outcomes. Based on the predictions from the model, the enterprise makes business decisions and takes action.

Figure 12.16: Model Implementation

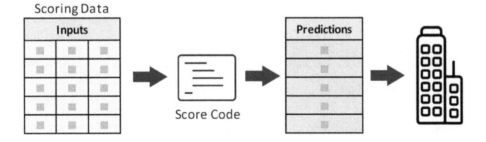

There are two types of score code that Model Studio nodes can create: **DATA step** or **analytic store** (also known as **ASTORE**). To generate score code for an entire pipeline, the score code for each node producing Node score code is appended together into a single DATA step. When the nodes in a pipeline produce multiple analytic stores, or one or more analytic stores and DATA steps score code, an **EP score code file** is created. EP score code represents the score code produced by these pipelines. To run this code outside Model Studio, see "Running Your Score Code from Analytic Store Models" in SAS documentation.

Model Studio: Scoring

Figure 12.17: Scoring Your Models

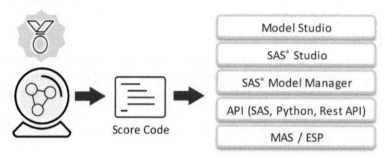

Model Studio creates two types of SAS language score code for the purpose of scoring new data:

- DATA Step
- Analytic Store (ASTORE)

Table 12.1 summarizes which Model Studio nodes produce score code, as well as the types of code that they produce.

Table 12.1: Scoring Nodes

DATA Step	Analytic Store (ASTORE)	
Clustering	Imputation	Anomaly Detection
Decision Tree	Linear Regression	Bayesian Network
Ensemble	Logistic Regression	Forest
Feature Extraction	Neural Network **	Gradient Boosting
Filtering	Replacement	SVM
GLM	Transformations	Text Mining

** DATA step for networks with fewer than six layers, analytic store for networks with six or more layers.

Model Studio: Scoring

After you download the score code, there are several model deployment options in SAS Viya:

- The Score Data node in Model Studio enables you to score a data table with the score code that was generated by the predecessor nodes in the pipeline. The scored table is saved to a caslib. By default, the scored table is temporary, exists only for the duration of the run of a node, and has local session scope. The Score Data node enables you to save the scored table to disk in the location that is associated with the specified output library. After it is saved to disk, this table can be used by other applications for further analysis or reporting.

- Models that create ASTORE code can be scored in SAS Studio using the ASTORE procedure.

- You can also run a scoring test in SAS Model Manager. This is shown later.

- Model Studio creates API for score code to be called from SAS or Python or through a REST API. Within a project in Model Studio, you can go to the Pipeline Comparison tab and click the **Project pipeline** menu (three vertical dots) in the upper right and select **Download score API**. The code that it provides can be used directly in other applications. (You just need to modify the CAS server and port that you are calling, the data source that you want to score, and the name of the output caslib and scored output table.) Even when you call the score code through the API from a Python program, the score code runs in CAS not in Python.

- Score code can also be published to Micro Analytics Services (web service) and to SAS Event Stream Processing.

Model Studio: Scoring

SAS Model Manager streamlines analytical model management and administration. Analytical models enable better decision making. SAS Model Manager provides a web-based environment to support life cycle management and governance of models. You can easily manage modeling processes and identify champion models for deployment. Performance monitoring and alerting automate the model updating process to address model degradation and ensure that models reflect current conditions.

Figure 12.18: SAS Model Manager

- Store SAS and open source models within projects or as stand-alone models.
- Develop and validate candidate models.
- Assess and compare candidate mod for champion model selection.
- Then publish and monitor champio and challenger models to ensure optimal model performance.

Demo 12.3: Exploring the Features for Scoring and Running a Scoring Test in Model Manager

In this demonstration, you place the champion model selected by Pipeline Comparison in Model Studio into the SAS Model Manager tool in SAS Viya. The model will be deployed on a scoring data set.

1. In Pipeline Comparison, click the **Project pipeline** menu (three vertical dots). Notice that the Manage Models option is now available because the champion model has been registered. Select **Manage Models**.

You are redirected to the Manage Model tool. A window containing a list of files is shown, which includes codes for training and scoring the model. Click the second icon assigned to **Projects** in the left pane of the window. This icon takes you to the SAS Model Manager projects.

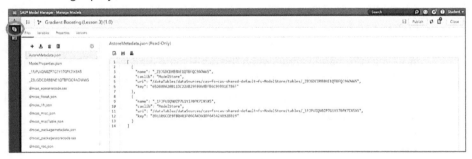

The SAS Model Manager project named Demo is based on the Model Studio project of the same name. Also in this project are models that were registered within Model Studio. Select the **Demo** project (Step 1 in the figure below) and click the **Open** shortcut button in the upper right corner (Step 2), or click the project name.

2. Models within the Demo project that have been registered are shown in the figure below.

There is currently a single model in the Demo project, a gradient boosting model. The name of the model, **Gradient Boosting (Lesson 3)**, is based on the champion model and pipeline name that the model came from in Model Studio.

Across the top of the page is a series of tabs. These tabs are used during the entire model management process, which goes beyond just model deployment.

The **Models tab** shows registered models within the Model Manager project.

The **Variables tab** is where input variables and output variables can be added to both project and model objects.

The **Properties tab** contains the project metadata. Project metadata includes information such as the name of the project, the type of project, the project owner, the project location, and which tables and variables are used by project processes, such as scoring. Project properties are organized into General, Tags, and User Defined.

The **Scoring tab is** where scoring tests can be run and also where published models can be validated.

The **Performance tab** shows performance monitoring reports, which are generated from scored data.

The **History tab** shows the history of how the project and model have been used, including information about when the project and models were created, when champion models were defined, and when the model was last deployed.

3. Click the name of the model. (Do not click the selection check box in front of it.)
4. Select **dmcas_epscorecode.sas** in the column on the left.

This file is the score code generated by the model and the other data preparation nodes contained within the pipeline. The score code can be exported to deploy the model in production considering distinct environments and platforms.

5. Click the **Close** button in the upper right corner of the score code window.
6. Click the second icon for **Projects** on the left pane of the window to return back to the projects view.

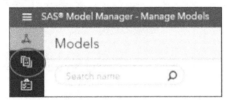

7. If the check box next to the name of the model is not already selected, click it.

8. Click the **Scoring** tab.

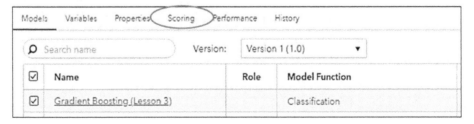

9. Click **New Test** to create and run a scoring test on the selected model.

Create and run a test on a model.

New Test

10. Enter **CPML_GB** as the name and **This is the champion model from the CPML class.** as the description in the New Test window.

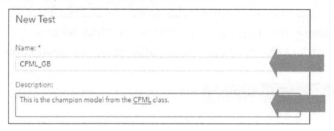

New Test

Name: *

CPML_GB

Description:

This is the champion model from the CPML class.

11. Select **Choose Model** in the **Model** field, and select the **Gradient Boosting (Lesson3)** model from the Choose a Model window.

New Test

Name: *

CPML_GB

Description:

This is the champion model from the CPML class.

Model: *

Gradient Boosting (Lesson 3) (1.0)   Choose Model

12. Select **Browse (Open** shortcut button) in the **Data Source** field.
13. Click the **Import** tab.

Choose a Data Source

Available   Data Sources   Import

Filter

14. Select Local Files and then navigate to the CPML pipeline data folder.
15. Select **score_commsdata.sas7bdat** and then click **Open.**

16. Click **Import Item**.

17. When the table is successfully imported, click **OK**.
18. The New Test window should appear as follows:

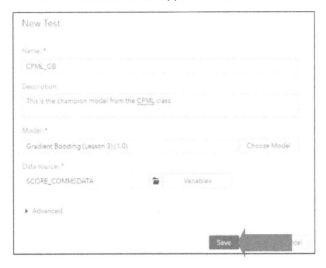

19. Click **Save**.
20. Select the check box next to **CPML_GB**.

21. Click **Run** in the upper right corner of the window.

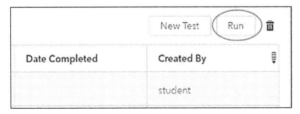

22. Observe that the Status column has a green check mark and that the table icon appears under the Results column. This indicates that the test ran successfully.

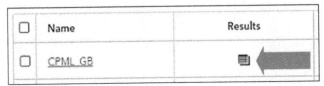

	Name	Results	Status	Model Name
☐	CPML_GB	🔲	✓	Gradient Boosting (Lesson 3) (1.0)

23. Click the table icon in the Results column.

	Name	Results
☐	CPML_GB	🔲 ⬅

24. Click **Output** under Test Results in the left pane to see the predicted scores.

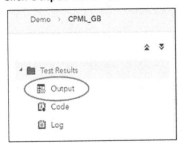

25. Click the **Options** button and then select **Manage columns**.

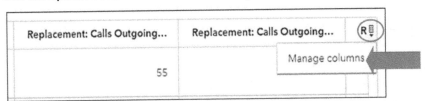

26. Move all of the variables listed under **Displayed columns** to **Hidden columns** by clicking the **Move All** shortcut button in the middle of the window.

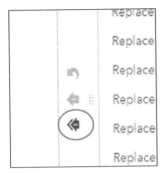

27. Select the following variables associated with scored output and the Primary Key (which is the Customer ID variable). Click the **Add** shortcut button in the middle of the window to move them from **Hidden columns** to **Displayed columns**. (Hold down the Ctrl key to select multiple variables at the same time.)

    ○ **Into: churn**

    ○ **Predicted: churn = 0**

    ○ **Predicted: churn = 1**

    ○ **Primary Key**

    ○ **Probability for churn = 1**

    ○ **Probability of Classification**

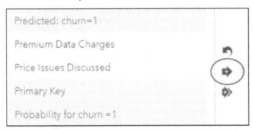

Displayed columns should appear as follows:

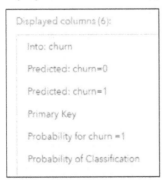

28. Click **OK** and observe the Output table.

By default, this table is created in the Public library and can be consumed for business use.

29. Close the **Output Table** window.

End of Demonstration

Monitoring and Updating the Model

After a model has been deployed, you need to closely monitor its accuracy and performance over time. Models are trained on static snapshots of data. After the model is deployed, the environment inevitably changes and becomes less and less like the conditions that were captured in the training data. As a result, the model's predictions typically become less accurate over time. Thus, a model must be revisited and re-evaluated in light of new data and changing circumstances. For example, consider a movie recommendation model that must adapt as viewers grow and mature through stages of life. After a certain period, the error rate on new data surpasses a predefined threshold, and the model must be retrained or replaced.

Champion-Challenger Testing

Champion-challenger testing is a common model deployment practice. This method compares the performance of a new challenger model with the performance of the deployed model on a historic data set at regular time intervals. If the challenger model outperforms the deployed model, the challenger model replaces it. The champion-challenger process is then repeated.

Figure 12.19: Champion-Challenger Testing

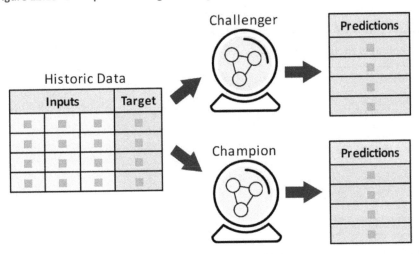

Another approach to refreshing a trained model is through online updates. Online updates continuously change the value of model parameters or rules based on the values of new, streaming data. It is prudent to assess the trustworthiness of real-time data streams before implementing an online modeling system.

Figure 12.20: Online Updates

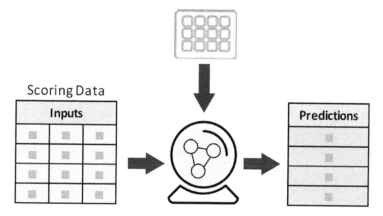

Quiz

1. Which of the following statements is true regarding the ROC curve?
   a. The vertical axis is the sensitivity, and the horizontal axis is specificity.
   b. The C-statistic equals the percent of concordant cases plus one-half times the percent of tied cases.
   c. A strong model has an ROC curve that follows a line that has a 45-degree angle going through the origin.
   d. The ROC curve has no upper bound on the Y axis.
2. When you have an interval target, which of the following fit statistics can you use to select the champion model?
   a. area under the curve (C-statistic)
   b. average squared error
   c. cumulative lift
   d. misclassification

Chapter 13: Additional Model Manager Tools and Open-Source Code

Introduction

There are several additional tools available in Model Studio that have not been covered in previous chapters. This section discusses three of these tools: the Save Data node, the SAS Code node, and the Open Source Code node. But first, here are some other useful tools.

Model Studio: Useful Tools

- Batch Code: The Batch Code node is a Supervised Learning node. It enables you to import external SAS models that are saved in batch code format. For example, you can import SAS Enterprise Miner batcchaph code into Model Studio. There are some details and limitations to consider. For example, the batch code needs to be generated from a Score node in SAS Enterprise Miner, and the score code must either be SAS DATA step code or ASTORE-based (HPForest or HPSVM). This eliminates Text Mining flows because their score code does not run in CAS. Credit Scoring flows are currently not supported because there is no equivalent of the Credit Scoring product in SAS Viya yet. For more information, see https://go.documentation.sas.com/?cdcId=vdmmlcdc&cdcVersion=8.3&docsetId=vdmmlref&docsetTarget=p11yvlxj5rkkjzn1x04rlk9usv8o.htm&locale=en.

- Score Code import: The Score Code Import node is a Supervised Learning node that enables you to import external models that are saved as SAS score code. For example, you can import SAS Enterprise Miner score code into Model Studio. For more information, see https://go.documentation.sas.com/?cdcId=vdmmlcdc&cdcVersion=8.3&docsetId=vdmmlref&docsetTarget=n0gbgjfngxnan3n15xy1jbgsoimr.htm&locale=en.

Model Studio: Useful Tools

- Ensemble: The Ensemble node is a Postprocessing node. It creates new models by combining the posterior probabilities (for class targets) or the predicted values (for interval targets) from multiple predecessor models.

Model Studio: Save Data Node

The Save Data node is a Miscellaneous node that enables you to save the training table that is produced by a predecessor node to a caslib. This table could be partitioned into training, validation, or test sets based on the project settings. In that case, the table contains the **_partind_** variable that identifies the partitions.

Figure 13.1: The Data Save Node

The Save Data node is used to save data exported by a node in a pipeline to a caslib.

By default, the training table produced by a pipeline is temporary and exists only for the duration of the run of a node and has local session scope. The Save Data node enables you to save that table to disk in the location associated with the specified output library. This table can then be used later by other applications for further analysis or reporting. The default output caslib in which tables are to be saved can be specified in the Output Library Project settings. You can overwrite this location using the **Output library** property. In addition, you can load the table in memory and promote this table to have global scope in the specified caslib. This enables multiple CAS sessions to access this table. If you run the node, the results consist of an output table that contains information about the saved table, including a list of variables and their basic attributes.

Model Studio: Save Data Node

The properties of the Save Data node are as follows:

- **Output library** specifies the output caslib where the table will be saved on disk. Use **Browse** to navigate to the proper library. If the user has specified an output library under Project Settings, then this library is used by default.

- **Table name** specifies the name for the CAS table being saved. The default value is **tmpSaveData**.

- **Replace existing table** specifies whether to override an existing CAS table with the same name when saving. By default, this option is deselected.

- **Promote table** specifies whether to load the table in memory and promote the table to global space. By default, this option is deselected.

Figure 13.2: Properties Panel

After running the node, you can open the Results window. Two tabs are in the Results window: Properties and Output.

- **Properties** specifies the various properties selected before running the node. These include the output library, the table name, whether to replace or promote the table, and the CAS session ID.

- **Output** displays the SAS output of the saved data run.

Model Studio: The SAS Code Node

The SAS Code node is a Miscellaneous node that enables you to incorporate new or existing SAS code into Model Studio pipelines. The node extends the functionality of Model Studio by making other SAS procedures available for use in your data mining analysis. You can also write SAS DATA steps to create customized scoring code, conditionally process data, or manipulate existing data sets. The SAS Code node is also useful for building predictive models, formatting SAS output, defining table and plot views in the user interface, and for modifying variables' metadata. The node can be placed at any location within a pipeline (except after the Ensemble or Model Comparison nodes). By default, the SAS Code node does not require data. The exported data that are produced by a successful SAS Code node run can be used by subsequent nodes in a pipeline.

Figure 13.3: SAS Code Node

The SAS Code node is used to run SAS code.

To indicate that the SAS Code node produces a model that should be assessed, right-click the **SAS Code** node and select **Move ▶ Supervised Learning**. If a SAS Code node that is marked as a Supervised Learning node does not generate any score code, either as DS1 or as an analytical store (ASTORE), then no assessment reports or model interpretability reports are generated. If the node produces score code that does not create the expected predicted or posterior probability variables, then the node will fail.

Model Studio: The SAS Code Node

The SAS Code node properties are as follows:

- **Code editor** invokes the SAS Code Editor.

- **Train only data** specifies whether the node should receive the training observations only if the data are partitioned. By default, this option is deselected. Currently, this property is unavailable for this node. To specify that the node receive only training data, add the following WHERE clause to your code:

```
where &dm_partitionvar.=1;
```

Figure 13.4: Properties Panel

The code editor window is opened from a property in the properties panel. The code editor window enables the user to view a Macros table and a Macro Variable table from the left column, which contain a list of macros and macro variables, respectively, that are available to the SAS session.

Model Studio: The SAS Code Node

Figure 13.5: Code Editor

Additional options are available as shortcut buttons on the top of the editor window. These options enable you to do the following:

- browse
- control settings, which include general (such as showing line numbers and font size) and editing (such as enabling autocomplete and auto indention) code options
- undo and redo
- cut, copy, and paste
- find and replace
- clear all code

User-written code is saved using a shortcut button (the good old 3.5-inch floppy disk icon) in the upper right corner of the editor window.

Model Studio: SAS Enterprise Miner

SAS Enterprise Miner and Model Studio are two solutions that you can use to create predictive and classification models. SAS Viya users have access to more power than they might realize. All SAS Enterprise Miner and SAS/STAT procedures are included with a SAS Visual Data Mining and Machine Learning license in SAS Viya. This means that by using the SAS Code node in a pipeline, users have access to the SAS Enterprise Miner procedures that are specific to that product and to the entire suite of tools available with SAS/STAT in SAS 9.

Model Studio: SAS Enterprise Miner

The in-memory CAS table would require being copied to a location accessible by these procedures in the form of a SAS data set.

In Model Studio, there are a few nodes (such as the Open Source Code node and the Batch Code node) that bring down sampled data from CAS. These nodes have a set of properties under the Data Sample property group that control the number of data and how the sample is created. But if you are licensed to run SAS 9.x procedures, you can run those PROCs using the SAS Code node where the data are downloaded automatically.

In the paper titled "SAS® Enterprise Miner™ and SAS® Visual Data Mining and Machine Learning Hand Shake," the authors show that although these applications have different architectures and run in different environments, you can integrate models generated in one environment and compare them with models produced in the other. For more information, go to https://www.sas.com/content/dam/SAS/support/en/sas-global-forum-proceedings/2019/3616-2019.pdf.

If you have been a SAS 9 user and are new to SAS Viya, read the technical paper titled "SAS® 9.4 and SAS® Viya® Functional Comparison" for a handy comparison at http://support.sas.com/resources/papers/sas-94-sas-viya-functional-comparison.pdf.

Model Studio: Executing Open-Source Code

Open source in SAS Viya supports Python and R languages and requires Python or R and necessary packages to be installed on the same machine as the SAS Compute Server. The server downloads data samples from SAS Cloud Analytic Services for use in Python or R code and transfers data by using a data frame or CSV file using the Base SAS Java Object.

Figure 13.6: Executing Open-Source Code

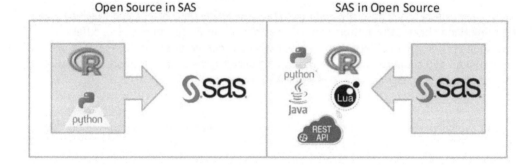

The Open Score Code node enables you to import external code that is written in Python or R. The version of Python or R software does not matter to the node, so any version can be used as the code is passed along. The Python or Rscript executable must be in a system path on Linux, or the install directories can be specified with PYTHONHOME or RHOME on Windows.

Figure 13.7: Open Source Code Node

- The Open Source Code node is used to run Python or R code in a pipeline.

- Requires Python or R and necessary packages to b installed on the same machine as the SAS Comput Server.

- Cannot be part of an ensemble.

- Does not support registering, publishing, or downloading scoring code or scoring APIs.

- Enables the comparison of Python or R models within a Model Studio pipeline.

Model Studio: Executing Open-Source Code

The node enables the user to prototype machine learning algorithms that might exist in open-source languages but have not yet been vetted to be included directly as a node in Model Studio. This node can subsequently be moved to a Supervised Learning group if a Python or R model needs to be assessed and included to be part of model comparison. The node can execute Python or R software regardless of their versions.

After selecting the language (Python or R) from properties, use the **Open** button to enter respective code in the editor. Because this code is not executed in CAS, a data sample (10,000 observations by default) is created and downloaded to avoid movement of large data. Use **Data Sample properties** to control the sample size and method. Apply caution and do not specify full data or a huge sample when the input data is large. When performing model comparison with other Supervised Learning nodes in the pipeline, note that this node might not be using full data.

Figure 13.8: Properties Panel

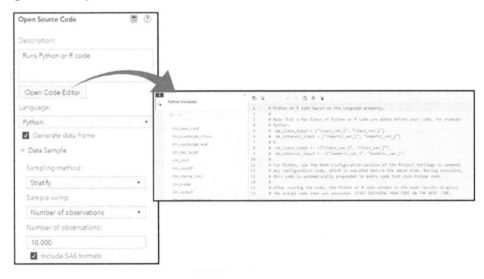

Input data can be accessed by the Python or R code via a CSV (comma-separated values) file or as a data frame. When **Generate data frame** is selected, a data frame is generated from the CSV, and input data is available in **dm_inputdf**, which is a pandas data frame in Python or an R data frame. When data are partitioned, an additional data frame, **dm_traindf**, is also available in the editor. That frame contains training data. If a Python or R model is built and needs to be assessed, corresponding predictions or posterior probabilities should be made available in the **dm_scoreddf** data frame. To do so, right-click and select **Move ▶ Supervised Learning** to indicate that model predictions should be merged with input data and model assessment should be performed. Note that the number of observations in **dm_inputdf** and **dm_scoreddf** should be equal for successful merge to occur.

Model Studio: Executing Open-Source Code

Note that this node cannot support operations such as **Download score code**, **Register models**, **Publish models**, and **Score holdout data** from the Pipeline Comparison tab because it does not generate SAS score code.

Properties of the Open Source Code node are as follows:

- **Code editor** invokes the SAS Code Editor.

- **Language** specifies the open-source language to be used. Available options for this property are R and Python. The default setting is R.

- **Generate data frame** specifies whether to generate an R data frame or a pandas data frame in Python. In addition, categorical inputs are encoded as factors in R. If this option is disabled, the input data should be accessed as a CSV file. By default, this option is enabled.

- **Data Sample** controls sampling of the data. By default, this property is collapsed. The Data Sample property has been expanded in Figure 13.8. When expanded, the subcategories are shown. The subcategories are as follows:

  ○ **Sampling Method** specifies the sampling method. When the input data has a partition variable or a class target (or both), the sample is stratified using them. Otherwise, a simple random sample is used. The available settings are **None**, **Simple Random**, and **Stratify**. The default setting is Stratify.

  ○ **Sample using** specifies whether to sample using the number of observations or the percent of observations from input data. The available settings are **Number of observations** and **Percent of Observations**. The default setting is Number of observations.

  ○ **Number of Observations** or **Percent of Observations** depends on the setting for the **Sample using**. When **Sample using** is set to **Number of Observations**, this property specifies the number of observations to sample from input data. The default in this case is 10,000, and the user can enter numeric values manually. When **Sample using** is set to **Percent of Observations**, this property specifies the percent of observations to sample from input data. In this case, a slider bar appears that ranges from 1 to 100 and the default setting is 10.

  ○ **Include SAS formats** specifies whether to include SAS formats in input data to downloaded CSV files, when passing data to open-source software. By default, this option is enabled.

Like the SAS Code node, for the Open Source Code node, the code editor window is opened from a property in the properties panel. The code editor window enables the user to view a list of R variables or Python variables, depending on what open-source language is being used, that are available to the editor session.

Model Studio: Executing Open-Source Code

Additional options are available as shortcut buttons that are identical to those described earlier in this section of the SAS Code node.

Further information about the Open Source Code node in Model Studio, including a short video illustrating use of the node, can be found here: https://communities.sas.com/t5/SAS-Communities-Library/How-to-execute-Python-or-R-models-using-the-Open-Source-Code/ta-p/499463.

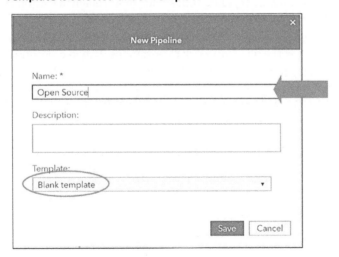

Demo 13.1: Adding Open-Source Models into a Model Studio Project

There might be times when it is beneficial to add components of open-source technologies into Model Studio. In this demonstration, you use the Open Source Code node available for Python and R scripts that help you explore data or build models within a pipeline. You create forest models in R and Python.

1. Ensure that the **Demo** project is open. Reopen the project if you have closed it. Click the plus sign next to the previous pipeline tab.

2. In the New Pipeline window, name the pipeline **Open Source**. Ensure that **Blank Template** is selected under **Template**.

3. Click **Save**.

4. Right-click the **Data** node and select **Add child node ▶ Data Mining Preprocessing ▶ Imputation**. Leave the settings of the Imputation node at the defaults. Many open-source packages do not like missing values.

    Note: Both Python and R packages sometimes do not support missing values in data. It is your responsibility to prepare the data as necessary for these packages. It is highly recommended that you add an Imputation node before the Open Source Code node to handle missing values. If the training data does not contain missing values but if either the validation or test data does contain missing values, consider enabling the **Impute non-missing variables** property in the Imputation node.

5. Right-click the Imputation node and select **Add child node ▶ Miscellaneous ▶ Open Source Code**.

6. Right-click **Open Source Code** node and rename the node **Python Forest**. Your pipeline should look like the one below.

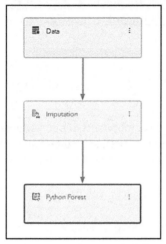

7. In the properties panel of the Open Source Code node (now renamed **Python Forest**), verify that the language is set to **Python**.

8. Expand the **Data Sample** properties. Clear the check box for **Include SAS formats**. This property controls whether the downloaded data sent to the Python or R software should keep SAS formats. It is strongly recommended that you keep SAS formats, and this should work in most cases. However, some numeric formats such as DOLLAR*w.d* add a dollar sign and change the data type of the variable when exporting to CSV. In such cases, these formats must be removed.

Note: We are sampling to use 10,000 observations, but you have the option to use all the data. The data sample is downloaded from CAS as a CSV file (**node_data.csv**). The default is stratified sampling, and stratification is done by partition variable or class target when applicable. This node uses a sample when performing model comparison.

Note: The **Include SAS formats** property either keeps or removes SAS formats for all variables in the data set. If input or target variables have SAS or user-defined formats that significantly modify the data, it is not recommended that you deselect this option because the model that is built might not be comparable to other models.

9. Under **Code editor**, select **Open** to invoke the SAS code editor. Copy and paste the code provided in the **Python_Forest.txt** file in your example code and data.

    Note: You can leverage nodes previously saved to the Exchange to alleviate copying and pasting. Right-click the node that you want to save and select **Save as**. Enter a name for the node in the Save Node to the Exchange window.

```python
from sklearn import ensemble

# Get full data with inputs + partition indicator
dm_input.insert(0, dm_partitionvar)
fullX = dm_inputdf.loc[:, dm_input]

# Dummy encode class variables
fullX_enc = pd.get_dummies(fullX, columns=dm_class_input, drop_first=True)

# Create X (features/inputs); drop partition indicator
X_enc = fullX_enc[fullX_enc[dm_partitionvar] == dm_partition_train_val]
X_enc = X_enc.drop(dm_partitionvar, 1)

# Create y (labels)
y = dm_traindf[dm_dec_target]

# Fit RandomForest model w/ training data
params = {'n_estimators': 100, 'max_depth': 20, 'min_samples_leaf': 5}
dm_model = ensemble.RandomForestClassifier(**params)
dm_model.fit(X_enc, y)
print(dm_model)

# Save VariableImportance to CSV
varimp = pd.DataFrame(list(zip(X_enc, dm_model.feature_importances_)), columns=['Variable Name', 'Importance'])
varimp.to_csv(dm_nodedir + '/rpt_var_imp.csv', index=False)

# Score full data
fullX_enc = fullX_enc.drop(dm_partitionvar, 1)
dm_scoreddf = pd.DataFrame(dm_model.predict_proba(fullX_enc), columns=['P_CHURN0', 'P_CHURN1'])
```

This code fits a random forest classifier model in Python. The default values for the parameters that control the size of the trees (for example, **max_depth (default=none)**, **min_samples_leaf (default=1)**) lead to fully grown and unpruned trees, which can be very large data sets. To reduce memory consumption, the complexity and size of the trees are controlled by setting parameter values like the ones in the code above.

The code that needs to be changed for different data sets is line 29, how your predictions are named using the **P_ + "*target*"** naming convention.

Note: Remember that we are just modeling the data here. Currently, there is not a way to do data preparation within the Open Source Code node so that a subsequent node will recognize it. If this is necessary, either prepare data before Model Studio, or perform both of the following: (1) open-source data preparation with the Open Source Code node (in preprocessing group), and (2) modeling with the Open Source Code node (in supervised learning group).

10. Save the code and close the Code Editor window.
11. Run the Python Forest node.

12. Repeat the previous steps for fitting a forest model in R. Right-click the **Imputation** node and select **Add child node ▶ Miscellaneous ▶ Open Source Code**.

13. Right-click the **Open Source Code** node and rename it **R Forest**. Your pipeline should look like the one below.

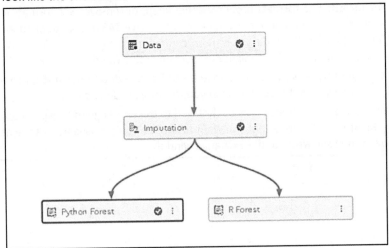

14. In the properties panel of the Open Source Code node (now renamed **R Forest**), set the language to **R** and clear the check box for **Include SAS formats**.

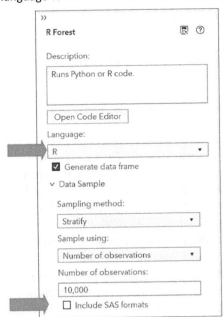

15. Under **Code editor**, select **Open** to invoke the SAS Code Editor. Copy and paste the code provided in the **R_Forest.txt** file in your example code and data.

```
1    library(randomForest)
2
3    # RandomForest
4    dm_model <- randomForest(dm_model_formula, ntree=100, mtry=5, data=dm_traindf, importance=TRUE)
5
6    # Score
7    pred <- predict(dm_model, dm_inputdf, type="prob")
8    dm_scoreddf <- data.frame(pred)
9    colnames(dm_scoreddf) <- c("P_ CHURN0", "P_ CHURN1")
10
11   # Print/plot model output
12   png("rpt_forestMsePlot.png")
13   plot(dm_model, main='randomForest MSE Plot')
14   dev.off()
15
16   write.csv(importance(dm_model), file="rpt_forestIMP.csv", row.names=TRUE)
17   |
```

This code fits Breiman and Cutler's random forest classifier model in R.

The code that needs to be changed for different data sets is line 9, how your predictions are named using the **P_ + "*target*"** naming convention.

Note: It is a good practice to execute the node in an empty state to validate whether Python or R is correctly installed and configured. In addition, you can view the precursor code that is added as part of the executed code. The code that is added depends on the combination of properties selected. The precursor code is part of the node results.

Note: Model assessment is performed automatically if the following are true:

- ○ Predictions are saved in the **dm_scoreddf** data frame or the **node_scored.csv** file.

- ○ Prediction variables are named according to following convention:

   P_<*targetVarName*> for interval target

   P_< *targetVarName* ><*targetLevel*> for class targets
   (All target level probabilities should be computed.)

16. Run the **R Forest** node.

17. Open the results of either the R Forest node or the Python Forest node.

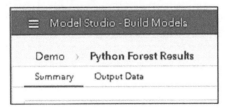

Why does the Open Source Code node not have assessment results even though it was successfully executed?

18. For model assessment, you need to move the nodes to the supervised learning group. Right-click the **R Forest** node and select **Move ▶ Supervised Learning**. A **Model Comparison** node is automatically added to the pipeline.

    Repeat the same for the Python Forest node.

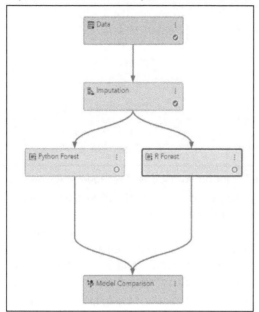

The color of both the nodes has changed to green, showing that these nodes have changed to the group of Supervised Learning nodes. Notice also that the nodes need to be rerun.

19. Run the **Model Comparison** node.

20. Open the results of the Python Forest or the R Forest node (or both). Click the **Assessment** tab in the upper left corner.

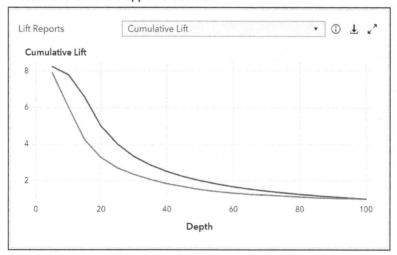

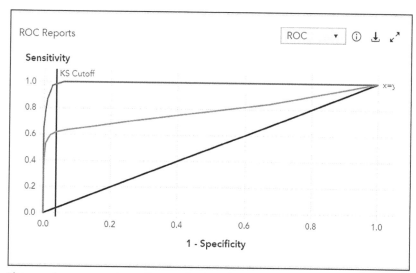

The usual assessment results are displayed. Close the results.

21. Open the results of the Model Comparison node.

Champi...	Name	Algorith...	KS (You...	Misclas...
⊡	R Forest	Open Source Code	0.5920	0.0717
	Python Forest	Open Source Code	0.5859	0.0740

You can also compare these open-source models with the models that you fit in Model Studio using the Pipeline Comparison tab.

Note: Results from Python or R execution can be viewed in the node when saved with the **rpt_** prefix.

○ Files with the **.csv** extension are displayed as tables where the first row is the header (**rpt_VariableImportance.csv**).

○ Files with a **.png, .jpeg/.jpg,** or **.gif** extension are displayed as images (**rpt_MeanSquareErrorPlot.png**).

○ Files with the **.txt** extension are displayed as plain text (**rpt_GLMOutput.txt**).

Remember that the **rpt_** prefix is not case-sensitive and that the **rpt_** prefix and file extensions (**.csv, .txt, .png, .jpeg, .jpg, .gif**) are key in identifying which files to display.

So, keep running open source within SAS or running SAS inside an open-source environment!

End of Demonstration

Appendix A

A.1: CAS-Supported Data Types and Loading Data into CAS

Caslibs

All data are available to the CAS server through caslibs, and all operations in the CAS server that use data are performed using caslibs. A caslib provides access to files in a data source, such as a database or a file system directory, and to in-memory tables. Access controls are associated with caslibs to manage access to data. You can think of a caslib as a container where the container has two areas in which data are referenced: a physical space that includes the source data or files, and an in-memory space that makes the data available for CAS action processing. Authorized users can add or manage caslibs with the CASLIB statement. Caslib authorization is set by your administrator. In some instances, such as when you copy native CAS tables that are not in-memory, a caslib is required although data is not copied to the caslib.

Load Data to a Caslib

You can load a SAS data set, database tables, and more to a caslib. A DATA step, the CASUTIL procedure, and CAS actions can be used to load data into CAS. After the data are in a caslib, you can use a DATA step, procedures, CAS actions, PROC DS2, or PROC FEDSQL operations on the CAS table. Tables are not automatically saved when they are loaded to a caslib. You can use PROC CASUTIL to save tables. Native CAS tables have the file extension .sashdat.

For information about file types that are supported in CAS, see "Path-Based Data Source Types and Options" in *SAS® Cloud Analytic Services 3.3: User's Guide* (available at http://go.documentation.sas.com/?cdcId=pgmsascdc&cdcVersion=9.4_3.3&docsetId=casref&docsetTarget=n0lgusu0v43zxwn1kc5m6cvtnzey.htm&locale=en#n1ed54an76245rn1xp0i7ms1jk3d) and the free video tutorial "Accessing SAS® Viya® Tasks in SAS® Studio or SAS® Enterprise Guide®" (available at: https://video.sas.com/detail/video/5714378981001/accessing-sas®-viya®-tasks-in-sas®-studio-or-sas®-enterprise-guide®).

Data Types

The CAS server supports the VARCHAR, INT32, INT64, and IMAGE data types in addition to the CHARACTER and NUMERIC data types, which are traditionally supported by SAS.

Variables that are created using the VARCHAR data type vary in width and use character semantics, rather than being fixed-width and using the byte semantics of the traditional

CHARACTER data type. Using the VARCHAR data type in the DATA step in the CAS server has some restrictions.

For more information, see "Restrictions for the VARCHAR Data Type in the CAS Engine" in SAS® Cloud Analytic Services 3.3: User's Guide (available at: http://go.documentation.sas.com/?cdcId=pgmsascdc&cdcVersion=9.4_3.3&docsetId=casref&docsetTarget=p00irrg1pxzro6n1aadfcb1p3cag.htm&locale=en#p0r5w4ptr4r7rzn1dcd37vofyraq).

Variables that are created or loaded using the INT32 or INT64 data types support more digits of precision than the traditional NUMERIC data type. All calculations that occur on the CAS engine maintain the INT32 or INT64 data type. Calculations in DATA steps or procedures that run on the SAS 9 engine are converted to NUMERIC values.

The CHARACTER and NUMERIC data types continue to be the supported data types for processing in the SAS Workspace Server.

The DS2 language supports several additional data types (available at: http://go.documentation.sas.com/?cdcId=pgmsascdc&cdcVersion=9.4_3.3&docsetId=ds2ref&docsetTarget=n1k7ka2deld03vn1dtr7dlszu985.htm&locale=en) . On the CAS server, DS2 converts non-native data types to CHARACTER, NUMERIC, or VARCHAR.

For information about data types that are supported for specific data sources, see "Data Type Reference" in *SAS® 9.4 DS2 Language Reference* (available at http://go.documentation.sas.com/?cdcId=pgmsascdc&cdcVersion=9.4_3.3&docsetId=ds2ref&docsetTarget=n1k7ka2deld03vn1dtr7dlszu985.htm&locale=en).

The CAS language (CASL) determines the data type of a variable when the variable is assigned.

In the following table, the letter Y indicates the data types that are supported for programming on the CAS server. In the last column, Y indicates data types that are supported on the SAS Workspace Server.

Table A.1: Variable Data Types Supported

Data Type	CAS Actions	CASL	Data Connectors	Procedures and DATA Step	DS2	FedSQL	Workspace Server Processing
BIGINT			Y		Y		
BLOB		Y					
BOOLEAN		Y	Y				
CHARACTER (CHAR)	Y	Y	Y	Y	Y	Y	Y
DATE		Y	Y		Y		

Data Type	CAS Actions	CASL	Data Connectors	Procedures and DATA Step	DS2	FedSQL	Workspace Server Processing
DATETIME		Y	Y				
DOUBLE	Y	Y	Y	Y	Y	Y	
FLOAT			Y		Y		
IMAGE	Y						
INTEGER			Y		Y		
INT32		Y	Y			Y	
INT64		Y	Y			Y	
ITEMS		Y					
LISTS		Y					
NCHAR			Y		Y		
NUMERIC (NUM)			Y				Y
NVARCHAR			Y		Y		
SMALLINT			Y		Y		
STRING UTF-8		Y					
TABLE		Y					
TIME		Y	Y		Y		
TIMESTAMP			Y		Y		
TINYINT			Y		Y		
VARCHAR	Y	Y	Y	Y	Y	Y	

Additional data types are supported by the data connectors. These data types are first converted to data types that can be processed on the CAS server. Check the data connector documentation for your data source to ensure that a data type is supported.

For more information, see "Data Connectors" in SAS® *Cloud Analytic Services 3.3: User's Guide* (available at: http://go.documentation.sas.com/?cdcId=pgmsascdc&cdcVersion=9.4_3.3&docsetId=casref&docsetTarget=n01iumvu56308zn1bud38udhg8w5.htm&locale=en). .

A.2: Rank of a Matrix

The rank of a matrix is the maximum number of linearly independent row (or column) vectors in the matrix. A vector r is said to be linearly independent of vectors r1 and r2 if it cannot be expressed as a linear combination of r1 and r2.

$$r \neq ar_1 + br_2$$

Consider the three matrices below:

$$A = \begin{matrix} 1 & 3 & 7 \\ 2 & 6 & 14 \end{matrix} \qquad B = \begin{matrix} 1 & 2 & 3 \\ 4 & 5 & 6 \\ 5 & 7 & 9 \end{matrix} \qquad C = \begin{matrix} 1 & 0 & 2 \\ 0 & 2 & 1 \\ 1 & 1 & 0 \end{matrix}$$

- In matrix A, row **r2** is a multiple of **r1**, *r2 = 2 r1*, so it has only one independent row. **Rank(A) = 1**
- In matrix B, row **r3** is a sum of **r1** and **r2**, *r3 = r1 + r2*, but **r1** and **r2** are independent. **Rank(B) = 2**
- In matrix C, all 3 rows are independent of each other. **Rank(C) = 3**

Transpose of a Matrix

The transpose of a matrix can be defined as an operator that can switch the rows and column indices of a matrix—in other words, it flips a matrix over its diagonal. To calculate the transpose of a matrix, simply interchange the rows and columns of the matrix—in other words, write the elements of the rows as columns and write the elements of a column as rows.

A.3: Impurity Reduction Measures

Impurity Reduction Measures for Class Targets

Figure A.3.1: Impurity Reduction Measures

X1: <38.5	<38.5	≥38.5		ΔGini	Δentropy	Logworth *
1	293	71				
7	363	1		.197	.504	140
9	42	294				

X10: <0.5	<0.5	1-41	42-51	≥51.5	ΔGini	Δentropy	Logworth
1	9	143	65	147			
7	221	88	1	54	.255	.600	172
9	1	4	16	315			

* ΔGini and Δentropy are impurity reduction measures. Logworth is based on the χ^2 from an *n-way* table. For all, higher is better.

After a set of candidate splits is determined, a splitting criterion is used to determine the best one. In some situations, the worth of a split is obvious. If target distributions are the same in the child nodes as they are in the parent node, then no improvement was made, and the split is worthless. In contrast, if a split results in pure children, then the split is definitely the best.

In classification trees, the three most well-known splitting criteria are based on the Gini index (BFOS 1984), entropy (Quinlan 1993), and the chi-square test (Kass 1980). Well-known algorithms and software products associated with these three splitting criteria are CART (classification and regression tree); C5.0 (developed by the machine learning researcher Quinlin); and the CHAID algorithm (chi-squared automatic interaction detection).

Details: Impurity Reduction Measures for Interval Targets

Regression trees endeavor to partition the input space into segments where the target values are alike. (That is, each segment or node has low variability.) All target values would be equal in a pure node. In other words, the variance of the target would be zero within a pure node.

The split-search considerations and the *p*-value adjustments are the same as with classification trees. However, the appropriate splitting criteria are different. The default splitting criterion for a regression tree is change in response variance. CHAID and F Statistic are also available as splitting methods.

Entropy and the Gini index are measures of variability of nominal variables. When the target distribution is continuous, the sample variance is the obvious measure of impurity (Morgan and Sonquist 1963, Breiman et al. 1984).

$$i(t) = \frac{1}{n_t} \sum_{j=1}^{n_t} \left(y_{jt} - \bar{y}_t \right)^2$$

Note: The denominator is *ni*, not *ni*-1. This is the MLE and not the usual unbiased estimate of sample variance.

The *F* test can be used analogously to the chi-square test for regression trees. A split at a node can be thought of as a one-way analysis of variance where the *B* branches are the *B* treatments. Let

$$\bar{y}_{i\cdot} = \frac{1}{n_i} \sum_{j=1}^{n_i} y_{ij}$$

be the mean of the target in each node and $\bar{y}_{\cdot\cdot}$ be the mean in the root node (the overall mean).

The between-node sum of squares ($SS_{between}$) is a measure of the distance between the node means and the overall mean. The within-node sum of squares (SS_{within}) measures the variability within a node. Large values of the *F* statistic indicate departures from the null hypothesis that all the node means are equal. When the target values, conditional on the inputs, are independently, normally distributed with constant variance, then the *F* statistic follows an *F* distribution with $B - 1$ and $n - B$ degrees of freedom. The *p*-value of the test is used in the same way as the *p*-value for a chi-square test for classification trees.

The total sum of squares (SS_{total}) can be considered fixed with regard to comparing splits at a particular node. Thus, it follows from the ANOVA identity

$SS_{total} = SS_{between} + SS_{within}$ that the *F* test statistic can be thought of as either maximizing the differences between the node means or reducing the within-node variance. This latter interpretation indicates the equivalency between the *F* statistic and the reduction in impurity (variance) splitting criterion.

$$\Delta \mathrm{var} = \frac{SS_{total}}{n} - \sum_{i=1}^{B} \left(\frac{n_i}{n} \right) \left(\frac{SS_i}{n_i} \right) = \frac{1}{n} \left(SS_{total} - SS_{within} \right) = \frac{SS_{between}}{n}$$

Thus, using D*variance* is equivalent to **not** adjusting the *F* test for degrees of freedom (number of branches).

A.4: Decision Tree Split Search

Understanding the details of an algorithm used for building trees enables you to better use SAS Visual Data Mining and Machine Learning to build a tree and interpret your results. The description presented here assumes a binary target, but the algorithm for interval targets is similar. (The algorithm for categorical targets with more than two outcomes is more complicated and is not discussed.) In Model Studio, the algorithm described here is known as *chi-square*.

The first part of the algorithm is called the *split search*. The split search starts by selecting an input for partitioning the available training data. If the measurement scale of the selected input is *interval*, each unique value serves as a potential split point for the data. If the input is *categorical*, the average value of the target is taken within each categorical input level. The averages serve the same role as the unique interval input values in the discussion that follows.

For a selected input and fixed split point, two groups are generated. Cases with input values less than the split point are said to *branch left*. Cases with input values greater than the split point are said to *branch right*. The groups, combined with the target outcomes, form a 2x2 contingency table with columns specifying branch direction (left or right) and rows specifying target value (0 or 1). A Pearson chi-squared statistic is used to quantify the independence of counts in the table's columns. Large values for the chi-squared statistic suggest that the proportion of 0s and 1s in the left branch is different from the proportion in the right branch. A large difference in outcome proportions indicates a good split.

Because the Pearson chi-squared statistic can be applied to the case of multiway splits and multi-outcome targets, the statistic is converted to a probability value, or *p*-value. The *p*-value indicates the likelihood of obtaining the observed value of the statistic assuming identical target proportions in each branch direction. For large data sets, these *p*-values can be very close to zero. For this reason, the quality of a split is reported by *logworth* = -*log*(chi-squared *p*-value).

Note: At least one logworth must exceed a threshold for a split to occur with that input. By default, this threshold corresponds to a chi-squared *p*-value of 0.20 or a logworth of approximately 0.7.

Figure A.4.1: Decision Tree Split Search

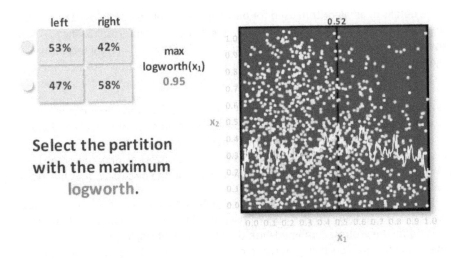

The best split for an input is the split that yields the highest logworth.

Several peripheral factors make the split search somewhat more complicated than what is described above.

First, the tree algorithm settings disallow certain partitions of the data. Settings, such as the minimum number of observations required for a split search and the minimum number of observations in a leaf, force a minimum number of cases in a split partition. This minimum number of cases reduces the number of potential partitions for each input in the split search.

Second, when you test for the independence of column categories in a contingency table, it is possible to obtain significant (large) values of the chi-squared statistic even when there are no differences in the true, underlying proportions between split branches. In other words, if there are many ways to split the variable that labels the rows of the table (and thus many Chi-square tables and tests), then you are likely to get at least one with a very small *p*-value even when the variable has no true effect. As the number of possible split points increases, the likelihood of obtaining significant values also increases. In this way, an input with a multitude of unique input values has a greater chance of accidentally having a large logworth than an input with only a few distinct input values.

Statisticians face a similar problem when they combine the results from multiple statistical tests. As the number of tests increases, the chance of a false positive result likewise increases. To maintain overall confidence in the statistical findings, statisticians inflate the *p*-values of each test by a factor equal to the number of tests being conducted. If an inflated *p*-value shows a significant result, then the significance of the overall results is assured. This type of *p*-value adjustment is known as a *Bonferroni correction*.

Because each split point corresponds to a statistical test, Bonferroni corrections are automatically applied to the logworth calculations for an input. These corrections, also called *Bonferroni adjustments*, penalize inputs with many split points by reducing the logworth of a split by an amount equal to the log of the number of distinct input values. This is equivalent to the Bonferroni correction because subtracting this constant from logworth is equivalent to multiplying the corresponding chi-squared *p*-value by the number of split points. The adjustment enables a fairer comparison of inputs with many and few levels later in the split-search algorithm.

Third, for inputs with missing values, two sets of Bonferroni-adjusted logworths are generated. For the first set, cases with missing input values are included in the left branch of the contingency table and logworths are calculated. For the second set of logworths, missing value cases are moved to the right branch. The best split is then selected from the set of possible splits with the missing values in the left and right branches, respectively.

The partitioning process is repeated for every input in the training data. Inputs whose adjusted logworth fails to exceed the threshold are excluded from consideration.

Figure A.4.2: Decision Tree Split Search – Repeat the Partitioning Process

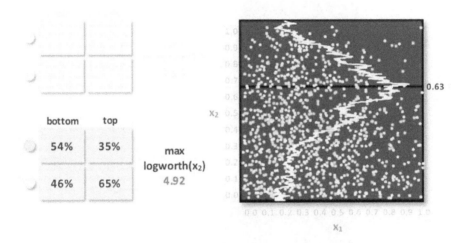

Again, the optimal split for the next input considered is the one that maximizes the logworth function for that input.

After you determine the best split for every input, the tree algorithm compares each best split's corresponding logworth. The split with the highest adjusted logworth is deemed best.

Figure A.4.3: Decision Tree Split Search – Partiioning the Training Data using the Best Split Rule

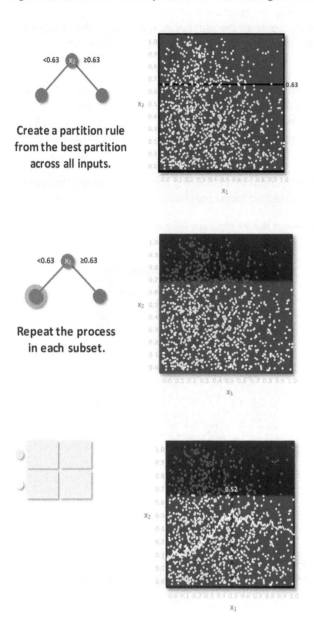

Create a partition rule from the best partition across all inputs.

Repeat the process in each subset.

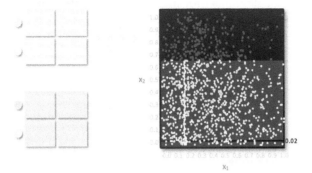

The training data are partitioned using the best split rule.

The logworth of the *x2* split is negative. This might seem surprising, but it results from several adjustments made to the logworth calculation. (The Bonferroni adjustment was described previously. Another, called the *depth adjustment*, is outlined later in this section.)

The split search continues within each leaf. Logworths are compared as before.

Figure A.4.4: Decision Tree Split Search – Comparing Logworths

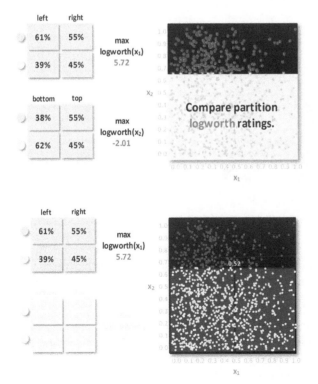

Because the significance of secondary and subsequent splits depends on the significance of the previous splits, the algorithm again faces a multiple comparison problem. To compensate for this problem, the algorithm increases the threshold by an amount related to the number of splits above the current split. For binary splits, the threshold is increased by $log10(2)$ $d \approx 0.3 \cdot d$, where d is the depth of the split on the decision tree. This is known as the *depth adjustment*.

By increasing the threshold for each depth (or equivalently decreasing the logworths), the tree algorithm makes it increasingly easy for an input's splits to be excluded from consideration.

Figure A.4.5: Decision Tree Split Search – Creating Partition Rules

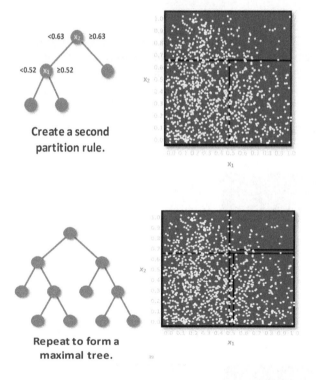

The data are partitioned according to the best split, which creates a second partition rule. The process repeats in each leaf until there are no more splits whose adjusted logworth exceeds the depth-adjusted thresholds. This process completes the split-search portion of the tree algorithm.

The resulting partition of the input space is known as the *maximal tree*. Development of the maximal tree is based exclusively on statistical measures of split worth on the training data. It is likely that the maximal tree fails to generalize well on an independent set of validation data. The maximal tree is the starting place for how complexity of the model will be optimized. Optimizing the complexity of a tree is done through pruning, and this is covered in the next section.

Appendix B: Solutions

Practice Solutions

Note: Due to the distributed nature of the SAS Viya environment, results might not be reproducible. Your results and answers to the questions in the practices could be different from those provided below.

Chapter 7

Building a Decision Tree

1. Build a decision tree using the Autotune feature. Add a Decision Tree node to the Lesson 3 pipeline, below the Variable Selection node. Use the Autotune feature. Explore the settings that are made available when **Autotune** is selected.

   a. On the Starter Template pipeline, right-click the **Variable Selection** node and select **Add child node ▶ Supervised Learning ▶ Decision Tree**.

   b. In the properties pane, turn on the **Perform Autotuning** option. The default properties show starting values and ranges that are tried for each property in the decision tree model.

   c. Right-click the **Decision Tree** node and select **Run**. This process might take few minutes.

   d. When the execution is over, right-click the **Decision Tree** node and select **Results**.

   e. Examine the Results window. Maximize the Autotune Results window and notice the different evaluations performed. Restore the Autotune Results window.

Evaluation	Maximum Tree Levels	Number of Bins	Criterion	Kolmogorov-Smirnov Statistic	Time in Seconds
0	17	20	GAIN	0.5647	0.5863
19	12	93	GAIN	0.5776	1.0119
46	11	98	GAIN	0.5750	1.1528
25	17	126	CHISQUARE	0.5746	2.3289
49	12	91	GAIN	0.5731	1.9069
51	13	93	GAIN	0.5709	2.3574
37	19	173	CHISQUARE	0.5715	3.7630
50	14	106	GINI	0.5704	1.9425
52	12	93	GINI	0.5704	0.9319
40	20	93	GAIN	0.5695	3.1531
17	11	110	GAIN	0.5690	0.8117

f. Scroll down and maximize the Output window. This output shows the set of parameters selected for the final decision tree model.

The SAS System

The TREESPLIT Procedure

Model Information	
Split Criterion	GAIN
Pruning Method	Cost Complexity
Max Branches per Node	2
Max Tree Depth	11
Tree Depth Before Pruning	11
Tree Depth After Pruning	11
Number of Leaves Before Pruning	426
Number of Leaves After Pruning	159

g. Click the **Assessment** tab. Scroll down and observe the Fit Statistics window. The average squared error for the Autotune model is 0.0573 on the VALIDATE partition.

Target ...	Data Role	Partitio...	Formatt...	Sum of ...	Averag...
churn	TRAIN	1	1	39,590	0.0548
churn	VALIDATE	0	0	16,967	0.0573

2. What criteria were selected for the champion model?

    o   Split criteria: **Gain**

    o   Pruning method: **Cost Complexity**

    o   Maximum number of branches: **2**

    o   Maximum tree depth: **11**

3. How does the autotuned decision tree compare to the other models in the pipeline, particularly to the decision tree model built during the demonstration? Consider the fit statistics average squared error for this comparison.

    It performed better than the decision tree built during the demonstration.

Chapter 8

Building a Gradient Boosting Model

1. Build a gradient boosting model using the Autotune feature. Add a Gradient Boosting node to the Lesson 3 pipeline, below the Variable Selection node. Use the Autotune feature. Explore the settings that are made available when **Autotune** is selected.

   a. On the Starter Template pipeline, right-click the **Variable Selection** node and select **Add child node ▶ Supervised Learning ▶ Gradient Boosting**.

   b. In the properties pane, turn on the **Perform Autotuning** option. The default properties show starting values and ranges that are tried for each property in the gradient boosting model.

   c. Right-click the **Gradient Boosting** node and select **Run**. This process might take few minutes.

   d. When the execution is over, right-click the **Gradient Boosting** node and select **Results**.

   e. Examine the Results window. Maximize the Autotune Results window and notice the different evaluations performed. Restore the Autotune Results window.

Evaluation	Number of Variables to Try	Learning Rate	Sampling Rate	Lasso	Ridge	Kolmogorov-Smirnov Stati...	Time in Seconds
3	12	0.1000	0.5000	0	1	0.5943	4.9236
11	14	0.1000	0.5000	5	1	0.5952	16.1654
43	15	0.1072	0.5133	0.1294	1.2895	0.5948	19.0498
27	6	0.1795	0.8461	1.4259	4.1695	0.5946	17.7240
10	14	0.1000	0.5000	3	1	0.5943	0.0000
32	5	0.2563	1	9.5405	7.4917	0.5943	9.4615
34	14	0.1000	0.9500	0	1	0.5941	14.3920
30	4	0.1514	0.9774	7.1430	2.9574	0.5940	14.2125
16	5	0.5050	1	5	5	0.5939	13.9294
54	14	0.1000	0.5000	10	1	0.5939	15.0415
23	7	0.5663	0.6970	9.4279	6.3806	0.5935	17.3961

f. Scroll down and maximize the Output window. This output shows the set of parameters selected for the final gradient boosting model.

The SAS System	
The GRADBOOST Procedure	
Model Information	
Number of Trees	150
Learning Rate	0.1
Subsampling Rate	0.5
Number of Variables Per Split	14
Number of Bins	50
Number of Input Variables	14
Maximum Number of Tree Nodes	31
Minimum Number of Tree Nodes	19
Maximum Number of Branches	2
Minimum Number of Branches	2
Maximum Depth	4
Minimum Depth	4
Maximum Number of Leaves	16
Minimum Number of Leaves	10
Maximum Leaf Size	15402
Minimum Leaf Size	5
Seed	12345

g. Click the **Assessment** tab. Scroll down and observe the Fit Statistics window. The average squared error for the Autotune model is 0.0560 on the VALIDATE partition.

Target ...	Data Role	Partitio...	Formatt...	Sum of ...	Averag...
churn	TRAIN	1	1	39,590	0.0560
churn	VALIDATE	0	0	16,967	0.0560

2. What criteria were selected for the champion model?

o Number of trees: **150**

o Number of variables per split: **14**

o Number of bins: **50**

o Maximum number of branches: **2**

o Maximum depth: **4**

3. How does the autotuned gradient boosting compare to the other models in the pipeline, particularly to the gradient boosting model built during the demonstration? Consider the fit statistic average squared error for this comparison.

The gradient boosting model built earlier in the lesson demonstration performed better on average squared error than the autotuned model. However, the autotuned model performed better than the earlier model based on other fit statistics (for example, KS).

Building a Forest Model

1. Build a forest using the Autotune feature. Add a Forest node to the Lesson 3 pipeline, below the Variable Selection node. Use the Autotune feature. Explore the settings that are available when **Autotune** is selected.

   a. On the Starter Template pipeline, right-click the **Variable Selection** node and select **Add child node** ▶ **Supervised Learning** ▶ **Forest**.

   b. In the properties pane, turn on the **Perform Autotuning** option. The default properties show starting values and ranges that are tried for each property in the Forest model.

   c. Right-click the **Forest** node and select **Run**. This process might take few minutes.

   d. When the execution is over, right-click the **Forest** node and select **Results**.

   e. Examine the Results window. Maximize the Autotune Results window and notice the different evaluations performed. Restore the Autotune Results window.

Evaluation	Number of Trees	Number of Variables to Try	Bootstrap	Maximum Tree Levels	Kolmogorov-Smirnov Statistic	Time in Seconds
0	100	14	0.6000	21	0.5732	7.6856
43	70	3	0.9000	30	0.5911	16.2677
37	76	4	0.6870	28	0.5909	18.7825
46	114	2	0.9000	30	0.5901	15.9216
52	29	2	0.9000	30	0.5900	10.7234
34	114	2	0.9000	21	0.5896	11.6642
5	49	2	0.9000	21	0.5899	6.7459
27	75	4	0.7297	28	0.5894	19.0429
20	90	4	0.8964	27	0.5889	23.652
49	20	2	0.9000	30	0.5875	3.2938
1	78	5	0.7222	30	0.5871	21.8239

f. Scroll down and maximize the Output window. This output shows the set of parameters selected for the final forest model.

The SAS System	
The FOREST Procedure	
Model Information	
Number of Trees	70
Number of Variables Per Split	2
Seed	12345
Bootstrap Percentage	90
Number of Bins	20
Number of Input Variables	14
Maximum Number of Tree Nodes	2935
Minimum Number of Tree Nodes	1783
Maximum Number of Branches	2
Minimum Number of Branches	2
Maximum Depth	29
Minimum Depth	29
Maximum Number of Leaves	1468
Minimum Number of Leaves	892
Maximum Leaf Size	10825
Minimum Leaf Size	5
OOB Misclassification Rate	0.06643092

g. Click the **Assessment** tab. Scroll down and observe the Fit Statistics window. The average squared error for the Autotune model is 0.0577 on the VALIDATE partition.

Target ...	Data Role	Partitio...	Formatt...	Sum of ...	Averag...
churn	TRAIN	1	1	39,590	0.0486
churn	VALIDATE	0	0	16,967	0.0577

2. What criteria were selected for the champion model?

   o Number of trees: **70**

   o Number of variables per split: **2**

   o Number of bins: **20**

   o Maximum number of branches: **2**

   o Maximum depth: **29**

3. How does the autotuned forest compare to the other models in the pipeline, particularly to the forest model built during the demonstration? Consider the fit statistic average squared error for this comparison.

   The forest built in the lesson demonstration performs slightly better than the autotuned forest based on average squared error (and other fits statistics, such as KS).

Chapter 11

Building a Support Vector Machine Model

1. Build a support vector machine using the Autotune feature. Add an SVM node to the Lesson 5 pipeline, connected to the Variable Selection node. Use the Autotune feature. Explore the settings that are made available when **Autotune** is selected, but keep all properties at their defaults, *except the polynomial degree*. Under the autotune properties, set the maximum value for the polynomial degree to be 2.

   a. On the Lesson 5 pipeline, right-click the **Variable Selection** node and select **Add child node ▶ Supervised Learning ▶ SVM**.

   b. In the properties pane, turn on the **Perform Autotuning** option. The default properties show starting values and ranges that are tried for each property in the SVM model.

   c. Under **Polynomial Degree**, change the maximum range by changing **To** from 3 to **2**.

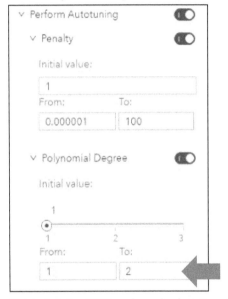

   d. Right-click the **SVM** node and select **Run**. This process might take few minutes.

   e. When the execution is over, right-click the **SVM** node and select **Results**.

f. Examine the Results window. Maximize the Autotune Results window and notice the different evaluations performed. Restore the Autotune Results window.

Evaluation	Penalty (C)	Polynomial Degree	Kolmogorov-Smirnov Statistic	Time in Seconds
0	1	1	0.5516	2.2635
26	12.7206	2	0.5665	44.7761
48	13.1826	2	0.5663	46.7929
39	13.4671	2	0.5660	39.5490
16	9.0764	2	0.5657	39.0414
25	9.2961	2	0.5657	44.5981
51	10.7621	2	0.5656	26.3379
46	9.7229	2	0.5655	44.1293
1	17.1111	2	0.5654	32.1260
4	88.8689	2	0.5652	32.0754
45	9.4847	2	0.5652	44.3701

g. Scroll down and maximize the Output window. This output shows the set of parameters selected for the final support vector machine model.

The SAS System

The SVMACHINE Procedure

Model Information	
Task Type	C_CLAS
Optimization Technique	Interior Point
Scale	YES
Kernel Function	Polynomial
Kernel Degree	2
Penalty Method	C
Penalty Parameter	12.7205947141729
Maximum Iterations	25
Tolerance	1e-06

h. Click the **Assessment** tab. Scroll down and observe the Fit Statistics window. The average squared error for the Autotune model is 0.1760 on the VALIDATE partition.

Target ...	Data Role	Partitio...	Formatt...	Sum of ...	Averag...
churn	TRAIN	1	1	39,590	0.1758
churn	VALIDATE	0	0	16,967	0.1760

2. What Kernel was selected during the autotune process? What is the value of the penalty parameter and is it much different from the default value (1) used for the other SVMs?

A polynomial kernel with degree of 2 was selected. The penalty term is 12.72, which is very different from the default value of 1. The number of iterations was 25.

3. How does the autotuned SVM compare to the other models in the pipeline? Consider the fit statistic average squared error for this comparison.

The autotuned SVM was considerably worse than the last model tuned during the demonstrations on ASE.

Quiz Solutions

Chapter 1

1. After you create your new project, Model Studio takes you to the Data tab. What can you do in the Data tab? (Select all that apply.)

      a. Modify variable roles and measurement levels.

      b. Manage global metadata.

      d. Manage columns to display the Variables table.

Chapter 2

1. The Data Exploration node in Model Studio enables you to do which of the following? (Select all that apply.)

      a. Profile a data set.

      b. Observe the most important inputs or suspicious variables.

2. Which of the following statements is true while defining metadata in Model Studio?

      c. Metadata properties can be defined either on the Data tab or in the Manage Variables node and then can be invoked by using an appropriate node.

Chapter 3

1. Which of the following statements is true about the Text Mining node?

      d. It creates topics based on groups of terms that occur together in several documents. Each term-document pair is assigned a score for every topic.

Chapter 4

1. Why bin an input?

      d. All of the above.

Chapter 5

1. What is the range of the logit function?

      a. $(-\infty, +\infty)$

Chapter 6

1. Which of the following statements is true regarding decision trees?

      a. To predict cases, decision trees use rules that involve the values or categories of the input variables.

Chapter 7

1. Which of the following statements is true regarding decision trees?

      d. The logworth of a split can sometimes be negative.

2. Which of the following statements is true regarding decision trees?

> **b.** Accuracy is obtained by multiplying the proportion of observations falling into each leaf by the proportion of those correctly classified in the leaf and then summing across all leaves.

Chapter 8

1. Which of the following statements is true regarding tree-based models?

> **a.** Small changes in the training data can cause large changes in the topology of a tree.

Chapter 9

1. Which of the following statements is true regarding neural networks?

> **c.** Neural networks are most appropriate for pure prediction tasks.

Chapter 10

1. Which of the following statements is true regarding neural networks?

> **d.** There are two optimization methods available for neural networks in Visual Data Mining and Machine Learning: limited memory Broyden-Fletcher-Goldfarb-Shanno (LBFGS) and stochastic gradient descent (SGD).

Chapter 11

1. Because only the observations closest to the separating hyperplane are used to construct the support vector machine, the curse of dimensionality is reduced.

> - True

Chapter 12

1. Which of the following statements is true regarding the ROC curve?

> **b.** The C-statistic equals the percent of concordant cases plus one-half times the percent of tied cases.

2. When you have an interval target, which of the following fit statistics can you use to select the champion model?

> **b.** average squared error

References

Alpaydin, E. and F. Gürgen. 1996. "Comparison of Statistical and Neural Classifiers and Their Applications to Optical Character Recognition and Speech Classification." in *Neural Network Systems: Techniques and Applications*, Leondes, ed. San Diego, CA: Academic Press.

Banks, R. B. 1994. *Growth and Diffusion Phenomena: Mathematical Frameworks and Application*. New York: Springer-Verlag.

Bartlett, P. L. 1997. "For Valid Generalization, the Size of the Weights is More Important than the Size of the Network." In *Advances in Neural Information Processing Systems Volume 9* (Mozer, Jordan, and Petsche, eds.). Cambridge, MA: The MIT Press.

Bauer, E. and R. Kohavi. 1999. "An Empirical Comparison of Voting Classification Algorithms: Bagging, Boosting, and Variants." *Machine Learning* 36:105–139.

Beck, A. 1997. "Herb Edelstein discusses the usefulness of data mining." DS Star. Vol. 1: No. 2.

Berger, J. 1980. *Statistical Decision Theory*. New York: Springer-Verlag.

Berk, K. N. and D. E. Booth. 1995. "Seeing a Curve in Multiple Regression." *Technometrics* 37:4.

Bishop, C. M. 1995. *Neural Networks for Pattern Recognition*. New York: Oxford University Press.

Blake, C., E. Keogh, and C. J. Merz. 1998. UCI Repository of machine learning databases. Irvine, CA: University of California, Department of Information and Computer Science. Available at http://archive.ics.uci.edu/ml/.

Box, G. E. P. and G. M. Jenkins. 1976. *Time Series Analysis: Forecasting and Control*. San Francisco: Holden-Day Inc.

Breiman, L. 1996a. "Technical Note: Some Properties of Splitting Criteria." *Machine Learning* 24:41–47.

Breiman, L. 1996b. "Bagging Predictors." *Machine Learning* 24:123–140.

Breiman, L. 1998. "Arcing Classifiers (with discussion)." *Annals of Statistics* 26:801–849.

Breiman, L., J. H. Friedman, R. A. Olshen, and C. J. Stone. 1984. *Classification and Regression Trees*. New York: Chapman & Hall.

Broomhead, D. S. and David Lowe. 1988. *Radial basis functions, multi-variable functional interpolation and adaptive networks* (Technical report). RSRE 4148.

Broyden, C. G. 1970. "The Convergence of a Class of Double-rank Minimization Algorithms." *Journal of the Institute of Mathematics and Its Applications* 6:76–90.

Byrd, R. H., P. Lu, J. Nocedal, and C. Zhu. 1995. "A limited memory algorithm for bound constrained optimization." *SIAM Journal on Scientific Computing*. 16, 1190–1208.

Bryson, A. E. and Y. C. Ho. 1969. *Neural Networks: Computers with Intuition*. Singapore: World Scientific.

Cai, Z. and C. L. Tsai. 1999. "Diagnostics for Nonlinearity in Generalized Linear Models." *Computational Statistics and Data Analysis* 29:445–469.

Carroll, R. J. and D. Ruppert. 1988. *Transformation and Weighting in Regression*. New York: Chapman & Hall.

Chatfield, C. and J. Faraway. 1998. "Time Series Forecasting with Neural Networks: A Comparative Study Using the Airline Data." *Applied Statistics* 47:231–250.

Chester, D.L. 1990. "Why Two Hidden-Layers are Better than One" in IJCNN-90-WASH-DC. *Lawrence Erlbaum* Vol. 1:265–268.

Cuellar, M. P., M. Delgado, and M.C. Pegalajar. 2006. "An Application of Non-Linear Programming to Train Recurrent Neural Networks in Time Series Prediction Problems." *Enterprise Information Systems* VII:95–102.

Cybenko, G. 1988. *Continuous Valued Neural Networks with Two Hidden Layers Are Sufficient*. Medford, MA: Technical Report. Dept. of Computer Science. Tufts University.

Dasu, T. and T. Johnson. 2003. *Exploratory Data Mining and Data Cleaning*. New York: John Wiley and Sons.

David Shepard Associates. 1999. *The New Direct Marketing: How to Implement a Profit-Driven Database Marketing Strategy*. New York: McGraw-Hill.

De Vries, B. and J. C. Principe. 1992. "The Gamma Filter: A New Class of Adaptive IIR Filters with Restricted Feedback." *IEEE Transactions on Signal Processing* 41(2):649–656.

De Vries, B. and J. C. Principe. 1992. "The Gamma Model - A New Model for Temporal Processing." *Neural Networks* 5:565–576.

De Vries, B. and J. C. Principe. 1992. *Short Term Memory Structures for Dynamic Neural Networks*. Princeton, NJ: David Sarnoff Research Center.

Dorffner, G. 1996. "Neural Networks for Time Series Processing." *Neural Network World* 6:447–468.

Efron, B. 1983. "Estimating the Error Rate of a Prediction Rule: Improvement on Cross Validation." *Journal of the American Statistical Association* 78:316–331.

Efron, B., T. Hastie, I. Johnstone, and R. Tibshirani. 2004. "Least Angle Regression (with Discussion)." *Annals of Statistics* 32: 407–499.

Ellingsen, B. K. 1994. "A Comparative Analysis of Backpropagation and Counterpropagation Neural Networks." Department of Information Science. University of Bergen: Bergen, Norway.

Elman, J. L. 1990. "Finding Structure in Time." *Cognitive Science* 14:179–221.

Ezekiel, M. 1924. "A Method for Handling Curvilinear Correlation for any Number of Variables." *Journal of the American Statistical Association* 19:431–453.

Falhman, S. E. 1988 "Faster-learning variations on back-propagation: an empirical study." In *Proceedings of the 1988 Connectionist Models Summer School*, D. Touretzky, G. E. Hinton, and T. J. Sejnowski, eds., pp. 31–51. San Mateo, CA. Morgan Kaufmann.

Fahlman, S. E. and C. Lebiere. 1990. "The Cascade-Correlation Learning Architecture." in *Advances in Neural Information Processing Systems Volume 2*, D. Touretzky, ed. San Mateo, CA: Morgan Kaufmann.

Fan, J. and I. Gijbels. 1996. *Local Polynomial Modeling and its Applications*. New York: Chapman & Hall.

Fletcher, R. 1970. "A New Approach to Variable Metric Algorithms." *Computer Journal* 13:317–322.

Fletcher, R. 1987. *Practical Methods of Optimization*. New York: Wiley.

Freund, Y. and R. E. Schapire. 1996. "A Decision-Theoretic Generalization of On-Line Learning and an Application to Boosting." *Journal of Computer and System Science* 55:119–139.

Friedman, J. H. 1991. "Multivariate Adaptive Regression Splines (with discussion)." *Annals of Statistics* 19:1–141.

Friedman, J. H. 1994. "An Overview of Predictive Learning and Function Approximation." In *From Statistics to Neural Networks. Theory and Pattern Recognition Applications*, Cherkasy, Friedman, Wechsler, eds. New York: Springer-Verlag.

Friedman, J. H. 1997. "On Bias, Variance, 0/1-Loss, and the Curse-of-Dimensionality." *Data Mining and Knowledge Discovery* 1:55–77.

Friedman, J. H. 2001. "Greedy function approximation: A gradient boosting machine." *The Annals of Statistics* 29:1189–1232.

Friedman, J. H. 2002. "Stochastic gradient boosting." *Computational Statistics & Data Analysis* 38:367–378.

Friedman, J. H. and W. Stuetzle. 1981. "Projection Pursuit Regression." *Journal of the American Statistical Association* 76:817–823.

Furnival, G. M. and R. W. Wilson. 1974. "Regression by Leaps and Bounds." *Technometrics* 16: 499–511.

Georges, J. E. 2003. "Beyond Expectations: Quantifying Variability in Predictive Models." *Proceedings of the M2003 SAS Data Mining Conference*. Cary, NC: SAS Institute Inc.

Georges, J. E. 2004. "Qualities to Quantities: Using Non-numeric Data in Parametric Prediction." *Proceedings of the M2004 SAS Data Mining Conference*. Cary, NC: SAS Institute Inc.

Goldfarb, D. 1970. "A Family of Variable Metric Updates Derived by Variational Means." *Mathematics of Computation* 24: 23–24.

Hand, D. J. 1997. *Construction and Assessment of Classification Rules*. New York: Wiley.

Hand, D. J. 2005. "What you get is what you want? – Some dangers of black box data mining." *M2005 Conference Proceedings*. Cary, NC: SAS Institute Inc.

Hand, D. J. 2006. "Classifier technology and the illusion of progress." *Statistical Science* 21:1–14.

Hand, D. J. and W. E. Henley. 1997. "Statistical classification methods in consumer credit scoring: A review." *Journal of the Royal Statistical Society A* 160:523–541.

Hand, D., H. Mannila, and P. Smyth. 2001. *Principles of Data Mining*. Cambridge, MA: The MIT Press.

Harrell, F. E. 2006. *Regression Modeling Strategies*. New York: Springer-Verlag New York, Inc.

Harrell F. E., K. L. Lee, and D. B. Mark. 1996. "Multivariate Prognostic Models: Issues in Developing Models, Evaluating Assumptions and Adequacy, and Measuring and Reducing Errors." *Statistics in Medicine* 15:361–387.

Harrison, D. and D. L. Rubinfeld. 1978. "Hedonic Prices in the Demand for Clean Air." *Journal of Environmental Economics and Management* 5:81–102.

Hassibi, B. and D. G. Stork. 1993. "Second Order Derivatives for Network Pruning: Optimal Brain Surgeon." In *Advances in Neural Information Processing Systems, Volume 5*, Hansen, Cowan, and Giles, eds. San Mateo, CA: Morgan Kaufmann.

Hastie, T. J. and R. J. Tibshirani. 1986. "Generalized Additive Models (with discussion)." *Statistical Science* 1:297–318.

Hastie, T. J. and R. J. Tibshirani. 1990. *Generalized Additive Models*. New York: Chapman & Hall.

Hastie, T. J. and R. J. Tibshirani, and Jerome Friedman. 2001. *The Elements of Statistical Learning: Data Mining, Inference, and Prediction*. New York: Springer-Verlag New York, Inc.

Hebb, D. O. 1949. *The Organization of Behavior*. New York: Wiley.

Hecht-Nielsen, R. 1987. "Counterpropagation Networks." *Applied Optics* 26:4979–4984.

Hertz, J., A. Krogh, and R. G. Palmer. 1991. *Introduction to the Theory of Neural Computation*. Redwood City, CA: Addison-Wesley Publishing Co.

Hettich, S. and S. D. Bay. 1999. The UCI KDD Archive. Irvine, CA: University of California, Department of Information and Computer Science. Available at http://kdd.ics.uci.edu.

Hinton, G. E., S. Osindero, and Y. W. Teh. 2006. "A Fast Learning Algorithm for Deep Belief Networks." *Neural Computation 18*. MIT. 1527–1554.

Hinton, G. E., N. Shrivastava, and K. Swersky. 2013. "Overview of Mini-Batch Gradient Descent" Video from Coursera - University of Toronto - Course: Neural Networks for Machine Learning: Published on Nov 5, 2013. Available at https://www.coursera.org/course/neura.

Hoaglin, D. C., F. Mosteller, and J. W. Tukey. 1983. *Understanding Robust and Exploratory Data Analysis*. New York: Wiley.

Hoerl, A. E. and R. W. Kennard. 1970. "Ridge Regression: Biased Estimation for Nonorthogonal Problems." *Technometrics* 12:55–67.

Hogg, R. V. 1979. "Statistical Robustness: One View of Its Use in Applications Today." *The American Statistician* 33:108–115.

Holden, K. 1995. "Vector Autoregression Modeling and Forecasting." *Journal of Forecasting* 14:159–166.

Holland, J. H. 1976. "Studies of Spontaneous Emergence of Self-Replicating Systems Using Cellular Automata and Formal Grammars." In *Automata, Languages, Development*. (A. Lindenmayer and G. Rozenberg, eds.) Amsterdam: North-Holland.

Holland, J. H. 1992. *Adaptation in Natural and Artificial Systems: An Introductory Analysis with Applications to Biology, Control, and Artificial Intelligence*, 2nd Edition. Cambridge, MA: The MIT Press.

Huber, P. J. 1964. "Robust Estimation of a Location Parameter." *Annals of Mathematical Statistics* 35:73–101. *IDC Digital Universe Study*, sponsored by EMC, May 2010.

Jacobs, R. A., M. I. Jordan, S. J. Nowlan, and G. E. Hinton. 1991. "Adaptive Mixture of Local Experts." *Neural Computation* 3:79–87.

Jaeger, H. 2001. "The 'echo state' approach to analyzing and training recurrent neural networks". *GMD Report 148*. GMD - German National Research Institute for Computer Science.

Jaeger, H. 2002. "Tutorial on training recurrent neural networks, covering BPPT, RTRL, EKF and the echo state network approach." *GMD Report 159*. Fraunhofer Institute AIS.

Jaeger, H. 2007. "Echo state network." *Scholarpedia* 2(9):2330.

Johnson, D. E. 1998. *Applied Multivariate Methods for Data Analysis*. Pacific Grove, CA: Druxbury Press.

Johnson, G. 1991. *In the Palaces of Memory*. New York: Vintage Books/ Random House.

Jordan, M. I. and R. A. Jacobs. 1994. "Hierarchical Mixture of Experts and the EM algorithm." *Neural Computation* 6:181–214.

Kass, G. V. 1980. "An exploratory technique for investigating large quantities of categorical data." *Applied Statistics*. 29:119–127.

Kohavi, R., D. Sommerfield, and J. Dougherty. 1996. "Data Mining using MLC." *International Journal on Artificial Intelligence Tools*. 6:234–245.

Landwehr, J. D., D. Pregibon, and A. C. Shoemaker. 1984. "Graphical Methods for Assessing Logistic Regression Models (with discussion)." *Journal of the American Statistical Association* 79:61–83.

Larsen, W. A. and S. J. McCleary. 1972. "The Use of Partial Residual Plots in Regression Analysis." *Technometrics* 14:781–790.

LeCun, Y., P. Y. Simard, and B. Pearlmutter. 1993. "Autonomic learning rate maximization by on-line estimation of Hessian's eigenvectors" In *Advances in Neural Information Processing Systems,* S. J. Hanson, J. D. Cowan, and C. L. Giles, eds. Vol. 5:156–163. San Mateo, CA: Morgan Kaufmann.

LeCun Y., L. Bottou, G. B. Orr, and K. R. Müller. 1998. "Efficient BackProp." In *Neural Networks: Tricks of the Trade. Lecture Notes in Computer Science*, G. B. Orr and K. R. Müller, eds. Vol. 1524. Berlin: Springer.

Leisch, F., A. Trapletti, and K. Hornik. 1999. "Stationarity and Stability of Autoregressive Neural Network Processes." In *Advances in Neural Information Processing Systems 11,* Kearns, Solla, Cohn, eds. Cambridge, MA: The MIT Press.

Loh, W. and Y. Shih. 1997. "Split Selection Methods for Classification Trees." *Statistica Sinica* 7:815–840.

Loh, W. and N. Vanichsetakul. 1988. "Tree-Structured Classification Via Generalized Discriminant Analysis (with discussion)." *Journal of the American Statistical Association*. 83:715–728.

Lukosevicius, M. and H. Jaeger. 2010. "Reservoir Approaches to Recurrent Neural Network Training." *Computer Science Revue* 3(3):127–149.

Lukosevicius, M. 2012. "A Practical Guide to Applying Echo State Networks." In *Neural Networks: Tricks of the Trade, 2nd ed.*, G. Montavon, G. B. Orr, and K. R. Müller, eds. *Springer LNCS* 7700:659–686.

Maass W., T. Natschlaeger, and H. Markram. 2002. "Real-time computing without stable states: A new framework for neural computation based on perturbations." *Neural Computation* 14(11):2531–2560.

Maldonado, M., J. Dean, W. Czika, and S. Haller. 2014. "Leveraging Ensemble Models in SAS® Enterprise Miner™." *Proceedings of the SAS Global Forum 2014 Conference*. Cary, NC: SAS Institute Inc. Available at http://support.sas.com/resources/papers/proceedings14/SAS133-2014.pdf.

Masters, T. 1993. *Practical Neural Network Recipes in C++*. Boston: Academic Press Inc., Harcourt Brace & Co. Publishers.

Melssen, W., R. Wehrens, and L. Buydens. 2006. "Supervised Kohonen networks for classification problems." *Chemometrics and Intelligent Laboratory Systems* 83:99–113.

McCullagh, P. and J. A. Nelder. 1989. *Generalized Linear Models, Second Edition*. New York: Chapman & Hall.

McLachlan, G. J. 1992. *Discriminant Analysis and Statistical Pattern Recognition*. New York: Wiley.

Minsky, M. 1986. *The Society of Mind*. New York: Simon and Schuster.

Mitra, S. 2000. "Neuro-Fuzzy Rule Generation: Survey in Soft Computing Framework." *IEEE Transactions on Neural Networks*. Vol. II, No. 3 (May).

Moody, J. 1994. "Prediction Risk and Architecture Selection for Neural Networks." In *From Statistics to Neural Networks. Theory and Pattern Recognition Applications*, Cherkasy, Friedman, Wechsler, eds. New York: Springer-Verlag.

Morgan, J. N. and J. A. Sonquist. 1963. "Problems in the Analysis of Survey Data, and a Proposal." *Journal of the American Statistical Association*. 58:415–434.

Mosteller, F. and J. W. Tukey. 1977. *Data Analysis and Regression*. Reading, MA: Addison-Wesley.

Murthy, S. K., S. Kasif, and S. Salzberg. 1994. "A System of Induction of Oblique Decision Trees." *Journal of Artificial Intelligence Research* 2:1–32.

Murthy, S. K. and S. Salzberg. 1995. "Lookahead and Pathology in Decision Tree Induction." *Proceedings of IJCAI-95, Montreal*, pp. 1025–1031.

NC Health and Human Services. North Carolina State Center for Health Statistics. "Statistics and Reports." Available at http://www.schs.state.nc.us/data/archivedvitalstats.cfm#vol1.

Nielson, M. 2015. *Neural Networks and Deep Learning*. Determination Press.

Ng, A. 2013. "Stochastic Gradient Descent" Video from Coursera - Stanford University - Course: Machine Learning: Published on Nov 1, 2013. Available at https://www.coursera.org/course/ml.

Olah, C. "Understanding LSTM Networks." Available at http://colah.github.io/posts/2015-08-Understanding-LSTMs. Posted Aug 27, 2015. Accessed March 7, 2016.

Pao, Y. 1989. *Adaptive Pattern Recognition and Neural Networks*. Reading, MA: Addison-Wesley.

Parker, D. B. 1985. *Learning Logic: Technical Report TR-47*. Center for Computational Research in Economics and Management Science. Cambridge, MA: MIT.

Patil, G. P. and C. Taillie. 1982. "Diversity as a Concept and its Measurement (with discussion)." *Journal of the American Statistical Association*. 77:548–567.

Pearlmutter, B. 1995. "Gradient calculations for dynamic recurrent neural networks: A survey." *Neural Networks*. IEEE Transactions. 6(5):1212–1218.

Piatesky-Shapiro, G. 1998. "What Wal-Mart might do with Barbie association rules." *Knowledge Discovery Nuggets* 98:1. Available at http://www.kdnuggets.com/.

Poh, H., J. Yao, and T. Jasic. 1998. "Neural networks for the Analysis and Forecasting of Advertising and Promotion Impact." *International Journal of Intelligent Systems in Accounting, Finance, and Management* 7:253–268.

Potts, W. J. E. 1999. "Generalized Additive Neural Networks." In *KDD-99 Proceedings,* Chaudhuri and Madigan. ACM.

Prechelt, L. 1996. "A Quantitative Study of Experimental Evaluations of Neural Network Learning Algorithms: Current Research Practice." *Neural Networks* 9:457–462.

Prechelt, L. 1997. "Investigation of the CasCor Family of Learning Algorithms." *Neural Networks* 10:885–896.

Prechelt, L. 1998. "Automatic Early Stopping Using Cross Validation: Quantifying the Criteria." *Neural Networks* 11:761–767.

Principe, J.C., N. R. Euliano, and W. C. Lefebvre. 2000. *Neural and Adaptive Systems*. New York: Wiley.

Quinlan, J. R. 1993. *C4.5: Programs for Machine Learning*. San Mateo, CA: Morgan Kaufmann.

Raftery, A. E. 1995. "Bayesian Model Selection in Social Research (with discussion)." In *Sociological Methodology 1995* (Marsden ed.) New York: Blackwell.

Rao, J. S. and W. J. E. Potts. 1997. "Visualizing Bagged Decision Trees." *Proceedings of the Third International Conference on Knowledge Discovery and Data Mining*, Heckerman, Mannila, Pregibon, and Uthurusamy, eds. Menlo Park, CA: AAAI Press.

Rendle, S. 2010. *Factorization Machines*. Osaka, Japan: The Institute for Scientific and Industrial Research, Osaka University.

Rendle, S. 2012. "Factorization Machines with libFM." *ACM Transactions on Intelligent Systems and Technology*, vol. 3, no. 3, article 57.

Ridgeway, Greg. 1999. "The State of Boosting." *Computing Science and Statistics*. 31:171–181.

Riedmiller, M. and H. Braun. 1993. "A direct adaptive method for faster back propagation learning: The RPROP algorithm." *Proceedings of the International Conference on Neural Networks*. San Francisco, CA. pp. 586–591.

Riedmiller, M. 1994. "Supervised Learning in Multi-layer Perceptrons – From Backpropagation to Adaptive Learning Algorithms." *Int. Journal of Computer Standards and Interfaces* 16.

Ripley, B. D. 1996. *Pattern Recognition and Neural Networks*. New York: Cambridge University Press.

Rubin, D. 1987. *Multiple Imputation for Nonresponse in Surveys*. New York: John Wiley & Sons.

Rubinkam, M. 2006. "Internet Merchants Fighting Costs of Credit Card Fraud." AP Worldstream. The Associated Press.

Rud, O. P. 2001. *Data Mining Cookbook: Modeling Data, Risk, and Customer Relationship Management*. New York: Wiley.

Rumelhart, D. E., G. E. Hinton, and R. J. Williams. 1986. "Learning Representations by Back-Propagating Errors." *Nature* 323:533–536.

Runkle, D. E. 1987. "Vector Autoregressions and Reality (with discussion)." *Journal of Business and Economic Statistics* 5:437–454.

Sarle, W. S. 1994a. "Neural Networks and Statistical Models." *Proceedings of the Nineteenth Annual SAS® Users Group International Conference*, pp. 1538-1550. Cary, NC: SAS Institute Inc.

Sarle, W. S. 1994b. "Neural Network Implementation in SAS® Software." *Proceedings of the Nineteenth Annual SAS® Users Group International Conference*, pp. 1550-1573. Cary, NC: SAS Institute Inc.

Sarle, W. S. 1995. "Stopped Training and Other Remedies for Overfitting." *Proceedings of the 27th Symposium on the Interface*.

Sarle, W. S., ed. 1997. Neural Network FAQ. Available at ftp://ftp.sas.com/pub/neural/FAQ.html.

Sarle, W. S. 1999. "How to Measure the Importance of Inputs?" Available at ftp://ftp.sas.com/pub/neural/importance.html.

Sarle, W. S. 2000. (Revised June 23, 2000.) "How to measure importance of inputs?" Cary, N.C. Available at ftp://ftp.sas.com/pub/neural/importance.html.

SAS Institute Inc. 2016. *SAS® Enterprise Miner 14.2: High-Performance Procedures*. Cary, NC: SAS Institute Inc.

Scheffe, H. 1959. *The Analysis of Variance*. New York: Wiley.

SCHS: North Carolina State Center for Health Statistics. 2012. "Selected Statistics for 2000 and 1996-00." Available at http://www.schs.state.nc.us/data/vital/volume1/2000/nc.html.

SCHS: North Carolina State Center for Health Statistics. 2003. "Selected Statistics for 2001 and 1997-2001." Available at http://www.schs.state.nc.us/data/vital/volume1/2001/nc.html.

Schwarz, G. 1978. "Estimating the Dimension of a Model." *Annals of Statistics* 6:461–464.

Seber, G. A. F. and C. J. Wild. 1989. *Nonlinear Regression*. New York: Wiley.

Shanno, D. F. 1970. "Conditioning of Quasi-Newton Methods for Function Estimation." *Mathematics of Computation* 24:647–656.

Shannon, C. E. 1948. "A Mathematical Theory of Communication." *The Bell System Technical Journal*. 27:379–423.

Suykens, J., B. D. Moor, and J. Vandewalle. 2008. "Toward optical signal processing using photonic reservoir computing." *Optics Express* 16(15):11182–11192.

Tibshirani, R. and G. E. Hinton. 1995 "Coaching variables for regression and classification." *Statistics and Computing* 8:25–33.

Tsukimoto, H. 2000. "Extracting Rules from Trained Neural Networks." *IEEE Transactions on Neural Networks*. Vol. II, No. 2 (March).

Vapnik, V. N. 1995. *The Nature of Statistical Learning*. New York, NY: Springer.

Vapnik, V., S. Golowich, and A. Smola. 1997. "Support Vector Method for Function Approximation, Regression Estimation, and Signal Processing." In *Advances in Neural Information Processing System 9*. 281-287. Also in *Proceedings of the 1996 conference on Neural Information Processing Systems*. Cambridge, MA: MIT Press.

Vracko, M. 2005. "Kohonen Artificial Neural Network and Counterpropagation Neural Network in Molecular Toxicity Studies." *Current Computer-Aided Drug Design* 1:73–78.

Wasserman, P. D. 1993. *Advanced Methods in Neural Computing*. New York: Van Nostrand Reinhold.

Weigend, A. S. and N. A. Gershenfeld. 1994. *Time Series Prediction: Forecasting the Future and Understanding the Past*. Reading, MA: Addison-Wesley.

Weiss, S. M. and C. A. Kulikowski. 1991. Computer Systems That Learn: Classification and Prediction Methods from Statistics, Neural Nets, Machine Learning, and Expert Systems. San Mateo, CA: Morgan Kaufmann.

Werbos, P. 1974. *Beyond Regression: New Tools for Prediction and Analysis in the Behavioral Sciences*. Ph.D. Thesis. Harvard University.

Wold, H. 1966. "Estimation of Principal Components and Related Models by Iterative Least Squares". In *Multivariate Analysis*, P.R. Krishnaiaah, ed., pp. 391-420. New York: Academic Press.

Wolpert, D. 1996. "The Lack of A Priori Distinctions between Learning Algorithms." *Neural Computation*, pp. 1341–1390.

Wujek, B., P. Hall and F. Güneş. 2016. Best Practices for Machine Learning Applications. SAS Institute Inc.: Cary, NC.

Zahavi, J. and N. Levin. 1997. "Applying Neural Computing to Target Marketing." *Journal of Direct Marketing* 11:5–22.

Zhou, Z.-H. 2012. *Ensemble Methods: Foundations and Algorithms*. Boca Raton, FL: Chapman & Hall/CRC.

Ready to take your SAS® and JMP® skills up a notch?

Be among the first to know about new books,
special events, and exclusive discounts.
support.sas.com/newbooks

Share your expertise. Write a book with SAS.
support.sas.com/publish

 sas.com/books
for additional books and resources.

 **§.sas.**
THE POWER TO KNOW®

CPSIA information can be obtained
at www.ICGtesting.com
Printed in the USA
BVHW010229070922
646402BV00009B/251

9 781951 685300